MUSIC IN AMERICAN LIFE

TENEMENT SONGS

MARK SLOBIN

TENEMENT SONGS

THE POPULAR MUSIC OF
THE JEWISH IMMIGRANTS

UNIVERSITY OF ILLINOIS PRESS

Urbana   Chicago   London

Volumes in the series
MUSIC IN AMERICAN LIFE
are listed at the end of this book.

LIBRARY OF CONGRESS CATALOGING IN PUBLICATION DATA

Slobin, Mark.
Tenement songs.

(Music in American life)
Includes index.
1. Songs, Yiddish—United States—History and
criticism.   2. Music, Jewish—United States—History
and criticism.   3. Music, Popular (Songs, etc.)—
United States—History and criticism.   4. Musical
revue, comedy, etc.—United States—History and
criticism.   I. Title.   II. Series.
ML3776.S6   784.5'0089924   81–4932
ISBN 0–252–00893–6   AACR2
ISBN 0–252–00962–2 (audio cassette)
ISBN 0–252–00965–7 (set)

To my grandmother,

SEMA LIEPAH (1889–1979),

who heard Mischa Elman's grandfather

play wedding dances in

the streets of Uman'

PREFACE

In 1973, having reached a pause in my work on the music of Afghanistan and Central Asia, I decided to look into a field much closer to home, both literally and emotionally: the musical heritage of the Eastern European Jews. I was enthusiastically adopted as a member of the "Yiddish Renaissance," especially by Barbara Kirshenblatt-Gimblett, who gave me access to the most stimulating research and people in the field of Yiddish studies and who has read all my work with her critically constructive eye.

The present book is the fruit of some five years of work, supported in part by two sabbatical semesters from Wesleyan University, one of which was spent in residence at the Max Weinreich Center for Advanced Jewish Studies at YIVO (Jewish Research Institute, New York). Earlier versions of sections of this study have been given as working papers or conference papers, some of which have been or will be published.

I would like to thank the staff of YIVO, particularly Marek Web and Dina Abramowicz, for their willingness to adopt an intellectual immigrant. I am very grateful to Khane Mlotek and Meir Noy, inexhaustible sources on Yiddish song, for sharing materials. Nahma Sandrow chipped in good ideas about Yiddish theater, and Richard Spottswood gave me perspective on ethnic recordings. The American Studies people at Wesleyan, particularly Richard Slotkin, Jeanine Basinger, and Neely Bruce, were very nice about taking me in and helping to shape my understanding of popular culture. Herbert Gutman and Russell Sanjek have also provided ideas and encouragement.

One methodological point needs to be made. I have deliberately excluded the folk and art music worlds from this book, for the most part. This is not because I undervalue their great importance to the development of ethnic identity and Jewish expressive life, the main topics of the study. The decision was made first because the popular culture of the immigrants has been so neglected, and second due to space considerations. We need full-length volumes on both folk and art musics that go well beyond the presently available sources.

MARK SLOBIN
Middletown, CT

CONTENTS

PROLOGUE

During the peak of Eastern European Jewish emigration to America (1901), the great Yiddish writer Y. L. Perets wrote a story called "A gilgul fun a nign." *Gilgul* is a wonderful word, which can mean migration, reincarnation, or (maybe best for our purposes) transmigration: the rebirth of a soul in another life, one of a chain of lives before the eventual release to a "nirvana." *Nign* is also a complicated word, meaning "tune," "melody," or even "song," if it is a spiritual sort of song.

Perets's story tells how a tune lived through one cycle and began another. The tale goes like this: Chaim, the small-town fiddler, is asked by the rich Katsners to go to the city in search of a tune suitable to be played at their daughter's wedding. He is to get an *El mole rakhmim,* a prayer for the dead that forms part of the complex ritual symbolism of the traditional Jewish wedding. But when Chaim gets to the city, Pedotsur, the great musician, has just left. Chaim does manage to pick up one of the master's tunes from a street band which happens by, accompanying an orphan bride to her wedding with a doleful melody.

Although Pedotsur's tune inspires Chaim to new heights, it is distorted into a dance ditty by rich guests from Kiev, the Jewish metropolis. Via one of these guests the tune is transported to the Yiddish stage, where it lives a sinful life as a sensual love duet. It is then picked up by a young girl who has been kidnapped from her wealthy parents' home and forced to perform with wandering acrobats. The showmen leave her for dead when she catches typhus. Blind, she wanders the streets as a beggar, chanting the imploring tune.

A would-be religious scholar has his thoughts interrupted by the beggar, and he curses the girl. The melody sticks in his mind obsessively. He seeks the aid of a traveling holy man and is forced to sing the tune at the Sabbath dinner among the rabbi's disciples. Sanctified, the tune is thus regenerated and reborn. As penance for insulting the beggar girl, the scholar finds her a suitable match. A few years later it turns out that she was the daughter of the Kiev folks who took the tune from the Katsner wedding—she was kidnapped while they were at the Yiddish theater. The story ends this way: "But now it was impossible to return the daughter. The mother had long been dead and the father had long since emigrated to America."

And, presumably, the tune lived on in both worlds.

Over the last two thousand years the Jews have lived in not just one Diaspora, but many: Babylonia, Spain, Germany, Eastern Europe, America . . . Some of these "exiles" were favorable to the flowering of Jewish culture, while others could only be graded on a sliding scale of horror. This book deals with a period that saw massive migration from one place of dispersion to another—from Eastern Europe to America. Both areas were in a state of extreme turmoil at the time. Industrialization, urbanization, violent social movements, and rapid secularization led the way into the twentieth century on both sides of the Atlantic. Despite this background and the trauma of being uprooted, some immigrants sensed that America could be one of the happy lands of exile. As one leader picturesquely put it in 1907: "In the great palace of American civilization we shall occupy our own corner, which we will decorate and beautify to the best of our taste and ability, and make it not only a center of attraction for the members of our family, but also an object of admiration for all the dwellers of the palace." [1]

It is hard to say whether American Jews' success has been quite as spectacular as this flamboyant prophecy; yet by the third generation in "the golden land" Jews enjoyed a blend of tolerance, affluence, and communal stability rarely seen in previous homelands. They did this in great measure by casting off their Europeanisms as the tattered cloaks of an earlier Diaspora. American problems eventually found American solutions. How did the early generations manage before they reached that point of self-confidence? How did they keep their footing on these slippery shores? I will argue that popular culture, especially the music that lay at the heart of public and private entertainment, played a significant role in giving the immigrants a sense of identity, both in terms of where they came from and where they were headed.

Song was an important part of Eastern European Jewish folk culture, even in the small communities we call the *shtetl*. As one folksinger reports, "The town was small, after all. If a guest visited, everyone got together. People who came to visit brought songs. When we used to go to another town, we learned new songs and brought them back. We always sang—while we worked, while we walked, when we got together. Sabbath and holidays the family sang *zmires* [table songs]." [2]

Starting from this firm foundation in folk life, which included folk drama, a group of cultural activists created the Yiddish theater. These men, led by Abraham Goldfadn in the 1870s, began life as thinkers and teachers, not clowns and minstrels. The leading musical figures of the movement were all trained in the synagogues as upholders of liturgical music, not as street singers. Goldfadn sought to elevate public taste and self-awareness while inserting pratfalls and belly laughs to hold his audience. As a result, a ban on Yiddish theater was included in the harsh edicts of 1882 that swelled a trickle of emigrants from Russia into a flood. "Entertainment" was a form of cultural self-expression that proved too potent for the czar. Suddenly actors, musicians, and their audiences all found themselves at Ellis Island as part of a mass movement that saw New York's Jewish population grow from 80,000 in 1880 to 1,250,000 by World War I. This meant that one more task fell to the entertainers: to explain America, and to define the problems of adjustment to a New World.

New York was the ideal place for such an experiment. The whole city was improvised, a patchwork of neighborhoods stitched together by horsecar (later, subway) lines. As ethnic groups jostled for scarce space, one could only hope that some day the foreign born, who were now in the majority, would create an orderly metropolis. The city stood for America as a whole, amorphous and expansive, exploiting the human and natural resources of a continent. Millions flocked into urban centers from the countryside or the cattle boats. For all of them, popular culture tried to make chaos coherent through shows and songs. New York was the great neon sign that flashed all of America's messages through households, dance halls, and dens of diversion. Everything was fair game for popular song: love, the latest fashions and scandals, the newest inventions, and even the arrival of the immigrants. At no other time was America so keen on finding new ways to entertain.

Our survey starts just as Edison is inventing the phonograph and ends as radio is sending out its first feeble signals. In between falls the heyday of sheet music, when hundreds of songs sold millions of copies each, while the moving picture grew from a toy to a necessity of American life. At the same time, recordings captured the sound of everything from Sousa to the synagogue. Natives and newcomers used song and story to symbolize their struggles, and the effort proved commercially viable.

Oldtimers like the Irish had already learned how to popularize their sentiments to themselves and to all America, with damp-eyed evocations of the Emerald Isle. The Irish, Germans, and others went to the extreme of putting on blackface for the minstrel show in order to be all-American, before rubbing off the burnt cork to show that even ethnics could be stars. For the Jews, self-expression and the idea of upward mobility through entertainment came naturally from their European experience. Street fiddlers' sons, like Mischa Elman, could become respected concert artists in imperial Russia. America reinforced this concept and held out a new, increased reward: national pop stardom. While America was shaping them, immigrant entertainers could help shape modern America. Products of the ghetto, rough-hewn Al Jolsons and Eddie Cantors preceded the "polite" envoys from the immigrant world, the writers, scholars, and statesmen. As Alfred Kazin has noted: "The positive creative role of the Jew as modern American, and above all as a modern American writer, was in the first years of this century being prepared not in the universities, nor even in journalism, but in the vaudeville theaters, music halls, and burlesque houses where the pent-up eagerness of penniless immigrant youngsters met the raw urban scene on its own terms." [3]

The scene was indeed raw. The bawdy balladeers of prostitutes and gangsters competed with genteel composers, just as they did in Warsaw and Odessa. There were types of immigrants to fit every niche America had to offer; all formed part of the popular culture message from which no one's ears were immune. The jammed, sprawling ghetto offered no hiding place. High and low rubbed shoulders along Hester Street and Second Avenue, as a turbulent mass sought desperately to build the "normal" life that had so long evaded their dreams.

Our heroes will not include the Mr. Goldfish who dubbed himself Goldwyn and made his MGM lion roar across America's silver screens. Instead, we will get to know men who never thought of updating names like Thomashefsky or Rumshinsky. We will touch only lightly on the Izzy Baline who became Irving Berlin by 1909 to sell songs caricaturing his co-religionists ("Yiddle on Your Fiddle, Play Some Ragtime"). Our protagonists will be men who faced the task of formulating and delivering messages about Americanization to the Yiddish-speaking masses. To them, the sinking of the *Titanic* was not a lesson in random disaster or earthly vanity, as it was to American songwriters, but a chance to play up a Jewish wife's devotion to her husband. (The image of Ida Straus choosing to go down with Isidor and the ship, rather than to seek safety in the lifeboats, was engraved on the minds of a generation via song.) We will follow the thinking of a composer who saw the Triangle Fire of 1913, with its massive toll of Jewish seamstresses, not as a step to politicize the proletariat, but as an event that created orphans and caused bereaved mothers to bewail their daughters "lying in shrouds instead of wedding gowns."

Both the short-term reactions to American events and the long-range maintenance of the values of European Judaism were packaged into the songs that shop girls took to their weekly piano lessons and that wandering minstrels brought to the courtyards of the Lower East Side. The songs themselves drew much of their cultural energy from that dynamo of the immigrant world, the Yiddish theater. Through much of its early history, the Yiddish stage relied heavily on songs to soften the audience for a play's message. When Goldfadn auditioned actors for his fledgling troupe, he had them sing. Arnold Perlmutter, a composer, sat in the corner and wrote down whatever the performer sang, whether operatic arias, liturgical music, or folksongs of any nationality. Later, Goldfadn wrote plays which took into account what the actors could sing, as well as how they could act—he simply plugged in their audition numbers, changing the text to suit his drama. This natural fit of actor to song led the audience to believe that music resided in the on-stage characters, that song and spectacle were inseparable: "I've sometimes happened to hear [writes Rumshinsky], when an actor has sung a lovely tune that tugs at the heartstrings, how a member of the audience remarks: 'Gevalt! Where does he [the actor] get such a smart head to make up such a heartfelt tune?'" [4]

For years it was unthinkable for a play not to have music. The same held true for Shakespeare in his day, for the popular comedy and melodrama of all of Europe and America in the nineteenth century, and for the various immigrant theater traditions of the United States. In ethnic drama, heart-warming tunes paved the way for song texts which sent messages about the values and hope of the group. Sometimes an entire play would hinge on a "punch-line tune," even if it had to be injected with all the grace of a sledgehammer—as in the case of the garden variety tearjerker:

> A mother sits rocking a cradle and weeping. Her child is
> dying. Enter the doctor. . . . The mother knows that her child
> is dying, but has heard that the doctor has a wonderfully sweet
> voice. She begs him, before her child dies, to sing her a little
> song. The doctor consents, comes down to the footlights, and
> switching to Americanese, addresses the orchestra leader with
> a brisk "Okay, Professor! Shoot!" The orchestra strikes up and
> [he] sings "A Mother is the Best of All Things." [5]

Even the great tragedian Jacob Adler, who loathed such musical histrionics, often used a song as emotional high point, as in Gordin's play

The Russian Jew in America: "Dying [the Russian Jew] has a vision . . . he lives through his whole life again, pictures of his old home appear before him, Russian fields, Moscow, pictures of America, too. And he dies in the strange land, singing quietly, 'Moscow, my Moscow, city of cities, streets of gold.' " [6]

The theater also combined the appeal of songs with a call to communal action:

> When news of the Kishinev pogrom [1903] horrified the world, the three-year-old Stella Adler stood center stage, arms thrown wide, and in a voice that carried to the farthest gallery cried:
> Jews, for the love of mercy,
> Give of your charity!
> For the dead, burial—
> For the living, bread!
> . . . At the last two lines, Adler would come down from the platform and go through the audience, stovepipe [hat] in hand. . . . People wept and emptied their pockets. Women with no money to give threw their wedding rings into his hat. [7]

An equally powerful symbol of music's power in the theater can be seen in Adler's approach to his most celebrated role, the Jewish King Lear. The memory of a song convinced him to take on the part: "Adler remembered a song in the Odessa wine cellars about an old father turned away by his children. He remembered how grown men had wept at that song. And he felt the play would be a success." [8] Songs reinforced the theater, and drama drove home the songs, which were hummed and sung across the entire Lower East Side after each new production. Some of these tunes stayed in the Jews' consciousness for decades, becoming folksongs as they returned to their roots in traditional culture. As a shared body of folklore, these songs spanned the Atlantic and united the entire Yiddish-speaking world.

A mother weeping for an expiring child; an alienated emigré dying while remembering Moscow; an appeal for alms—how do these gloomy topics fit with the optimistic assessment of American Jewish culture as a new flowering of Judaism, as a lovely corner of the American palace? The answer is that entertainment's success can be measured not in the fun it provides, but in its survival value. Popular culture's ability to sympathize with the bereaved, to comfort the rootless, or to unite the community in outrage against Jewish suffering gives it a special place in the history of immigrant adaptation. Music was a cultural adhesive, covering over the cracks in immigrant society and hardening its edges.

Above all, it helped frame a space that was purely for the in-group, and hence comfortable, in an alien world.

With time, of course, everything fell apart. Young Jews tired of the old formula. At first they could be held in line with more Americanized material, but each new generation forgot and even reviled the messages and songs of its parents. When Congress shut the door to immigration in the early 1920s, a great experiment in cultural continuity had to end. The all-consuming drive for constructive assimilation directed energy into new channels. Institutional music-making in synagogues, schools, and social movements mirrored the Jews' creation of a polity organized on strictly American lines; no longer could the old prima donnas sing arias bewailing Israel's abandonment of tradition. In the Yiddish theater of the 1920s, the petite Molly Picon offered the Peter Pan image of a sparkling entertainer from a Second Avenue Never-Never Land, who need never grow up and whose songs sounded increasingly like the hits American citizens should enjoy. With Broadway and Muzak's adoption of hits like "Bei mir bist du sheyn," ethnicity proved marketable. Much later, the Holocaust snapped the lifeline to the Old World. Postwar affluence and the creation of Israel eventually allowed the Jews to take on the other ethnics' habit of seeing Europe in a golden haze, and to raise the villager fiddler from the dust to the rooftop.

It is not our job here to judge the culture of American Jews. What will be argued, though, is that Jewish-Americans do not know the whole of their culture. In the songs the immigrants published, hawked, played, sang, and finally forgot, they poured the energy of people hungry for direction and hoping for the best. Few now remain who can remember that era, but its traces remain in the memoirs of musical activists, in the hundreds of tattered folios, and in the columns of yellowed newspapers. We will follow the trail of the songmakers from the Old World to the New, searching through the words, music, and illustrations of the songs for the messages of forty years of immigrants and reevaluating a legacy left in the piano bench.

NOTES

1. Quoted in E. Friesel, "The Age of Optimism in American Judaism, 1900–1920," in B. Korn, ed., *A Bicentennial Festschrift for Jacob Rader Marcus* (New York: KTAV, 1976), p. 143.
2. Quotation from unpublished interviews with Mariam Nirenberg by Barbara Kirshenblatt-Gimblett for the YIVO Jewish Folksong Project.

3. Alfred Kazin, "The Jews as Modern American Writers," in A. Chapman, ed., *Jewish-American Literature* (New York: New American Library, 1974), pp. 588–89.
4. J. Rumshinsky, "Baglaytvort," in Sholem Perlmutter, *Yidishe dramaturgn un teater-kompozitors* (New York: YKUF-ferlag, 1943), p. 315.
5. Lulla Rosenfeld, *Bright Star of Exile: Jacob Adler and the Yiddish Theatre* (New York: Crowell, 1977), p. 333.
6. Ibid., p. 321.
7. Ibid., p. 335.
8. Ibid., p. 265.

PART I

BEFORE ELLIS ISLAND

CHAPTER 1

THE MYTHIC
OLD WORLD

The time is the mid-1890s. In the provincial Russian city of Dvinsk lives Joseph Rumshinsky, a teenage musician working in liturgical music. The manager of the visiting German circus asks Rumshinsky to do him a favor: would he stage one of the new Yiddish biblical melodramas between the acrobats and the clowns in order to entice the local Jews and liven up business? Rumshinsky accepts his first conducting experience. In the process, while teaching the German girl Yiddish arias, he falls in love with the beautiful bareback rider Jeanette. A Jewish composer matures musically and emotionally before moving on to the next job offer. Eventually, in America, he will become known as "The Jewish Victor Herbert."

This is not what we think of as a story of "Old World" musical life. To accept this moment in Rumshinsky's career as part of the evolution of an immigrant music culture in America, one must throw off considerable mental ballast. For many of us, the "Old World" consists of Sholom Aleichem's village of Anatevka as filtered through the Broadway sensibilities of *Fiddler on the Roof.* It is largely a nostalgia-laden rural dream world of Sabbath candles and orthodoxy, broken by pograms and harsh edicts. Much of the conflict Sholom Aleichem left unresolved in his original stories is muted or omitted. The *Fiddler* writers drew heavily on the 1950s book *Life Is With People* to understand the European context of Jewish life. As a recent study [1] has shown, the research team (headed by Margaret Mead) which produced that book chose to depict a standardized community model, rather than to confront the complexity of Eastern European Jewish life.

Even Irving Howe's astute 1976 survey of the territory adds little: a brief look at the intellectuals of the secularizing "Jewish Enlightenment," and at the radicals of the early Jewish proletariat in the Russian cities. *Fiddler* had already flirted with the latter by portraying the radical student who makes off with one of Tevya's daughters. Both village and city tend to be stereotypes, piety versus progress.

Music is a wonderful wedge with which to split open this diorama of Eastern Europe. Through songs, fiddlers, and an emerging popular music we will survey an incredibly diverse world, one teeming with the eclecticism and paradox of a people hemmed in by hostile neighbors.

Rumshinsky was born in 1881, that critical year when the break-up of the old ways accelerated. The assassination of Czar Alexander III and the subsequent massive pogroms and restrictive legislation crystallized the hopeless situation of large masses of Jews, and full-scale migration to America began. Over 2.5 million Jews came to America in the ensuing forty years. Two points must be made if we are to understand the musical situation before and after this pivotal year. First, flight to the New World did not mean that the "Old World" disappeared. Second, we must realize that, at least musically, the "Old World" never really existed.

In his best-selling look at the world of his fathers, Irving Howe devotes twenty-five pages to the European antecedents of American Jewry, and seventeen more to their trans-Atlantic odyssey. After that, Europe fades out of the picture. In the following 600 pages one rarely senses the continual coming and going of Jews as they went "home" to Europe to seek brides or visit relatives, or the nonstop impact on American Jewry of new stimulation provided by successive waves of immigrants. Until 1939 there *was* a parallel Jewish culture in Europe; perhaps the shock of the Holocaust has blurred our vision so that we see an Old World destroyed before its time. Rumshinsky arrived only in 1906, and countless other major contributors to the immigrant musical world did not arrive on the first ships in 1881. This will become clear when we examine the life histories and repertoires of individual singers in the "folk" tradition. These men and women carried songs back and forth, enriching the musical environments of two continents, throughout the peak decades of immigration. By studying the European situation, we are studying America as well.

By saying there was no "Old World," I mean simply this: by the time of mass migration, European Jewish music had produced a sophisticated and multifaceted musical life, including both repertoires and musicians, in keeping with the latest developments of Industrial Age Europe. That music was based on folk traditions which showed a wide range of familiarity and interaction with whatever was most modern in

Europe, dating back at least to Renaissance times. To understand a Rumshinsky—or an Irving Berlin—we must dig into the musical infra-structure of Eastern European Jews (though of course to do so thor-oughly would be to write a separate volume). Very little has been studied of that complex musical world: even the first published collec-tions of Yiddish folksongs gathered from traditional performers is no older than the twentieth century.[2] Significantly, it was produced in 1901 in St. Petersburg, with an introduction in Russian, somewhat at a distance from the singers. Even more meaningfully, the *melodies* of the hundreds of folksongs sent in by mail were not notated—the actual music seemed of little importance at the time. What we can know of the musical life must be inferred, extrapolated from the written and live recollections of survivors of that bygone era and from the scattered writings of the few scholars who took music seriously in the years from 1901 to 1939, before the culture and the vast majority of its carriers disappeared forever.

For ethnomusicologists, those researchers who study music as a part of culture, there are four interlocking aspects to that lively organism we call a "music culture": 1) a belief system; 2) its embodiment as the social organization of music; 3) the material culture which produces the artifacts of music; and 4) what most of us would simply label "the music"—the repertoire of items which forms a people's heritage and which reflects the other three components. We will briefly survey each of the four. Of course, all facets of the music culture will be readjusted when the music migrates. In the realignment many items change, some disappear, and a few, which we will eventually look at in great detail, carry over to demonstrate the culture's continuity.

The Belief System. This aspect encompasses an enormous range of questions about music that the culture answers for its members, from the most abstract of cosmological queries ("Is music good or bad for man?") through more pragmatic, aesthetic tenets that tell one whether a song is beautiful and appropriate, or if the singer is going on a bit too long. In between are questions having to do with when, where, and by whom music is to be produced. Should it be rarely heard, especially as sung by women, as would be the case in Afghanistan? Or is music to be an important part of the daily acoustic environment, as in certain Indonesian settings or in the American city?

We can touch on only a few basic tenets of Eastern European Jewish musical life, as we can reconstruct it, in areas outside the metropolitan centers where Western European values took root. The rural-urban distinction is a necessary one. For example, as early as 1839, the Jews of

Odessa took the best seats in the opera house and behaved too demon-stratively, according to the report of a disgusted Russian governor.[3] This would hardly have been the case even fifty years later throughout much of the Russian Jewish network of villages and small towns.

One implicit principle seems to have been that musical talent could reside in any member of the community, which represents at least an implied affirmative answer to the question of whether music is a good thing. Even though few people (particularly women) could achieve fame and wealth through music, a gift for singing was supported, if only on an amateur level. Recently an impressive set of folksingers' biog-raphies was gathered for the YIVO Institute for Jewish Research by the eminent folklorist Barbara Kirshenblatt-Gimblett. Time and again, in hundreds of hours of taped interviews, the informants stressed how music got them through life, and how their reputations as above-average singers stood them in good stead in the community. One lady remembered how she was asked to sing for a group of women when they gathered for a joint chicken-plucking before the holidays; in re-turn, they plucked her chicken. Another recalled getting coveted oranges for her fellow passengers in steerage because she was able to sing German songs for the ship's crew. Many singers recounted how, in the difficult and lonely years of adjustment to America, this proclivity for song gave them strength.

Such a pattern is remarkable in that it directly conflicts with another basic tenet: music is dangerous. As in many Islamic settings, there was a traditional belief among Eastern European Jews that the sound of a woman's voice, like the sight of her hair, might lead a man astray from pure thoughts and upright behavior. As a result, women were generally allowed to sing only in front of men to whom they were already married or whom they could not marry due to incest rules, i.e., their nearest kin. In addition, over the centuries European rabbis fulminated against the sensuous seduction of the community's emerging arch-musician, the cantor, who led minds away from contemplation of the sacred texts by stressing the earthly beauty of his honeyed voice.

When implicit values are somewhat at odds, stresses on a culture will favor the ascendancy of the one which fits the emerging situation. In America the favorable (rather than the suspicious) view of music pre-vailed. And in late nineteenth century Europe the widening sphere of musical activity open to budding professionals like Rumshinsky left no doubt that talent, rather than reticence, would carry the day. Yet the old dichotomy persisted in the conflict between sacred and secular musical obligations. The major shapers of the secular, popular music tradition were nearly all involved in simultaneous work in the sacred field; in some cases, they may have viewed that activity as a counterweight for worldliness.

The distinction between vocal and instrumental music had profound and far-reaching consequences for Jewish music in both Europe and America. Like women, musical instruments were viewed as potentially dangerous components of the music culture. Instrumental music was regularly forbidden from services (though we know of some exceptions), resulting in the decades-long controversy within the modern branches of Judaism over the incorporation of the organ into the synagogue, an issue which caused schisms within American congregations in fairly recent times.

Outside of the general restriction of instrumental music to the non-liturgical world, musicians themselves were consigned to a social limbo, as we will see when we examine social organization. This status is confirmed by traditional and modern societies alike, as any American musician who has tried to get a low insurance rate or a credit card will have discovered. Even the barndance fiddler was considered an agent of the Devil in large parts of the Midwest as recently as the 1930s.

Social Organization. By discussing the musician's status, we have come to the second sphere of the music culture, which manifests the implicit principles of belief just outlined. Once it is understood how music and society fit together, roles and statuses are apportioned, niches are left to be filled, and rewards for performance are established. We have already touched upon one of the most fundamental aspects of social organization: the sexual division of music which marks most cultures. Here we need to survey several male categories of performers that will be of paramount importance to an understanding of immigrant music by virtue of their presence, absence, or adaptation: the *badkhn* (wedding entertainer), the *klezmer* (instrumental musician), the *khazn* (cantor, sacred singer), and the *meshoyrer* (choirboy, cantor's assistant).

The *badkhn* was once an extremely prominent performer, nearly indispensable at weddings. We need not linger over the long and tangled past of this central personage, save to note three main points. First, he is a direct link to late Renaissance German and Central European non-Jewish types of entertainers. Second, he functions as a transitional link between folk and popular musics in the late nineteenth century. Finally, he all but vanishes in America, save in ultra-orthodox Hasidic communities.

The *badkhn*'s primary function was to act as a one-man show at weddings, performing a mixed bag of entertainment ranging from acrobatics and crude practical jokes and insults directed at worthy guests through lofty moralizing—in improvised rhymes—on the subject of marriage as calamity, which evoked the instant tribute of copious tears from the assembled women. His antecedents seem to have been the German *marschalik*, and parts of his function can be seen in figures such as the *tysiatskii* (master of ceremonies) of the traditional North Russian folk wedding or the *lăutar* minstrel of Rumanian peasant nuptials, who sang the bride's lament for her. Through the extremely popular verses of such outstanding *badkhonim* as Eliokum Zunser, which were published, a transition from folk to popular performer was made. Zunser himself was a symbol of the decline of the *badkhn*'s role in America. He lived out his years as the proprietor of a printing shop on New York's Lower East Side, his old age beautifully described in Hutchins Hapgood's evocative work, *The Spirit of the Ghetto* (1902).

The three remaining roles are of greater importance for the emergent immigrant music culture. As can be imagined from the earlier mention of a vocal-instrumental dichotomy, the paths of the *klezmer* instrumentalists and the two types of sacred singers, *khazn* and *meshoyrer*, rarely crossed either in Europe or in America. Each must be considered as a separate, fascinating branch of the complicated musical structure we are investigating.

The *klezmer* belonged to an extremely tight-knit social group within Eastern European Jewish culture. Despite the fact that he often held down other part-time jobs in order to survive, his musicianship tended to define his social status. As folk musicians, *klezmorim* were considered somewhat outside the pale of regular community life. Distrusted and even feared for his unorthodox ways, the *klezmer* was often contemptuously called "gypsy." Indeed, his position in the Jewish world was quite similar to that of the gypsy in the general social environment. Mobile so as to maximize job possibilities, eclectic in repertoire for similar reasons, *klezmorim* and gypsies kept to themselves. The *klezmorim* even had their own argot (as did the gypsies), and were suspected of thievery and seduction as well.

Perhaps our best depictions of the *klezmer* and his role can be found in literary sources. We have already seen how Perets drew on the musician. Joseph Lateiner's 1897 melodrama "David's Violin" will be analyzed at length in a later chapter, in connection with music's role in the Yiddish theater; it deals with the transition from the "gypsy" *klezmer* role to that of the classical virtuoso. Here we turn to two first-rate fictional descriptions of the instrumentalist in his village setting, by Sholom Aleichem and by Chekhov.

In his early novel *Stempenyu*, Sholom Aleichem could draw on au-

thentic materials in describing the musician's life, since he himself
lived amongst *klezmorim* in his youth. He even introduces *klezmer*
argot, complete with Yiddish footnotes for the reader. The cultural and
musical situation of the *klezmer* is nowhere better summarized (albeit
somewhat romanticized) than in the following passages from the
novel's opening:

> Stempenyu? What sort of name is "Stempenyu?" It's not a
> name, folks, its a monicker he inherited from his father. His
> father, may he rest in peace, was called Berl Bas, or Berl Stem-
> penyer. He played the bass and was also a good *badkhn*, a fine
> rhymester . . . danced like a bear, imitated a Jewish woman
> giving birth . . . or hung a liver-and-lung on the mother-in-
> law's apron. . . .
>
> Berl's father, Mr. Shmulik Trumpet, played the trumpet,
> while his grandfather, Mr. Faybush Tsimbler, played the cim-
> balom [a hammered dulcimer], and his great-grandfather, Mr.
> Ephraim Faytl—in short, Stempenyu comes from ten genera-
> tions of *klezmorim*, and he's not ashamed of it.
>
> Among Jews it was considered a privilege to hear Nisi Bel-
> zer from Khmelnitsk sing, Gadik Badkhn from Gontiorsk de-
> claim, and Stempenyu from Mazepevka play. . . . Jews love
> music and understand melodies—even our enemies won't deny
> that. Say what you will, we're experts, keen experts, in singing
> and playing. . . . If a world-famous *khazn* comes to us, we run
> for tickets to hear him, and it's also our duty to hear a *klezmer*
> at a wedding.
>
> The public sits very respectfully, and the *klezmer* plays a sad
> piece . . . the fiddle cries, dissolves in the lower strings, and
> the other fellows support him very sadly. A bit of melancholy
> falls on the audience and everyone gets pensive . . . everyone is
> lost in thought and puts his nose down and, rubbing his fin-
> gers on the plate or kneading a crumb of the fresh bread,
> steeps himself in his thoughts, his sad thoughts, since prob-
> ably everyone has his worries, and a Jew doesn't need to bor-
> row trouble. . . .
>
> Oy, Stempenyu was an expert! He just grabbed the fiddle
> and made one pass with the bow, no more, and the fiddle be-
> gan to speak. What do I mean, speak? Really, with words, with
> a voice, like (forgive the comparison) a living person—speak-
> ing, discussing, singing weepingly in the Jewish manner, with
> power, with an outcry from deep in the heart, from the soul.

... as for the girls, the "mam'zelles," they stood rooted to the spot, like dolls, looking at Stempenyu with his magic fiddle, not moving a muscle, not blinking an eye. But somewhere, yonder on the other side of a corset, a heart was beating—tick, tick, tick—and often a buried sigh escaped from there.[4]

The linking together of the *klezmer*, *badkhn*, and *khazn* as the three main types of performers leaps out from this description, as does the strongly positive evaluation of the instrumentalist's (particularly the violinist's) art. The reference to the girls at the end is Sholom Aleichem's device for moving to a description of the heroine, Rokhl, who will fall in love with Stempenyu, propelling the plot forward.

Writing from outside the tradition, Chekhov shows us the *klezmer* from quite a different angle. His story is about a Russian villager whose brutal and pointless life is revealed to him after his wife's death, when he feels his own end is near. In addition to being the town gravedigger, Yakov (known as Bronza) also fills in as a violinist for a local Jewish band. He is disgusted by the Jews' behavior and music, and he brutalizes Rothschild, the ironically named poor Jewish flutist and fiddler:

At weddings in the town there usually played a Jewish orchestra, the conductor of which was the tinsmith Moses Ilyich Shakhkes, who kept more than half the takings for himself. As Yakov played very well upon the fiddle, being particularly skillful with Russian songs, Shakhkes sometimes employed him in the orchestra. . . . When Bronza sat in the orchestra he perspired and his face grew purple; it was always hot, the smell of garlic was suffocating; the fiddle whined, at his right ear snored the double bass, at his left wept the flute, played by . . . Rothschild. And even the merriest tunes this accursed Jew managed to play sadly. Without any tangible cause Yakov had become slowly penetrated with hatred and contempt for Jews, and especially for Rothschild.[5]

On his deathbed, Bronza's newly acquired perspective on life leads him to bequeath his treasured violin to Rothschild. Using a literary idea very close to that of Perets's contemporary "transmigration" story, Chekhov has Rothschild's fiddle (like Stempenyu's) take on special powers:

And now in the town everyone asks: Where did Rothschild get such an excellent fiddle? Did he buy it or steal it—or did he get it in pledge? Long ago he abandoned his flute, and now plays on the fiddle only. From beneath his bow issue the same mournful sounds as formerly came from the flute; but when he tries to repeat the tune that Yakov played when he sat on the threshold stone, the fiddle emits sounds so passionately sad and full of grief that the listeners weep. . . . But this new song so pleases everyone in the town that wealthy traders and officials never fail to engage Rothschild for their social gatherings, and even force him to play it as many as ten times.

What is of particular interest in this description is the inter-ethnic life of the local music, which goes beyond Perets's in-group metamorphoses since the two writers have different points to make. In Chekhov's story, the pain of both Russian and Jew suffuse the music and lend it its magical power. Almost ethnomusicologically, the Russian writer points out the strong non-Jewish component of the *klezmer* repertoire. Beregovski, the leading scholar of Jewish folk music between the two world wars, provided the scholarly counterpart to Chekhov in a careful study of Ukrainian-Jewish musical interaction and of the Ukrainian-Jewish *klezmer*, detailing the strong impact of Jewish and non-Jewish musicians on each other's repertoires. This situation held true for Rumania as well; as late as the 1960s, Rumanian bands in various parts of the country played Yiddish tunes for visiting researchers, explaining that they used to fill in at Jewish weddings when no *klezmorim* were available.[6] When we turn to the *klezmer*'s adjustment to America, this resilience of the instrumentalist will be stressed.

We turn next to the remaining key positions in the social organization of music: the *khazn* (cantor) and his assistant, the *meshoyrer*. The role of cantor shows a slow but steady rise throughout the Jewish experience in Europe. The rabbinical disapproval of this process parallels the outbursts of archbishops and popes against music's preempting of sacred texts for "sensual" musical purposes in Christendom. These protests were in vain. By the mid-nineteenth century the cantor had risen to extraordinary prominence, reigning as the musical star of the sacred world—indeed, of the musical culture as a whole. Of course, consistent with the belief system, the cantor as musician was held somewhat in disrepute; the most common Yiddish proverb about this figure was *ale khazonim zanen naronim* ("all cantors are fools.") Yet the *khazn* was respected, even adulated, if he attained star status. It is difficult to overrate the social importance of the cantor for the musical culture in the period under discussion.

Three points about the *khazn*'s musical role need stressing here. First, his repertoire, like that of the secular folksinger and the *klezmer*, was broadly eclectic; second, his role is of trans-Atlantic import throughout the period; and third, he is the main source of music education for most of the professional musicians at the core of early Jewish-American music.

The eclecticism is worth a closer look, since it nicely illustrates the complexity of Eastern European Jewish musical life. This catholicity of taste had different faces in varying social contexts. Both the small-town and the metropolitan *khazn* drew on multiple sources, yet those sources were not the same in both situations. Perhaps the best description of the small town–big city dichotomy is to be found in Mendele Mokher Sforim's novel *Fishke the Lame* (1869). The backwoods narrator is amazed at the cantor of the modern Odessa synagogue. Similarly, Sholom Aleichem tells us that Stempenyu traveled as far as Odessa, then turned homeward when he realized he had no place in the metropolis. Here is Fishke's commentary on the sacred side of the equation:

> A cantor indeed! He sat in a booth while a chorus sang the prayers! He did nothing at all. You wouldn't catch him sticking his finger down his throat or pulling on his cheek like our Reb Jerechmiel Weepsister, who shouted in low register, then skipped to a few piercing notes like pistol shots, then back to the low strings again, shifting the words up and down the scale, breaking into a thin falsetto for a sweet Rumanian shepherd song with which he tried to soften the Lord of Nations. "Oy, *tatenyu*, dear Father! Oy vay, woe is me, woe!" Reb Jerechmiel put his heart and soul into his singing and was soaking wet by the time he reached "Who is Blessed." But the cantor here? Did he work like that? God forbid! He hardly did a thing. As soon as he sang a note, the chorus caught up the cue and dished it out on a little platter, carried it up and down, mixed it with kasha and poppy seeds. That's what they called "services" here. And where was the Rumanian shepherd song? And where was the appeal to the Lord of Nations? [7]

Notice the hallmark of the cantor of Glupsk ("Dumbsville," Mendele's fictitious prototype of the small town): a Rumanian shepherd tune. It is typical of Jewish folk music that this patently "non-Jewish" item should stand for the downhome quality of the Glupsk musical scene. On the metropolitan side, the Odessa synagogue music is no more homegrown; it is simply that other sources of inspiration were available. Choral music on the Reformed German model was used for fashionable services in the city long before it had a foothold in other parts of the Russian Empire, and was doubtless influenced by secular music as well. As we have seen, as early as the 1830s Odessa Jews were known for their passionate love of opera. The opera-cantorial connection remained an important one throughout the nineteenth century, and is quite evident in the careers of choirboy-composers like Rumshinsky.

One can conveniently use the English word "choirboy" for the *meshoyrer*, but beyond this lexical match-up there is very little overlap between the two words' meanings. The role of *meshoyrer* was unlike that of the Christian choirboy of the late nineteenth century; rather, the Jewish choir was the nursery of musicians, as it had been for Christians in the Renaissance. The *meshoyrer* was apprenticed to a cantor at a very early age, making the nursery metaphor very nearly accurate. Training first by ear and later from notation provided the boy with all his musical knowledge. Luck, talent, and personal preference then decided the *meshoyrer's* fate: musical dropout, provincial cantor, star *khazn*, or a life in the budding Jewish or non-Jewish entertainment world.

One anecdote will suffice to indicate the complexity of the liturgical singer's place in the social organization of Eastern European music. It is the late 1870s, not long after Fishke was amazed at the Odessa cantor. The boy Boris Thomashefsky, future superstar of the Yiddish stage, has moved to Kiev with his parents after training as a *meshoyrer*. Jewish boarders who work in the Kiev Opera choir (and simultaneously sing in the synagogue chorus) take the boy to the director of the opera, an Italian, for an audition. The Italian, impressed by the prodigy, tells him to go back for more cantorial training; in a few years he may qualify for a spot in the opera.[8] The understanding on the part of the Italian director of a Russian opera house of the value of cantorial training, and his advice to continue it, indicate the multi-faceted nature of the Jewish musical world, and underscore once again the extent and the strategic value of eclecticism.

Material Culture of Music. Strangely enough, this component of Jewish music will interest us at length in America, but need not detain us in describing the European musical setting. Under "material culture" we include all physical embodiments of the music, including instruments, printed music, and such recent manifestations as sound recordings and their associated equipment. In Eastern Europe, the musical instruments of the Jews in no way differed from those of non-Jews. In fact, it almost appears that Jewish bands picked up their odd assortments of brass and stringed instruments (and costumes) from czarist army surplus, much as American southern black musicians collected discarded Civil War horns and trumpets. In terms of printed music, we will see the heyday of an internal Jewish publishing industry in New York, with little, if any, precursor in the Old World. Sound recordings, too, flourish in America and were probably more often exported to than imported from Europe.

Repertoire. At the World Congress on Jewish Music held in Jerusalem in 1978, one question kept turning up like a bad penny: What is Jewish music, anyway? Over the course of two thousand years of Diaspora, the Jews have crafted many musical cultures, each adapting to the local environment. The president of Israel went so far as to half-seriously offer a prize to anyone who could demonstrate a "proto-Jewish" music that underlies all the far-flung manifestations of world Jewish musical expression. He said he expected no takers. At the Congress, the musicologist Curt Sachs's dictum that Jewish music was music "made by Jews for Jews as Jews" was often quoted, but no one seemed eager to accept it as definitive. At least Sachs avoids the problem of identifying any particular repertoire as being purely Jewish by placing the Jewishness in the context (a very self-conscious context at that) of composers' and musicians' intents.

As they arrived in Eastern Europe over the course of some centuries, the Ashkenazic Jews brought with them a music influenced by Mediterranean and German stylistic features. To this was added a liberal dose of Southeastern European traits akin to those in the music of the Middle East, the original homeland of the Jews. So, by means of a grand circle, the European Jews found themselves near the roots of their own culture. One of the curious ironies of music history is that much of what passes for a "Jewish" sound in contemporary times, adapted from Palestinian (later Israeli) Jewish music, is in fact derived from Eastern Europe due to the stylistic affinity between the two adjacent regions. Perhaps the best-known international Jewish musical symbol is the dance tune "Hava Nagila," associated with Israel like the dance called the *hora.* Yet both tune and dance have roots in Eastern Europe, being brought to Palestine by European Jewish musicians.

This is not to say that there is no Jewish musical profile in Eastern Europe. Perhaps the best analogy to the music of that region is the language of the people who sang the songs. Emerging in late Carolingian times on the Romance-Germanic borderland along the Rhine, Yiddish evolved along with the population's shifts eastward, through Germanic and Slavic territory, eventually stretching from the North Sea to the Black Sea. Often called a "jargon" or "dialect," Yiddish is in fact a self-sufficient European tongue which, like English, is classified as a fusion language. Similarly, the fusion nature of East European Jewish music does not disqualify it from distinctiveness. Even the most blatantly non-Jewish material can change its character, when adopted for internal use.

As a case in point, let us see what happens when Lifsha Schaechter Widman, a folksinger of the YIVO project, sings the Schubert "Serenade," which she learned from a sister who knew many songs in German. While keeping the original German text, she alters Schubert's complex song structure. Instead of changing the music continually in what music theorists call a "through-composed" manner, Widman shapes it into the more familiar traditional Yiddish strophic style, making a new verse after each quatrain. In addition, she ends the melody while it is still in the minor key, avoiding the typically Schubertian modulation to the major. She performs the song in a "Yiddish" manner, with appropriate ornamentation and voice quality. Thus a "classical art song" becomes a Jewish folk song.

Thorough study of the entire European Jewish body of songs in Yiddish has not been undertaken, nor have the instrumental dance tunes been appropriately researched, so we do not have a well-considered view of how the European musical heritage was transformed by the Jewish filter. However, examples such as Widman's Schubert indicate that simple labels like "borrowing" will not wash. Particularly important for an understanding of "Yiddish" music is the existence of independent in-group networks of musical diffusion. It is significant, even typical, that Widman learned the Schubert song not from an "official" non-Jewish source, but from a relative: we cannot tell whether the adaptation is hers or whether it was already part of a communally evolved approach to the use of an outside repertoire, such as German art songs. We know that this pattern is an old one, since we have the case of the Yiddishization of the European ballad, which must have taken place some centuries earlier. As Eleanor Mlotek[9] has shown in a careful study, many of the ballads common to a number of European peoples were also widespread among Eastern European Jews. Certainly close parallels in, say, an English and a Yiddish ballad bear witness to old internalization of a general European stock, probably in late Renaissance times. What is important for our purposes is the clear evidence of conceptual change demonstrated by the Yiddish ballads. Lords and ladies frequently turn into ordinary folk, with the wicked queen becoming a mother-in-law as the scene changes from the court to the family hearth. Christian and supernatural elements fade away as more personal domestic situations are described.

These ballads form the oldest layer of the recoverable Yiddish song tradition. In a similar category, but less datable, are scores of lyric songs and children's songs. On the sacred side, we have the older liturgical repertoire and the tunes used for teaching Hebrew-Aramaic texts; here we must remember that exposure to the sacred began as early as age three for males. It is no surprise to find extensive overlap of "sacred" and "secular" musical motives within the folk tradition, and we will see this important trend continue into the popular music style in Europe and America. As Max Wohlberg has noted, "it is . . . difficult to ascribe a primordiality to either one or the other category, or to derive ultimate conclusions concerning melodic influence and cross-fertilization." [10] In other words, the streams of both sacred and secular music, as we know them from the late nineteenth century, flow from the same wellsprings in the European past. Both are modified by the accelerated pace of musical change so characteristic of the Industrial Age.

A second layer of repertoire begins in the 1860s, with the increasingly strong impact of that movement known as the Jewish Enlightenment (*Haskala*). That dynamic trend was born of Western philosophical ideals in late eighteenth century Germany and was nourished by Napoleonic political and social reform. Its radical energy penetrated Eastern Europe slowly but surely throughout the second half of the nineteenth century. At the risk of simplification, we can isolate some basic cultural features of the movement, features which will help explain musical developments of critical importance to the evolution of immigrant music some decades later.

First, the *Haskala* came to reluctantly espouse the use of Yiddish, rather than Hebrew, to convey the ideals of secularization to the Eastern European Jewish masses. This was no easy decision. As Dan Miron has shown in a brilliant study, [11] Yiddish was viewed by *Haskala* writers as a Caliban of a language—ugly, deformed, but useful for heavy work—as opposed to the Ariel-like Hebrew, in which lofty and significant messages could be sent. Writers went so far as to state that romantic love could not be depicted in Yiddish literature, since the intrinsic ugliness of the language (which they called "jargon") could not express noble sentiments. Yet they began to create prose and poetry for a broad readership, and met with a lively response. Important for us is the fact that many collections of short poems were designated as *lider* (songs) or even *folkslider* by the authors. Their hopes were sometimes fulfilled: many of these poems were in fact taken up as folksongs across the Yiddish-speaking world, resulting in a large repertoire of items generally termed "songs of literary origin."

Second, a group of adventurous entertainers began to spread *Haskala* songs in novel ways. Not themselves cloistered enlighteners, these wandering minstrels criss-crossed the street corners and wine cellars of Eastern Europe with a new brand of lively, topical, and satirical songs and skits tailored to an emerging middle-class audience. Indeed, the entertainers were dubbed *broderzinger* (singers from Brody) after one cosmopolitan crossroads of trade, Brody, in Austrian Galicia. Their field of operation moved farther and farther south and east, into Rumania and Russia, and included a variety of performers. They were to form the nucleus of the movement toward a new Yiddish theater and to lay the groundwork for a whole new conception: the Yiddish popular song.

Beyond the older folk and newer literary and popular layers of the repertoire, numerous contributions emerge with the changing times. Social movements emerge as the century wanes: various shades of socialism, communism, anarchism, Zionism, or general "national" trends spring up after the severe repression of the Jews in 1881. All of these share a musical approach common to new social movements the world over—older songs are adapted, and new means of musical expression are sought at the same time. Such movements may also create whole new aspects of social organization and context, as in the case of workers' choruses, Zionist singing societies, mandolin orchestras, and other innovations. These are fairly late to develop, crystallizing only after 1900, so they are contemporary with—and responsive to—the immigrant music. Rumshinsky is generally credited with the first well-known Jewish chorus, in Lodz (Poland) around 1900. Named Hazomir, the group is said to have inspired the later, larger Warsaw choruses. Their repertoire consisted largely of "national" Hebrew songs, which coexisted with Rumshinsky's work in the Yiddish theater.

At the same moment, not far away in Galicia, Jacob Shaefer was combining cantorial training with socialist ideas. These activities were to bear fruit in America, where he organized the first socialist choruses in Chicago in 1914. Meanwhile, Jewish workers and artisans were translating and adapting the songs of Russian revolutionaries, particularly at the time of the 1905 Revolution. Trans-Atlantic currents were quite visible in this trend as well. The songs of the sweatshops and factories of New York came back to Europe and were localized, even to the point of substituting Russian words for English in the basically Yiddish texts.[12]

In the final analysis, it is difficult to generalize about the music culture of the Eastern European Jews because individual experience varied so widely. Repertoires were shaped by environment and acquisition patterns; they were not the same even among members of the same family, due to fluctuating social and economic situations and to personal networks and affinities. Among the dozen key informants of the YIVO project, no two have the same song profiles or even similar backgrounds. Some of their stories will be detailed below. Here we can begin by citing oral histories of three Jewish women; all are roughly of the same generation (born 1895–1906), and all spent most of their youth in Europe. The first, Pearl Moscowitz, lived in a rural setting, and has fond recollections of peasant songs: "[On the estate] the peasants would come during the summer to rake the hay and cut the wheat . . . they would get twenty-five cents a day for working; and they used to sing those Russian songs. What impressed me as a child—when they used to go home before sunset, the sun was just setting, and they'd put their rakes on their shoulders and they would sing those sweetest songs. To me, that was music and they were so happy." [13]

The second woman, Anuta Sharrow, lived in a small town linked to Kiev. Both of her parents had strong social aspirations. Her father built the first middle-class house in the town, which he outfitted with a baby grand piano bought in Kiev and meant for Anuta to play: "He was an artist at heart . . . a musician; and thanks to him that I know so much about music. He was very musical himself; in the army, he played trombone and cornet. In fact, they had a little orchestra of amateurs in Goronstaypol. He encouraged [me]; that shows you that there was a sense of culture, of art. He loved to go and listen to the *chazan*." [14] Here we have a middle-of-the-road situation: amateur musicians with sketchy mainstream musical knowledge (military band) who are still attached to the central in-group musical figure, the *khazn*.

At the other end of the spectrum we find the third woman, Katya Govsky, who straightforwardly begins by saying, "In Russia, all of our relatives were rich." She lived in Ekatorinoslav, a large city. Her father owned coal mines and belonged to a Jewish elite. The mother was the major musical influence on the girl's early life, and Mama's taste suited her social standing: "[There] was no Yiddish culture in our family. Mama couldn't speak Jewish well. . . . Ma used to go to the opera and the symphony. . . . she used to take us to musical recitals to appreciate good music, libraries to appreciate good books. She used to pack up the kids and go traveling to France, to Germany, to Latvia, Lithuania, Turkey. We were all over Russia . . . we always had people from the theaters, from the opera, from the symphony. Twelve o'clock at night the life started." [15] Clearly, Katya Govsky's repertoire would be vastly different from either Pearl Moscowitz's or Anuta Sharrow's. What is interesting is how much music surfaces as a focus of the women's recollections, although the oral histories were not gathered by folklorists or ethnomusicologists. That music was both ubiquitous and positively valued is clear from these accounts.

The complexity revealed by the foregoing spectrum of personal musical patterns gives only a general sketch. Examining a given individual's pattern of song acquisition discloses an almost bewildering variety of influences on a private repertoire. Each Jew's song-world seems to have been distinctive. Let us take a glimpse at the musical profile of Mariam Nirenberg, a folksinger of the YIVO project who has been the subject of an entire disc. We begin with the older generation's influence:

> My grandfather raised me. He used to be a dairyman . . . he had cows and he sold the milk as well as the butter and cheese he made himself. He used to sing a lot too, and I learned songs from him.

> My father remarried . . . with a beautiful young woman from Bialostok . . . she did a good job of bringing me up. She used to sing all the time. She sang beautifully, mostly old songs. She used to sing songs in Russian too, but I never learned those songs. I only learned the songs she sang in Yiddish. She used to sing funny little [children's] songs to us when we were small . . . when I got older I learned her old love songs.[16]

Quite a different set of songs came from her local non-Jewish peer group:

> All the peasant girls used to be my girlfriends. We used to go to the fields. I used to sing with them. We worked together cutting wheat, gathering potatoes. . . . I learned a lot of songs from them. We became very friendly. We were like one family, because it was a small town. In the spring we would get up at four in the morning . . . I would go with the peasant girls to the forest. We would gather wild raspberries and strawberries. Then we walked the twelve *viorst* [ca. 7 miles] to Brisk, singing all the way. In Brisk we would sell the berries at the hospital, and made a little money.

The Jewish peer group, however, had different activities, especially as they grew older: "I used to get together with my friends, boys and girls. We had fun together. There were about twenty, twenty-five kids. We drank tea and ate cake and sunflower seeds. We would sing, dance, tell jokes. And we played games . . . other times when we got together we had a gramophone with a big horn. There was only one in the whole town. We would dance to that music. Otherwise we sang the tunes ourselves."

Here we see how popular music made its way into village life. We are remarkably ill informed as to what records the young people might have been listening to in the provinces, but, judging by available sheet music, we can guess at a broad mixture of Polish and Russian pop songs (of American, South American, French, German, or local origin) and perhaps Jewish theater and vaudeville hits, some probably pressed in

America and distributed abroad, with others manufactured in Poland, some of the latter being bought up and distributed in America by firms like Columbia.

The communal life of a village provided other sources of repertoire as well:

> We used to dance at weddings. If it's a wedding in a little town, everybody goes. It doesn't matter if it's Jews or if it's Gentiles. They brought the *klezmorim* from Brisk—Antshl the *klezmer* and his band. They played fiddle, drum, and trumpet, and sometimes there was a *tsimbl* [hammered dulcimer]. And a *badkhn* came too. We did all kinds of dances: *koketke, kozatske, krakovyak, shrayer, sher, broyges tants, mitsve tants,* quadrille, waltz, parade waltz, charleston, tango, polka, fox trot, and other ones. Sometimes they would invite me and my brother to sing. We'd sing songs with a marriage theme during dinner.

The listing of dances is truly encyclopedic, ranging from nineteenth-century ballroom through Jewish folk up to the latest imported American styles—all this in a peasant village.

Harvesting the memoirs of a folksinger like Mariam Nirenberg, one is amazed at the sheer vivacity of the musical life of a small community: "The town was small, after all. If a guest visited, everyone got together. People who came to visit brought songs. When we used to go to another town, we learned new songs and brought them back. We always sang—while we worked, while we walked, when we got together. Sabbath and holidays the family sang *zmires* [table songs]." So runs the testimony of a single village-dweller, supposedly isolated in the closed world of the *shtetl*, that mythic Jewish world beloved of social scientists and writers of musicals. Clearly Mariam Nirenberg's evidence will not allow us to believe in a simple Old World music culture; even the excerpts given here fall far short of giving a well-rounded picture of her acquisition patterns and repertoire.

In one sense, the Jewish experience in Eastern Europe is similar to that of other ethnic groups. In a thorough recent study, Stephen Erdely[17] has shown how the present-day repertoire of two Hungarian-American folksingers, like the women we have just cited, is strongly conditioned by disparities in their early experiences in Europe. Similar studies could surely be done for any group of the region. In areas most heavily settled by Jews, non-Jews were a far from homogeneous population. The tangled and tumultuous period from the 1880s through 1945 saw large and small invasions, realignments, and mass emigration across all of Eastern Europe. In this context, the Jews were just one of many peoples who had to find cultural—and musical—solutions to times of trouble. Even today, when national boundaries and population shifts have produced relatively clean cut settlement patterns, areas like Transylvania show ethnic groups in tight, at times conflicting contact involving multi-lingualism and multi-musicality.

Yet differences mark off the Jews from their neighbors before 1939. In musical terms, several factors are distinctive. First, the use of two internal languages (Yiddish and Hebrew) with nearly universal literacy in at least one language was anomalous for Eastern Europe. The spread of the songs of literary origin and of a broadside tradition must have been facilitated by this phenomenon. Interpenetration of sacred and secular song involving two languages was also part of this situation, resulting in internally bilingual songs alongside those adapted from other languages. Second, the particular evolution of the role of cantor and choirboy is unparalleled in Christian culture. Third, the existence of a circumscribed internal group of instrumentalists (the *klezmorim*) is opposed to the non-Jews' reliance on a similar stigmatized group (the gypsies) who are beyond the ethnic boundary. Finally, a somewhat less easily definable factor is the Jewish tendency to use music as a way out of restrictive social circumstances. For comparison, one thinks of the Neapolitans, a cosmopolitan group who were repeatedly invaded and repressed and who evolved a pleasing and marketable musical style—all Europe and America sang (and still sing) so-called Neapolitan songs ("O Sole Mio"). In Italy, opera has, since the seventeenth century, offered an upward and outward path for gifted and energetic musicians of poor background. Similar as this approach to music may by, the Jewish experience is radically different. It is not Jewish music that Heifetz, Rubinstein, and Irving Berlin produced to improve their lot, but the elite and popular music of the general Euro-American market.

One remaining key difference between the Jews and their neighbors involves the Holocaust. With the destruction of the culture and its carriers in Eastern Europe, it is extremely difficult for us to fully understand the Jews' musical life. Though Hungarians, Poles, and Rumanians (among others) suffered greatly, their research institutes have restocked the destroyed archives and have turned out voluminous recordings and publications that detail the older musical traditions. A scholar of Hungarian-American song like Erdely can find all the variants he needs in Budapest as a control on his study; in contrast, the student of Jewish-American music has no such resource available.

One final point regarding repertoire. Despite all the diversity of individual song profiles, we must also remember that some songs were shared by a large majority of Eastern European Jews. Along with ethnic food, clothing, and folkways, song is one of the great unifiers of an ethnic group. In 1979 a moving tribute was paid to Molly Picon, one of the great Jewish-American entertainers, on her eightieth birthday. An emotional high point was the audience's singing along with the song "Rozhinkes mit mandlen" ("Raisins and Almonds"), a folk-based theater song that became folklorized as a lullaby. Its use as a bedtime song put it right at the heart of the expressive culture, where it formed part of early memory; as a result, it is one of the most widely known songs among Eastern European Jews. Another classic lullaby, Sholom Aleichem's "Shlof mayn kind" ("Sleep, My Child"), has been traced by Mlotek from its first publication in Kiev.[18] Within six years the song had blanketed the Yiddish-speaking world in folklorized versions.

It is tragic that we know so little about the scope and diversity of the musical life of Eastern European Jews. What we can tell is that, despite some shared aspects, there was no simple, self-contained "Old World." It is also clear that there is no room for pat labels such as "Jewish," or even "folk." What we can sense, all too dimly, is a musical culture with a long and tortuous past of movement and change. New conditions called for novel musical solutions for unprecedented circumstances, particularly in the late nineteenth century, when the pace of change picked up. It is from this fertile musical soil that a generation of immigrant musicians will spring, ready to take on the challenges of a strange and musically uncharted continent. To understand how they bridged the trans-Atlantic gap, we must first survey their kaleidoscopic—if not checkered—careers in Europe, where the young vacillated between the altar and the music hall.

NOTES

1. Barbara Kirshenblatt-Gimblett, "The 'Shtetl' Model in East European Jewish Ethnography," paper delivered at the Conference on Jewish Folklore of the Association of Jewish Studies, May 2, 1977. The paper is based on notes of Margaret Mead's seminar which culminated in the production of *Life Is With People*. The deliberate selectivity of the book, and of the *shtetl* model of Eastern European Jewish culture it helped create, have influenced the self-perception of Jewish-Americans for nearly thirty years.
2. S. M. Ginzburg and P. S. Marek, *Evreiskie narodnye pesni v Rossii* (St. Petersburg: Voskhod, 1901).
3. Cited in Steve Zipperstein, "Jewish Enlightenment in Odessa: Cultural

Characteristics, 1794–1871," unpublished paper for YIVO Institute for Jewish Research, 1979.

4. *Stempenyu* has recently become available in a new English translation as part of an anthology called *The Shtetl*, ed. and trans. J. Neugroschel (New York: Richard Marek, 1979). The translation here is my own.

5. A. Chekhov, "Rothschild's Fiddle," *Rothschild's Fiddle and Other Stories*, (New York: Boni & Liveright, n.d.); passages quoted are from p. 2 and pp. 11–12.

6. I am grateful to Ghisela Suliţeanu, Mariana Kahane, and Elisabeta Cernea, Rumanian ethnomusicologists, for this information (1974).

7. Mendele Mocher Seforim, *Fishke the Lame*, trans. G. Stillman (New York, 1960).

8. The anecdote is in Thomashefsky's memoirs, *Mayn lebns-geshikhte/The Book of My Life* (New York: Trio Press, 1937), pp. 14–16.

9. Eleanor Gordon Mlotek, "International Motifs in the Yiddish Ballad," *For Max Weinreich on His Seventieth Birthday* (The Hague: Mouton, 1964), pp. 209–28.

10. Max Wohlberg, "The Music of the Synagogue as a Source of the Yiddish Folksong," *Musica Judaica* 2, no. 1 (1979): 21.

11. Dan Miron, *A Traveler Disguised: The Rise of Modern Yiddish Fiction in the Nineteenth Century* (New York: Schocken, 1973).

12. Sh. Z. Pipe, "Folklorizirungen fun D. Edelshtats 'Der arbeter,'" in D. and M. Noy, eds., *Folklore Research Center Studies* (Jerusalem: Hebrew University, 1971), II, 333–54.

13. S. Kramer and J. Masur, eds., *Jewish Grandmothers* (Boston: Beacon Press, 1976), p. 49.

14. Ibid., p. 78.

15. Ibid., p. 62.

16. This and the following four quotations are from unpublished interviews of Mariam Nierenberg by Barbara Kirshenblatt-Gimblett for the YIVO Jewish Folksong Project.

17. Stephen Erdely, "Traditional and Individual Traits in the Songs of Three Hungarian-Americans," *Selected Reports in Ethnomusicology* 3, no. 1 (Los Angeles: UCLA, 1978): 99–152.

18. Eleanor Gordon Mlotek, "America in East European Jewish Folksong," in U. Weinreich, ed., *The Field of Yiddish* (New York: Linguistic Circle of New York, 1954), pp. 184–85.

CHAPTER 2

PREFABRICATING A POPULAR MUSIC

> At that time the *shul* [synagogue]
> and the *khazn* [cantor] were, for Jews,
> the opera, the operetta, and the symphony.
>
> —JOSEPH RUMSHINSKY[1]

Brody, Friedsell, Gilrod, Mogulesco, Perlmutter, Rumshinsky, Wohl . . .
the names mean little now, outside a small circle of Yiddish theater
aficionados. Even there these pioneers are not accorded the respect paid
to their inheritors, the generation of Secunda, Olshanetsky, and Ell-
stein, the later composers of the 1920s–1950s. After all, the younger
group put the Yiddish sound on the American musical map through
songs like "Bei mir bist du sheyn," which can still be heard frequently at
Jewish events and occasionally in international background music. Yet
the success of the later Broadway-oriented musicians would have been
impossible without the existence of a specifically Eastern European
Jewish popular music, a style created by the group we will call the
choirboys. Their strictly musical development will be the subject of a
later chapter; for now, their biographies will provide a backdrop for the
remarkable flourishing of early immigrant music. They form the living
bridge between musical worlds.

When Sigmund Mogulesco (1856–1914) was first approached by
Abe Cahan, the powerful editor of the *Forverts* (the major Yiddish
newspaper), the great comedian and songwriter was surprised that
anyone might be interested in writing about his childhood.[2] His idea of a
memoir was to outline his role in the founding of the early Yiddish
theater in the late 1870s. Fortunately for us, Cahan was perceptive
enough to realize that the formative period of musicians like Mogulesco

lay far back in boyhood, since virtually every one of the men listed above began his professional life as a choirboy (*meshoyrer*). Among the many paradoxes of what is loosely called "Yiddish culture" is the flowering of a modern secular musical style grown from sacred roots, a paradox once again explained by the extraordinary interpenetration of musical spheres among Eastern European Jews.

Mogulesco's story, like that of many a colleague, begins in an obscure corner of the Russian Empire. His father, a humble mechanic, died when the future Sigmund, then Zeligl, was nine. It was his mother who saw him through. She had *yikhes*, that list of respected forebears so highly valued in her culture; but, more important, she was musical. Indeed, she then married a cantor, so Mogulesco encountered the world of professional music at home. Soon thereafter the little boy's singing ability was noticed (and probably encouraged), and his mother decided to apprentice him to a *khazn*. Simple necessity must have played a part in this decision—after all, where else could a mother farm out a child of nine and still feel that he was not only earning his keep, but also quite possibly beginning a lifelong career? As audition numbers for his future master, a boy like Zeligl could sing only the best-known tunes. In Mogulesco's case, a Ukrainian song first sprang to his lips when he faced the cantor; he switched to sacred songs only when asked. This small but revealing anecdote only confirms the close ties not only between sacred and secular, but also between Jewish and non-Jewish.

With the true showman's care for matters of payment, Mogulesco remembered the exact details of his first contract. He was to receive three years of free clothes, board, lodging, and a small salary with an escalator clause: five rubles the first year, ten the second, and fifteen the third. It is hard to know whether this was typical for the period, in the absence of statistically significant data on the *meshoyrer* system. What we can assume is that his mother could heave a sigh of relief at finding her nine-year-old son so well set up in life. An added stipulation should be mentioned: the new choirboy was not allowed to sit at table with the cantor's family until he became a soloist.

Mogulesco's good memory is also helpful in fixing the pattern of music education he considered normal for boys like himself. The novice began simply by listening, using the age-old process of aural learning common to folk music cultures the world over. The cantor seems to have spent little time with the *meshoyrer* at this stage, trusting to the boy's innate abilities to absorb the basic repertoire of the particular synagogue to which he was attached. Only after this stage of osmosis was past was the choirboy given permission to advance. His promotion was twofold: first the boy was allowed to enter the choir, and then he could learn to read music. The learning process for notation was expected to take quite a while. Mogulesco, always eager to rise, had the older boys teach him ahead of schedule, and was proud of learning to read music within four months. The surprised cantor gave the young choirboy the sobriquet "Zeligl der notnfresser" ("Little Zelig the Note-Gobbler"). This was apparently a standard epithet, since in his memoirs Joseph Rumshinsky flaunts the same term (in his case, "Yoshke der notnfresser").

Of this earlier period, Mogulesco has one striking memory. It happened that his first cantor took the choir to sing for a famous rabbi. The sage distributed coins to the choirboys, giving Zeligl twenty kopeks instead of the ten allotted the others. Going home, Mogulesco couldn't help spending five kopeks on watermelon, which meant he had to pass off the fifteen kopeks in change as the coins the rabbi had given him. So overwhelmed was his mother at the thought of having the money come to her directly from the rabbi's hand that she treasured the kopeks all her life, never spending them. Mogulesco's guilt at this seemingly slight deception is palpable in his telling of the story. Here a single anecdote illuminates two sides of the *meshoyrer* system: from the boy's point of view, we sense the conflict between duty to mother and the pull toward enjoying one's hard-earned professional pay; from the mother's vantage point, we feel how intense the satisfaction can be when her child acts as mediator between the rabbi's holiness and her humble self.

However, the more usual outcome of the system was the separation of parents and child—guilt and satisfaction had to be felt at a distance. Among the most talented boy singers, an itinerant lifestyle seems to have begun at an early age. Mogulesco had not yet reached the bar mitzvah age of thirteen before he was literally stolen away from his first master by a rival *khazn*. This competitor was none other than the celebrated Nisi Belzer, one of the best-known cantors of the late nineteenth century. Nisi was famous not so much for his extraordinary singing as for his innate musicality and his ability to put together exceptional choirs. No wonder, then, that he got his *meshoyrers* by hook or by crook. But Nisi's activities were not without redeeming features: he raised Zeligl's salary to sixty rubles a year plus 12 percent of whatever the choir earned on the side, a generous offer by any standards. Mogulesco now found himself in Kishinev, an important Jewish city in Rumania (now capital of the Moldavian SSR).

Training with Nisi could count for a great deal in a fledgling musician's career. (Boris Thomashefsky, later a grandee of the Yiddish stage, was initially received in America as a boy who had sung under Nisi Belzer.[3] The day his boat docked, little Boris, the only possible breadwinner in the family, was approached by a congregation who had simply heard that "a *meshoyrer* of Nisi's was on the ship.") Mogulesco seems to have spent only a little time with the great Nisi before he was again kidnapped, this time by a *khazn* named Kuper, who removed Zeligl to the metropolis of Bucharest. By the age of fourteen, Mogulesco was Kuper's choir director, running rehearsals and organizing concerts on his own.

So far we have dealt—with the exception of a Ukrainian song—with the internal musical world only. The stew thickens when various Rumanian spices are added. One way or another, Mogulesco was attracted to the Conservatory while doing his cantorial work; Jewish sacred song was apparently much appreciated in certain Christian precincts. One of the most interesting features of the memoir literature on the *meshoyrer* system is the depiction of apparent acceptance by the non-Jewish musical world of the training and performance standards of the cantorial milieu. In Mogulesco's case, he was able to attend classes at the Conservatory and simultaneously to perform at the Royal Opera House. French operettas were beginning to be translated into Rumanian around 1870; along with three other of Cantor Kuper's choirboys, Mogulesco was invited to perform secular European roles. Following this success, they toured Rumania as *Chor Israelit* ("Jewish Chorus").

Stepping even further beyond the bounds of Jewish music, Zeligl and his friends ventured into very dangerous ground by accepting Sunday jobs in Rumanian Orthodox churches. With boyhood trepidation still evident, Mogulesco described the time when the sexton of his synagogue nearly saw the future star of the Yiddish stage carrying an icon in a church procession. Even more risky was the offer of scholarships to study voice in Italy. The price tag of the forbidden musical fruit was high: conversion. The little band of *meshoyrers* almost took the bait; only at the last minute did Kuper's choirboys excuse themselves, during a pause in the conversion process, to retire to a cafe and think things over. Perhaps the sight of food reminded them that Yom Kippur was quickly approaching, and they decided to return to the synagogue to chime in for "Kol Nidre," the most solemn sacred song of the year. Fifty years later, the same choice would be played out on the silver screen in the pioneer talkie film, *The Jazz Singer*. Of course, Broadway instead of Italy was the bait for the character played by Al Jolson; but "Kol Nidre" was the decisive performance in question in both cases. In the movie, Jolson got to have the best of both worlds, "Kol Nidre" and Broadway fame, while Mogulesco stayed within the bounds of ethnic entertainment, albeit secular instead of sacred. The options change for later generations, but the conflict of tradition versus innovation marked the performer's life in both Europe and America.

The rest of Mogulesco's tale is, as they say, history. The acting talent he began to show at the Royal Opera House led him to the embryonic Yiddish professional theater being created in Rumania by Abraham Goldfadn. Goldfadn (1840–1908) had been extensively discussed in works on the Yiddish theater, of which he is invariably given as being the father. He fits right in with the other figures we are looking at: ". . . by nature he was a trouper, an artist, a dreamer, an intellectual, a hustler, a scrapper, a con man, a romantic, a dandy, an optimist, and a one-man band—and his child was a chip off the old block." [4] Goldfadn's musical role will be examined in detail in a later chapter. Though his status as founding father was unquestionably important, he took his duties too seriously: "Goldfadn ruled the members of his companies with a heavy paternal hand—not only their performances, but their lives. . . . In later years it turned out that they'd resented his authority bitterly all along and they made him pay." [5] So it was that Mogulesco and Goldfadn parted after a short collaboration. Zeligl, now Sigmund, ended up in New York in the early 1880s with the first massive wave of immigration, just in time to become the dominant figure of the early Yiddish stage. As the *Forverts* said in its obituary, "Mogulesco has always been the most talented, the central figure of the Yiddish theater." [6] He managed to combine comic acting of the highest order with a deceptively facile gift for tuneful, folksy melodies and texts that bridged the gap between the folk and cantorial worlds of Eastern Europe, with their strong imprint of variegated non-Jewish sources, and the emerging pop music of the Jewish-Americans.

Meanwhile, back in Russia, the strain of being a child professional, combined with the complexity of career choices, continued to mark the next generation of composers. This breathless pace of musical maturation makes the memoirs of Rumshinsky absorbing reading. [7] Fifteen years younger than Mogulesco, Rumshinsky came of age in the 1890s, when there was an already established Yiddish theater and a Jewish popular music style. It was also the heyday of pre-Revolutionary salon and cabaret music in Russia, and all these streams flowed through his musical life. Coming to America in 1906, Rumshinsky became the most prolific and influential of the operetta composers. He lived through the transition from the older European-based plots and musical styles to the advent of the lighter Americanized shows that set popular taste in the 1920s. In the jubilee book prepared for his fiftieth birthday in 1931, luminaries of the Jewish show business world shower praise on Rumshinsky for his thorough professionalism and his transformation of Jewish-American style. Looking at the early life of this key figure can help us to understand the evolution of mainstream immigrant music.

Unlike most movers and shapers of Yiddish popular culture, Rumshinsky came from the North, from Vilna, instead of from Galicia or the Ukraine. He himself notes that show people at first found his dialect hard to take, because they were unaccustomed to the sibilant sound of *litvak* (Lithuanian) Yiddish. Like Mogulesco and most other founders of Yiddish popular music, Rumshinsky did not inherit his musical calling directly, but fell into its path accidentally. This is an important point, since it distinguishes the choirboys from the children of *klezmorim* (instrumentalists). The latter's entry into a musical life tended to be more ascribed than achieved: their fathers were musicians. The category of *meshoyrer* seems to have been open to recruiting from the widest possible pool of talent. It is hardly surprising, then, that choirboys tended to be enterprising, and often freethinking, fellows. In this respect the figure portrayed in the Broadway and Hollywood versions of *The Jazz Singer* rings somewhat false, as his burden is said to be the heritage of four generations of cantors. Certainly it was possible for a *khazn* to train his son to follow in his path, yet it appears that the type of boy who would be interested in leaving home to become a jazz singer (or its equivalent in Russia) need not have been a cantor's son; indeed, he need not even have been directly in conflict with sacred song, since he could perform a variety of styles while still a boy. If the dilemma of freedom versus inherited career choice really did hold true in America, the New World was more old-fashioned than the Old.

Rumshinsky seems to have gotten his musical background in the usual folk way—through oral/aural transmission:

> My father . . . used to express his feelings by singing, together with his five or six workers, hatter-apprentices. When life was going along as usual, he would sing bits and proverbs from *Ethics of the Fathers*, which he knew by heart. He would start in Hebrew and then translate into Yiddish, then improvise the music in his own special way. . . . If circumstances were depressing, such as money matters or, God forbid, illness at home, father would sing chapters from the Psalms . . . with the harmony of the apprentices; it would melt your heart with its sweetness and sadness. And again, when Father had a good day at the market with the peasants, to whom he used to sell his hats . . . then he was the soloist, the *zapievala* as they call it in Russian, that is, he would begin, and everybody would

join in. The happy songs consisted of half-Russian, half-Polish, mixed in with Yiddish and Hebrew, and the work would follow along with the tempo and the mood of the music.

Rumshinsky's early aural training was particularly marked, since he suffered from some sort of disease which entailed his being planted in a bucket of sand to correct a leg problem. Immobilized until the age of six, he was all ears. As the above passage indicates, there was a lot to hear: song texts in four languages, music for all moods and times of the year, in-group and outside styles. The accurate use of the Russian term *zapievala* for the leader of the call-response style of song indicates how carefully the Jews performed their chosen repertoires. Success at the market logically accompanies the singing of market (i.e., peasant) songs.

Yet we have touched upon only half of Rumshinsky's childhood training. He goes on to say:

> Mother's musical career went farther than Father's . . . [she] was actually a teacher of singing. . . . Not, God forbid, for money! But women, unmarried girls, matrons, would come to Slova to sing with her, and really learn the songs they used to hear at weddings from the *badkhonim*. The eighties of the last century was the most magnificent period for the *badkhn*. . . . The greatest busy season my mother had . . . was when Eliokum Zunser published his ten songs. Everybody used to come with their booklets and mother would sing with the women.
>
> Even though my parents were not professional musicians, I still felt I was born into a musical atmosphere. I must confess that with all of my musical training . . . I have my parents to thank for my career as a composer because my successes, all the melodies which captured all those who spoke Yiddish, resulted from their influence.

Rumshinsky's account supports the outline of the music culture given earlier, with the stress on eclecticism and the positive value of amateur song. The mention of Zunser is significant, since his work falls between the folk world of the *badkhn* and the professionalism of the wandering minstrels who took the *badkhn*'s role of social critic and merry-maker onto the streets. Notice the mention of "booklets": the transformation of the folk music culture from strictly oral to at least partly literate is a symptom of the emergence of a popular music culture.

Little Yoshke Rumshinsky was inexorably drawn to performance as soon as he could use his legs. By the age of seven or eight he was taken to the Vilna city cantor for an audition. He sang a bit of sacred song and two Zunser compositions. That evening he heard a full chorus for the first time, singing a composition of Lewandowski, an extremely popular cantorial composer who used a highly Westernized style. Yoshke nearly fainted from the terror and pleasure of so much concentrated music. From that point on it became inevitable that the boy would drift into a musical life. The pace of the action picked up dramatically upon the death of his mother and the entrance of a wicked stepmother. (This sort of life crisis often precipitates a move toward music. We have seen how the arrival of Mogulesco's stepfather came just before his mother apprenticed the boy. An unfeeling stepmother also seems to have served as the impetus for the young Al Jolson to take to the streets in song. The important perspective here is one which views American musicians' experiences as similar in many ways to those of European Jewish artists; after all, Jolson and Rumshinsky both belong to the generation of the 1880s.)

The next stage in Yoshke's development deviates from Mogulesco's. The boy heard how successful certain Jewish singers could become, even singing before the czar, if they had a Russian education. Yoshke convinced his father to enroll him in a kind of prep school which differed markedly from the traditional *kheydr* classroom. In the latter "the smells were of Jewish foods and the sounds were loud; here the smells were of pork and it was quiet." Within a month the boy learned to read music and was introduced to a kind lady who taught him some piano. This woman, Mrs. Trotsky, had been a student at the St. Petersburg Conservatory. In short, the musical life of a modern city like Vilna, close to the centers of Russian music, offered a broad range of experiences. For instance, the first concert at which Rumshinsky sang a solo was an event combining all the educational institutions of the city, ranging from the Russian school through the Jewish Teachers' Seminary, held at the palace of the governor-general. Yoshke's solo fell in the Russian soldier's song "Ekh ty zimushka zima," in which he and a Russian colonel's son sang alternate verses.

One more anecdote of these earliest years is worth retelling. For a time Rumshinsky was sent to a village to stay with his brother, who lived not far from a Polish church. Spellbound by the sound of the organ, he was easy prey for the church musician, who brought the boy into the church and promised to teach him harmony. Here the biography parallels Mogulesco's, indicating a striking similarity in career development. Younger than Mogulesco when he was tempted by the Gentile, Rumshinsky was roundly scolded by his brother and shipped out of the village before he could come to spiritual harm. The musical ethnic boundary stopped not at the door of the opera house, as for Mogulesco, but at the church gates. Leaving the village, the wavering Rumshinsky was beset by one last appeal. The sound of peasant girls singing "gripped me. I had the feeling that I was sinning again, because everything that was *goyish* [Gentile] appealed to me. I began to sing, out loud, my mother's song 'In der Sokhe' [a Zunser song], and Yankel said, 'This is much prettier. . . . Yoshkele, this way I'd like to travel with you all the way to America.' "

His journey to the New World was still fourteen years away. During that time Rumshinsky faced and resolved many questions of career choice, too numerous to detail here. A brief outline will indicate the wealth of possibilities open to a gifted young Jewish musician in the last decades of the Russian Empire, and will indicate the Old World training that an immigrant composer could fall back upon when encountering America.

Sacred music. The initial impetus for Rumshinsky to leave his native Vilna was, as usual, a contract for apprenticeship to a noted *khazn*—in this case, Razumny of Odessa. Though he never made it to Odessa, "jumping ship" on the way with a band of Yiddish theater folk, Yoshke kept signing on with cantors at various times in his career, doing part-time work while absorbing himself—often on the sly—in several varieties of secular music. Later in life, Rumshinsky came to feel that he should put more time into sacred song and he wrote numerous choral compositions. In this impulse he was not alone. Nearly all the figures listed at the beginning of this chapter spent part of their time writing for the synagogue, with several musicians (e.g., Wohl) devoting a great deal of energy to liturgical music. The younger generation of popular composers, like Secunda, did the same. In this drive to balance the secular with the sacred they were joined by various outstanding singers, such as Jan Peerce and Richard Tucker, who always found time to officiate for the High Holidays and to put out records of religious music while keeping up busy opera careers. One is tempted to make an analogy to the world of jazz, in which many great performers (Duke Ellington, Mary Lou Williams) pay tribute to the church at one time or another while devoting their lives to secular music.

Yiddish theater music. The world of the theater, which irresistibly pulled Yoshke away from Cantor Razumny, was to be Rumshinsky's life's work. Writing fifty years after first seeing *Shulamis*, Goldfadn's music drama set in biblical times, Rumshinsky was able to describe his awed excitement in full detail. Little by little he heard the call of the theater louder than any of the competing musical voices in his life. He spent some time with the finest early Polish troupe, that of the great actress Esther-Rokhl Kaminska, but it was too hard to make a living writing for the Yiddish stage in Europe. Since the czar had proscribed Yiddish theater, it inhabited a social limbo, masquerading as German drama or getting temporary licenses. Even in America, Rumshinsky was slow to break into the tightly controlled guild of Jewish thespians, and his impact began to be felt only after 1910.

Yet what is clear in the memoirs is the interplay between all sorts of sacred and secular music. Leading singer-actors of the Yiddish stage doubled as choir soloists—adult *meshoyrers*—in major synagogues. The Grodno cantor, being up-to-date, not only allowed Yoshke to sing in the Russian theater, but was grateful for free tickets to the shows. It is the much-too-clear vision of hindsight that has allowed us to erect barriers between these musical worlds.

Secular Non-Jewish Music. By the time of his bar mitzvah, Rumshinsky had already had a great variety of European musical experiences. While "the entire Jewish theater with its songs simply enchanted" him, "a close second was the Russian operetta, especially the tenor Mikhailov. . . . Mikhailov came to love me as if I had been his own child. He actually wanted to adopt me. As for Demidovich, the director of the Russian operetta, I have a lot to thank him for in my musical career."

Intra-Jewish networks were also important in the Europeanization of the *meshoyrer.* In Yiddish culture, non-Jewish vocabulary and co-territorial songs passed from Jew to Jew in separate and distinct patterns of diffusion. A Russian or German word or song might be learned from a Jewish relative or friend, rather than from a member of the appropriate non-Jewish ethnic group. Popular and classical musical styles were also transmitted within Jewish circles; we have already seen that Rumshinsky's first brush with piano came from a Jewish conservatory graduate, Mrs. Trotsky. Now the singer-composer Rozhansky taught him the Russian operetta repertoire, along with popular songs. Rozhansky, like more prominent Jewish urban composers (Shteinberg, Fel'dman) wrote songs in the gypsy vein which would sell to the parlor piano players of Russia. Another profitable market was the military band of the local czarist garrison, which played music for skating on the river in winter.

The Jewish penchant for filling every available niche in the musical ecology was learned early, and the lesson carried over to America. Rozhansky came to New York and teamed up with a partner to found the large piano establishment of Perlman and Rozhansky. This duo made recording history before 1910 by founding the first independent

Jewish label, and perhaps the first in-group ethnic record label in the United States: the Hebrew Disc and Cylinder Company. Such commercialism had its price: "In spite of the comfortable living he made in America he [Rozhansky] was a disappointed, unhappy, dissatisfied man. He missed the music and theater very much."

Rumshinsky's brush with the German circus of Bialostok, which hired him to direct Goldfadn among the acrobats, has already been cited. Moving to Dvinsk at the behest of the Bialostok Jewish musicians, who wanted to save Rumshinsky from the circus, things changed little. He carried on with a *femme fatale* Russian actress and a young revolutionary girl who was sent to Siberia, while simultaneously working for the synagogue and the Yiddish theater. Finally, he published his first composition ("Eastern Echoes," a skating waltz) as a farewell to Dvinsk before shoving off for Elizavetgrad. And so it went. From station to station of his career, the young composer tacked on more and more varied types of repertoire, outlook, and training. In the booming industrial city of Lodz he helped shape an altogether new type of musical organization.

Jewish "National" Music. In Lodz, Rumshinsky founded an amateur chorus named *Hazomir* ("Nightingale"). This group, which faced considerable parental opposition because of its progressive caste, was dedicated to the performance of nationalistic songs, mainly in Hebrew: "A thirst began to be felt for a Jewish song, Jewish notes, especially among the young people with progressive, national Jewish feelings. This included teachers, bookkeepers, doctors, clerks. They envied the German and Polish singing group, which had been in existence for the past fifty or sixty years." Realizing that to flaunt Jewish ethnicity was to court disaster in the form of czarist police repression, a lawyer named Shapiro petitioned the government to charter the new singing group in a roundabout way. He sought permission "to set up a Jewish song group in order to win young people away from the godless revolutionary notions and meetings which were poisoning their minds. . . . 'Let the whippersnappers amuse themselves with poetry and singing, and they'll have no thought of foolishness.' The idea appealed to the government, which issued a charter, and instructed the police not to disturb the meetings of the song group."

Rumshinsky's choir seems to have been a pioneering organization, and to have influenced the formation of similar groups in Warsaw and elsewhere. Opposition within the Jewish community was hardly absent, with the criticisms reflecting general cultural-political rifts. "The assimilationists complained: 'To whom do they think they're showing off their art? To the Polish group with a director . . . who got the

Rubinstein prize in Paris? . . . Or to the great German group? . . . And the Hasidic Jews simply shouted 'Gevalt! Young men and women together!' . . . The Zionist youth came to ridicule, and the assimilationists came to see how the little yids tried to ape the Gentiles."

Nevertheless, the idea of a national chorus gained momentum. This period, around 1900, also saw the birth of the movement toward a Jewish art music, an entire field of Jewish music we will have little space to discuss. Largely at the suggestion of Rimsky-Korsakov, who was surprised that his Jewish students used Russian instead of Jewish themes in their compositions, a group of Conservatory students began to write pieces with a marked ethnic flavor. They were also involved in the early collection of Jewish folksongs as they searched for musical roots. Some of these pioneers came to the United States, while others went to Israel, helping to found the national school of composition there. The striving of this group of composers toward a legitimate Jewish art music has not received the attention it deserves, though recent concerts and studies in America and Israel indicate a strong reawakening of interest in the early decades of Jewish "serious" music.

Rumshinsky's enthusiastic activities were brought to an abrupt halt in the usual manner: there arose the threat of being drafted into the czar's army. In short order he stole across the border, eventually found himself in London, by then almost a traditional stopping-place for Jewish actors and musicians, and later passed through the gates of Ellis Island. Now he would have to use his European knowhow in order to survive in America.

"Since I had already been in London, New York didn't surprise me much." Cosmopolitan training can count. In a very short time Rumshinsky found himself a congenial circle of writers and musicians, and he managed to find work as a hack arranger and piano teacher. His first paid job had nothing to do with either Jewish or American music, reinforcing the strategic value of eclecticism:

> While I was talking to Rusotto [an important immigrant arranger and composer], a lady came into the restaurant, a typical member of the Russian intelligentsia, Mrs. Eva Krantz. Rusotto explained to me . . . that she was playing the lead in Rubinstein's opera *The Demon*. . . . I told Rusotto I knew the opera, and that I had trained the choir to sing it at the Russian operetta in Dvinsk. . . . He told me that it would be hard for him to get enough music from Russia for the entire orchestra . . . so he asked me to arrange the entire opera . . . and to train the choir to sing it. He offered me forty dollars to do this.

So it was that a Russian-Jewish musician could start a career in America arranging a Russian opera. Rusotto, about whom very little is known, was quite a figure at that time. He had been director of the Vilna Choir School when Rumshinsky was a boy alto there. Marrying a girl named Rusotto, he changed his name from Nisvizhevsky—probably to sound more Italian, and hence more imposing, as a musician. His name and face stare out at us from dozens of sheet music folios of the immigrant period, since he was the staff arranger for various publishers. It is hard to tell how many works he actually composed; "by Rusotto" appears in many cases when the piece is clearly just an arrangement.

Rusotto did Rumshinsky another good turn by introducing him to a certain S. Goldberg. This gentleman owned an important music store on the Lower East Side and was one of the earliest immigrant music publishers, being included in the official Copyright Office index of sheet music in 1908. Just as Rozhansky teamed up with Perlman to sell pianos, so Rumshinsky joined forces with Goldberg to stimulate piano playing. Goldberg quickly saw the possibility of having Rumshinsky grind out easy pieces that could be published and displayed in the shop window. Then fledgling pianists could come to study with the composer himself, in a small room "upstairs back":

> Almost every poor working man that lived in more than two
> rooms had a piano. . . . Since Goldberg's music store was deco-
> rated with my compositions, he found it easy to supply me
> with students. The idea of having the composer also become
> the teacher appealed to many people, so I got busy, busy,
> busy. . . . From ten in the morning until three in the afternoon
> I taught young women, recently married, who wanted to show
> their husbands they could play piano. From three until seven I
> taught school children. And from then until ten or eleven in
> the evening I taught shop girls and office girls who wanted to
> get married. . . . In those days if you wanted to make a living
> as a piano teacher on the East Side, you had to take on a great
> many students at a quarter a lesson. However, since I was also
> the composer, they paid me fifty cents, seventy-five cents, and
> a few paid a dollar.

In short, Rumshinsky had stumbled into America during the heyday of the piano. As Arthur Loesser, historian of the piano's role in Western culture, has pointed out, "most of the enormous expansion of the American piano market took place between 1890 and 1910. . . . From 1900 to 1910 the rate of piano increase was 6.2 times as high as that of human beings." [8] Never again would the instrument be so much in demand. The high point of pianomania fell in the period when the choirboys' style set the pace for Jewish-American music and when Jewish sheet music began to proliferate.

On the surface, it would seem that the immigrants were only part of this vast wave of piano fever. It might also be assumed that, as ordinary European hack musicians, the choirboys were using the training that the Russian taste for the piano had required of them "back home." Yet such conclusions would be premature. Let us turn back to the Old World situation. How exceptional was the work of Rumshinsky & Co. in Russia? Loesser tells us that

> in 1910 Russian piano production and consumption amounted to less than six per cent of that of the United States, thus revealing the relative insignificance of the prosperous middle class in the vast empire. Serious professional music education hardly existed in Russia until . . . 1859. . . . Under the circumstances, it is interesting to contemplate the numbers of remarkable composers for the piano, and the outstanding virtuosos of the instrument that came forth from later Imperial Russia.[9]

Some of these concert artists (Josef Lhevinne, Artur Rubinstein) were upward-striving Jews. It seems that the group's traditional drive for an escape from the doldrums of Russian life led musically talented individuals both to compose and arrange popular music and to take to the concert stage for classical careers. Loesser's statistics show that it was just as difficult to succeed in one musical sphere as in another: becoming a skating-waltz composer or a piano virtuoso were both unlikely means of employment at that place and time, and Jews took both paths.

As to the American situation, Loesser's admirable study of the social history of the piano seems to sidestep a particular immigrant interest in the coveted middle-class instrument. Rumshinsky's description of East Side pianomania fits nicely with Loesser's judgement: "The piano was much bought and drummed; but it was not in 1887, nor did it ever afterward become, a possession of the 'masses.' There were, indeed, vast segments of the population—subsistence farmers, agricultural laborers, Southern Negroes, hillbillies, factory workers, mariners', fishermens', and loggers' families, and hordes of city workers in service occupations—to whom a piano and its use were foreign." [10] Though his list fails to exclude New York garment workers, Loesser does not raise the possibility that sales to urban working-class immigrants (Jews and others) may have helped account for the burst in piano ownership. Of course, without statistical support we cannot determine if a decided socio-ethnic buying pattern did exist, but the possibility at least seems worth raising. Later American musical history shows that strong family emphasis on piano lessons as a necessary ritual of Jewish-American childhood went hand in hand with a powerful urge to excel in commercial mainstream, piano-based music. What is being posited in this chapter is that this generation provides the logical link between the Russian and American versions of a similar Jewish musical impulse. Having made the breakthrough in Europe, even though they themselves did not, on the whole, move into purely American styles, the choirboys' activities and example laid the groundwork for the Berlin-Kern-Gershwin generation. On the classical side, the American-born Menuhins and Isaac Sterns belong just as clearly to a European Jewish musical genealogy, that of the Elman generation pioneers.

One more case study of a choirboy's career will both sharpen and broaden our perspective on the group's background and contribution. In his earliest years Jacob Shaefer, of the Rumshinsky generation, had a career which paralleled that of the others we have examined.[11] His father was an artisan, a carpenter whose Hasidic leanings led him to constantly sing those eloquent textless tunes called *nigunim*. Little Jacob sang so well that he was told he would be a cantor, and he was apprenticed to one at age ten. Yet his career later took interesting twists that helped shape a different type of Jewish-American music. Before examining those detours, it is worth pausing for one childhood anecdote which underscores both the prominence of the piano and the underdog status of the Jewish musician. As a small boy, Jacob had heard about an instrument called the piano, although he had never seen one. He tried hard to imagine what it might look and sound like, and he constantly walked around his town (Kremeniec in Galicia) on the lookout for the fabled piano. Finally his patience was rewarded: in the threatening non-Jewish quarter of town he heard a strange and wonderful sound which he instinctively felt must come from a piano. He ventured closer day by day until he was set upon by a guard and bitten by the watchdog. The incident is almost a metaphor for the Jewish love affair with Gentile secular music: until the Jews learned to lull the watchdog with familiar tunes, the street was dangerous. Throughout his growing years, this incident burned in Shaefer's mind, and it heavily influenced the beginning of his important musical activity in America. Not until 1910, in Chicago, could he scrape together the money for a piano of his own; then he made an enormous effort to master the instrument in the shortest possible time.

Shaefer's account of his *meshoyrer* years is a strong indictment of the choirboy system. His first disappointment came at thirteen, when a cantor claimed credit for one of his own early compositions. This was followed by a cruel abduction. Needing a *meshoyrer* in his new position in Brod, the cantor spirited young Jacob away. This was not an ordinary kidnapping of the Mogulesco variety; the cantor insisted on parental approval, disguised the trip to Brody as a brief tour, and then kept the boy against his will for three years. Without the necessary visas to cross the bound from Russian-ruled Galicia to Brody, in Austria-Hungary, the parents were powerless in the face of the cantor's machinations.

On his return to Poland, Shaefer found himself drawn to leftist discussion groups, perhaps due to his experience of exploitation. A lively interest in the oppressed led him away from the path of a Rumshinsky. (The latter was upset to see his girlfriend Sonia sent to Siberia, but made no attempt to identify overtly with radical causes.) Shaefer stayed out of both sacred and commercial secular music, following his father's trade (carpentry) through the period of emigration. His drive to master the piano seems to have reawakened his dormant interest in musical activity, and this urge led him to take a step avoided by the other choirboys: creation of a leftist music in America. Shaefer's workers' choruses in 1911 Chicago set the pace for a new, socially committed musical style in the United States, soon to be followed by the Workmen's Circle choirs of the mid-teens. What was Shaefer's model? Just as Rumshinsky was inspired by the non-Jewish singing societies of Poland to form his "national" chorus in Lodz, so Shaefer is said to have been influenced by the well-organized German workers' singing societies in Chicago.

As diverse as the response by the *meshoyrer* generations was to the complex stimuli of the Euro-American musical scene, certain characteristic origins and impulses should by now be clear. These include an early, non-hereditary drive toward music, initially channeled into sacred song; rudimentary music education derived from the cantorial world, possibly with some early exposure to classical music; an interest in and susceptibility to a broad range of Jewish and non-Jewish secular styles; and a drive toward combining all the basic musical materials in order to create a new, lively Jewish-American style. Just how that style was shaped will occupy much of the mid-section of the present study. First we must look at the main road and the ethnic byways of nineteenth-century American music in order to put the choirboys' achievement in its proper context.

NOTES

1. Quoted in Z. Zilbertsvayg, *Leksikon fun yidishn teatr*, III, column 2153.
2. Mogulesco's memoirs appear in the *Forverts*, February 5–7, 1914, and are the sole source for the following account of his life.
3. Material on Thomashefsky's life is taken from his memoirs, *Mayn lebns-geshikhte/Book of My Life* (New York: Trio Press, 1937).
4. Nahma Sandrow, *Vagabond Stars: A World History of the Yiddish Theater* (New York: Harper & Row, 1977), p. 40.
5. Ibid., p. 52.
6. *Forverts*, February 6, 1914, p. 1.
7. Material on Rumshinsky's life is taken from his memoirs, *Klangn fun mayn lebn* (New York: Biderman, 1944), in an unpublished translation for the present book by Judith and Norval Slobin.
8. Arthur Loesser, *Men, Women & Pianos* (New York: Simon & Schuster, 1954), p. 549.
9. Ibid., p. 592.
10. Ibid., p. 540.
11. The account of Shaefer's life is from Y. V. Beylin, *Yakov Sheyfer: zayn lebn un shafn* (New York: Yidisher muzikalisher arbeterfarband, 1938).

CHAPTER 3

MEANWHILE,
IN AMERICA . . .

Her father keeps a hock shop
With three balls on the door
Where the Sheeny politicians can be found . . .
—OLD VAUDEVILLE SONG[1]

On October 24, 1881, as severe repression raged in czarist Russia, a New York audience braved a chill rain to attend Tony Pastor's first evening of an amusement he called "vaudeville." [2] Pastor, an amiable impresario and singer, meant to present good clean fun so the ladies and kiddies would swell the crowd. The opening-night program is worth a close look, since it succinctly indicates the major types of entertainment available to audiences on the very eve of massive Jewish immigration. It was the kind of diversion to which the immigrants' children would flock by century's end, and which they would eventually dominate.

The evening opened with Frank McNish doing an acrobatic "dumb" act, vaulting over barrels and tables to the accompaniment of a musical medley. Next came Ferguson Mack, who specialized in a rough Irish act. Their song, dance, and character routine was "a feeder for their feature known as the bumps, or hard falls on neck, shoulder and head. They finished with Mack sinking a hatchet in Ferguson's skull."

These pseudo-Irish types were followed by refugees from the minstrel show, Lester and Allen, "eccentric blackface comics combining song and dance with crossfire or question-and-answer dialogue." Naturally, the succeeding number had to be a "class" act: the French Twin Sisters, "who dressed alike and made interesting costume changes." Lillie Western then appeared as warm-up for the head of the bill, Ella Wesner. Lillie, dressed in a boy's outfit, did tricky numbers on the banjo and xylophone, which nicely prepared the way for Ella's male impersonation routine. Her sketches included a drunk getting a haircut and a military man named Captain Cuff. Dan Collyer was the last featured act, running through a number of English music-hall items, and Tony Pastor himself closed out the evening, delighting the audience with favorites such as "The Strawberry Blonde" and "Lula, the Beautiful Hebrew Girl." Douglas Gilbert, to whom we are indebted for this survey, points out that no one knows much about the latter song: "It is an unusual song for the period when humors and sentiment were mainly Irish, Dutch [i.e., German] and Negro." Jews would be added to the list in the 1890s, when there were enough of them near Fourteenth Street to parody.

This, then, was a large part of the world of entertainment the Jews would encounter. It was a grotesque microcosm of American society where, in almost ritual form, the major subcultures were held up to public view as ridiculous effigies. There are two basic reasons for setting foot in this swamp of stereotypes. First, prevailing American varieties of entertainment have influenced the Jews' own commercial diversions, from the very first days down to the present. In his memoirs Boris Thomashefsky relates how seeing an American melodrama in the late 1870s inspired him to dream of the Yiddish stage. Second, Jews were very quick to adapt to mainstream custom, and they helped shape and polish American forms. By the 1890s a pair of Lower East Side boys named themselves Weber and Fields and created the short fat/tall thin act (later Laurel and Hardy, Abbott and Costello), influencing vaudeville through their spectacular productions. So it is worth a backward glance to fix the origin and trace the evolution of the amusements that informed and delighted Americans.

From the 1820s to the 1840s the major genres of entertainment crystallize, each built upon an ethnic stereotype. All of them previously existed in England; indeed, much of the impetus for the creation of native forms of amusement came from traveling English actors and comedians, keen observers of the American scene. To set the American scene in perspective, we can look at the contents of an important compendium of English repertoire, the *Universal Songster* of 1826. Its headings include "Irish," "Scotch," "Jews," etc., including blacks and Indians, clearly laying out the common caricatures that shaped the New World stage. The index of first lines summarizes the character of the ethnic stereotypes. All are in the first person, underscoring the identity of actor and group: "My name it is Pat, I was born in a bog"; "Molrooney's my name, I'm a comical boy"; "I am a Jew tailor but a very good man"; "Ve're a set of people at whom the folks frown"; "And I could weep! Th' Oneida chief his descant wildly thus began"; "Oh, I love my massa kind." [3]

A brief survey of the American evolution of these ethnic effigies will carry the story up to the immigrants' time and beyond.

The Indian. Even in pre-Revolutionary times some English ballad operas performed in America depicted comic, noble, and savage stage Indians. In 1828 Edwin Forrest chose *Metamora* from among the fourteen plays he had sponsored in a contest "for the best tragedy in five acts of which the hero shall be an aboriginal of this country." [4] Dozens of Indian plays followed, while Forrest portrayed the noble redman hundreds of times across the country. John Brougham's celebrated 1855 parody *Po-Ca-Hon-Tas* showed that the genre had reached maturity. Later we shall see how the Indians' image reached as far as Yiddish vaudeville in the 1890s.

The Country Bumpkin. Another English actor, Charles Matthews, perfected a comic stage Yankee in the late 1820s and 1830s, and was soon emulated by a galaxy of American comedians. [5] He drew on the English tradition of the stage Yorkshireman. Eventually, as the country grew, the type was generalized to a canny rustic who always outsmarts the city slickers, and his home shifted to Appalachia. This figure has had a lively career down to the days of "Beverly Hillbillies" and "Hee-Haw" on television. Yiddish parodies on the American rustic persist, and are enshrined in such songs as "Ikh bin an alter bok fun old Kentok" ("I'm an Old Goat from Kentucky").

The Black. The 1820s also saw the beginnings of that most formidable of early American amusements, the minstrel show. It is outside our province to detail the complex rise, flowering, and decline of that great American institution. As the immigrants grew in number from the 1840s on, blackface entertainers took notice by adding ethnic material to their routines. Of particular significance is the fact that virtually every Jewish-American stage personality, from Weber and Fields through Al Jolson, Sophie Tucker, and Eddie Cantor, first reached out to American audiences from behind a mask of burnt cork. The black character himself is a rare visitor within the Yiddish theater, but we will see him in the 1895 vaudeville that features Indians.

The "Dutch," or German. This stage caricature blossomed with the heavy German immigration of the 1840s to 1860s. It provided a good transition to the Yiddish comic of the '90s and beyond, since the Yiddish accent and the German share some common features. Replete with beer-swollen belly, surrounded by sausages and kraut, the dumb but harmless Dutchman graced American boards for decades, only receding with the general decline of German-American ethnic identity brought on by World War I. We know this type today principally in the comic figure of the mad German scientist and the sometimes dumb but always brutal Nazi.

The Irishman. The Irish present a special and extremely important case, as they are the first group to have a double entertainment image: the external, presented to general audiences, and their own home-grown brand of amusement that somewhat precedes and strongly parallels the Yiddish theater. We will examine both sides of the Irish image.

The Irishman is brought to America at roughly the same time (1830s) as the other caricatures, and is also introduced by English actors. With the major influx of Irish immigrants in the 1840s the figure achieves wide currency. There are two sides to the stereotype: on one hand, the Irishman is a brawling drunkard, simultaneously maudlin and pugilistic; on the other he can figure as the rustic hero, saving the heroine in the beloved midcentury melodramas of Boucicault ("The Shaughraun," "Arran-no-Poghue"). A third character, distinctly New York in origin and dialect, emerges in the Civil War period: Mose, the Bowery B'hoy, who goes beyond ethnicity to stand for the urban hooligan with a heart of gold. (This type later surfaces in Hollywood.) As the Irish progress socioeconomically, these varied caricatures grow in stature. Symbolic of the upward social climb is the victory of the polished Gentleman Jim Corbett, the "new" Irish-American from California, over the stereotypical street brawler John Sullivan in the 1892 fight for the heavyweight championship.

It is hard to overemphasize the importance of these bizarre "national" stereotypes. Collectively they create a very strong sense of "us" versus "them," forming a bulwark of nativism in the great age of turbulence which saw industrialization combine with massive immigration to create modern America. It is not merely songs and stage caricatures which tickled the New World muse, but widely distributed songbooks which brought the ethnic images into the parlors of a great many American homes. As almost random examples, one can look at listings from turn-of-the-century anthologies. One is the catalogue of Wehman Bros. joke books,[6] which were "handy pocket-size books for the millions. 10¢ each, or 6 copies for 50¢"—an early version of the mass-market paperback. Some titles are outspokenly ethnic: "Irish Jokes," "Minstrel Jokes," "Darkey Jokes and Funny Stories," "Scotch Jokes," "Combination Irish, Hebrew and Dutch Jokes." There is a volume of "Rube Jokes" mocking poor Reuben, the hayseed who comes to the city; the rustic was viewed both as hillbilly and as a type of immigrant. Then there are other pocket joke books which seem non-ethnic, but which were bound to contain caricatures. The cover for "Short Stories Between Drinks" shows slicked-back, cigar-smoking backroom boys, doubtless chuckling at the frailties of the foreign born and the dark skinned. In a companion series of "Popular Recitations" we find Jewish, German, Irish, and black bits interwoven with historical, patriotic, childlike, adventurous and, above all, sentimental American declamations.

Closer to the world of music, we find that home songbooks were similarly organized. The title page for *The Treasury of Song for the Home Circle* (1882)[7] indicates that national origin is a basic organizing principle for its contents, which have been "carefully selected from the best works of the American, English, Scotch, Irish, Welsh, Swiss, French, Spanish, German, Italian, African and Russian authors." Some of these items are caricature songs, while others attempt to represent national repertoires. The "African" material is drawn from that sung by the Fisk Jubilee Singers, the celebrated spiritual singers, rather than from the minstrel show. Yet one is acutely aware of "our" music and "theirs" throughout, stereotype or no. The pattern continues unabated into the twentieth century, as the extension of the piano into more and more American homes reached its peak. There is remarkably little variation in content or approach by the time of the landmark anthology of 1910, *Heart Songs*.[8] This volume was a compendium of submissions sent in by 25,000 Americans in response to a call from *The National Magazine*, so it represents the broadest spectrum of popular taste. The usual percentage of Scottish, Irish, German, and black items is present, with a nod to other groups: Italian, Spanish, Danish, Swedish, French, Portuguese, and even Chinese tunes are included. Some caricature items—such as the "Bavarian" song "Buy a Broom" (really of English origin)—date back to pre-Civil War days.

Toward the end of the period of peak immigration, attitudes toward ethnics seem to change. Two songs illustrate the prevailing social currents. One, a World War I appeal to all Americans to stand together and fight for Uncle Sam ("Let's All Be Americans Now"), was largely written by Irving Berlin, an immigrant musician who has been associated with patriotic songs all his life. It calls for ethnic Americans to substitute national goals for their ties to previous homelands:

> England or France may have your sympathy, or Germany
> But you'll agree that now is the time to fall in line.
> You swore that you would, so be true to your vow

This surprising acknowledgment of the pull between motherland (or Vaterland) and America frankly indicates the depth of the ethnics' quandry in the face of World War I, a particularly traumatic event for

German-Americans. The tone of the line meant to be the "clincher" is a bit ominous: "You swore that you would, so be true to your vow," an apparent reference to the naturalized citizen's promise to defend his adopted country. The implied "or go back to where you came from" seems just below the surface.

The second song is an outspoken statement of nativism, recorded by the star Nora Bayes in 1920:

Verse 1
Columbus discovered America in 1492.
Then came the English and the Dutch,
The Frenchman and the Jew.
Then came the Swede and the Irishman,
To help the country grow.
Still they keep on coming, and now everywhere you go:

Chorus
There's the Argentines, and the Portuguese, the Ar-
   menians, and the Greeks.
One sells you papers, one shines your shoes,
Another shaves the whiskers off your cheeks.
When you ride again in a subway train,
Notice who has all the seats
And you'll find they are taken by the Argentine,
   and the Portuguese, and the Greeks.

Verse 2
There's the Ritz Hotel, and the Commodore, and the Van-
   derbilt, and the rest
All of them are classy up-to-date hotels
That boast accommodations of the best.
When you ask the clerk for a room and bath
He looks at you sarcastically and speaks:
"Why, we're all filled up with the Argentines, and the Por-
   tuguese, and the Greeks."

Verse 3
There are pretty girls, there are witty girls,
There is every kind of a girl.
Some you like a little, some a little more,
But none of them will set your heart a-whirl.
When you really feel you've met your ideal
A girl who's smart and cheek,

You'll find she belongs to an Argentine, an Armenian,
   or a Greek.

Verse 4

There's the Argentines, and the Portuguese, the Armeni-
ans, and the Greeks.
They don't know the language, they don't know the law
But they vote in the country of the free.
And the funny thing, when we start to sing
"My Country 'Tis of Thee"
None of us knows the words but the Argentines,
   and the Portuguese, and the Greeks.[10]

The odd discrepancy between the ethnics who shine shoes but who
fill up the Ritz reveals the real point of the song, which is to knock the
rise of the non-native American. The stress on particularly exotic (and
not very visible) ethnics is coupled with the opening verse's praise of the
more usual targets of popular song. Most likely this is another tactic that
serves as screen for severe nativism: "The Argentines . . ." appeared
just as the end of mass immigration was in sight, capping a long
struggle against an unrestricted flow of newcomers. Even the immigrants' patriotism, which had been so strongly requested in "Let's All Be
Americans Now," here seems to count against them—they know the
words to "My Country 'Tis of Thee" too well, it appears.

We have seen the ethnics evaluated as both comic and threatening
figures in American popular entertainment. Either way, the newcomers
were under enormous pressure to become "straight" Americans, to
jettison those traits that kept them from rising in society. At one end of
the spectrum, the "anglo" imperative bluntly stated that everyone had
to look, talk, and act like the older settlers. This view was not widely
expressed in popular culture. Much more prominent was the position
which has been tagged "the melting pot." The term (suitably, for its
age) is an industrial metaphor, relating to the process of smelting by
which diverse components are dissolved under great heat to form a new
and tough alloy.

That we still recognize the term is due partly to the impact of a
product of popular culture: a 1908 play, *The Melting Pot*, which was
written by an English Jew, Israel Zangwill, and enthusiastically received in the United States.[11] Zangwill, who throughout his life wa-
vered from cause to cause, briefly took on the matter of America's
future, dedicating his play to Theodore Roosevelt, arch-believer in
America's manifest destiny as world cultural model. Zangwill's weakly
structured drama is of interest to us because its hero is a Jewish violinist

and composer named David. Unlike the hero of a Yiddish play we will examine later, who also is named David and plays the violin, the protagonist of *The Melting Pot* does not represent in-group history and sentiment; rather, he stands for the process of assimilation. This is boldly stated as complete surrender, a dizzying dive into "the crucible," as Zangwill's David terms America. All ethnic characteristics—including internal musics—must be offered up to the New America which will emerge from the universal cultural dissolve.

> DAVID. Here you stand, good folk, think I, when I see them at Ellis Island, here you stand in your fifty groups, with your fifty languages and histories, and your fifty blood hatreds and rivalries. But you won't be long like that, brothers, for these are the fires of God you've come to—these are the fires of God. A fig for your feuds and vendettas! Germans and Frenchmen, Irishmen and Englishmen, Jews and Russians—into the Crucible with you all! God is making the American!

At play's end, David has had the premiere of his *Sinfonia Americana*, and the curtain falls as the audience—made up of settlement house people, not Carnegie Hall concertgoers—sings "My Country 'Tis of Thee." Zangwill's use of an immigrant entertainer to carry his message of ethnic fusion repeats a pattern of many fictional and dramatic works in America. Consciously or unconsciously, authors realize that the performer carries the burden of his people.

The melting-pot ideal was basic to American thinking for decades, and was only "officially" expelled from our intellectual history by the widespread acceptance of a book titled *Beyond the Melting Pot* in the 1960s.[12] What had been clear to some historians since the 1920s now became apparent to all: that the ethnic groups had rightfully refused to jump into "the Crucible." In the 1960s and 1970s the post-immigrants from Europe created a new ethnicity on the basis of the doctrine of cultural pluralism and in response to black Americans' emphatic insistence on group pride and, particularly, its reflection in expressive culture.

How did the ethnics manage to hold onto their cultural individuality while in the double bind of the melting-pot ideology on the one hand and popular caricature on the other? Anthropologists speak of "ethnic boundaries," which set groups apart in a multi-ethnic society.[13] They usually mean factors of social organization, political and religious behavior, language, and material culture (dress, housing). Ethnomusicologists tend to think that music is every bit as important as the other elements just listed in helping people to define who they are. In the following chapters we will be largely concerned with defining just how it is that the Jews assembled coherent musical symbols of self-recognition. Yet we must first, at least briefly, see how other immigrant groups solved the same problem. This is still an unexplored area in American life; only now are there beginning to be studies of individual ethnic responses to the overall question of musical identity. For our purposes, we need merely to focus on a few guiding principles that can be used as yardsticks for the Jewish case. Because there are great overriding similarities in the responses of all ethnic groups to the American challenge, we will find Jewish solutions to be similar in many ways to those of preceding immigrant groups, like the Irish. Yet we will also see how the Jewish material can differ radically in content and social context.

In quickly surveying ethnic song-making in America, we will touch on two major themes: the topic of emigration/immigration, and the question of accommodation to the American song tradition. Both are matters which every ethnic group has had to face.

Songs of emigration/immigration. This topic has two sides. On the one hand we have the true folksong, sung in every European language, about the bitterness of leaving one's homeland and the dangers of the journey across the waters. A Polish song conveys the concerns of the folk:

> The mountaineer made the sign of the cross on his brow
> Preparing for his journey.
> Bidding farewell to father and mother
> And to his birthplace.
>
> He said goodbye to brothers and sisters
> And with a heavy heart
> He was leaving the house where he was born
> And his beloved Podhale.
>
> He bid farewell to the Tatra, its crests and woods
> To the green clearing in the forest
> To the swift waters of the stream
> And to his beloved village.
>
> And he left for the distant world
> Far from his beloved Tatra
> To live among strangers in America.[14]

This emigration song is typical of a whole group of ethnic American folksongs, emphasizing the intimacy and rootedness of the Old World environment and the pain of departure. An Irish song on the same topic, still sung today, is called "The American Wake," named after the custom of holding a memorial celebration for a person who has emigrated to the New World. One who leaves his native land is as good as dead to the community that stays behind.

This retrospective view of the Old World prepared the way for the more stylized song of ethnic nostalgia which eventually became an American popular staple. Virtually every song anthology for home use contains a number of such songs about European scenes, including, more often than not, mention of European girls left behind. Here we are on the borderline of our two concerns: emigration and accommodation. The immigrant's natural interest in nostalgia can be accommodated to the American song market so as to produce popular songs that can serve both audiences. "Kitty Neil" (1852) is a good example of this trend from the heyday of the stage Irishman, which coincided with the rise of the American parlor song. On the sheet music cover, the last line of the refrain is engraved in a shamrock, allowing for easy identification of topic in the music-shop window:

Ah sweet Kitty Neil, rise up from your wheel
Your neat little foot will be weary with spinning.
Come trip down with me to the sycamore tree;
Half the parish is there, and the dance is beginning.

The sun has gone down, but the full harvest moon
Shines sweetly and cool on the dew-whitened valley
While all the air rings with the soft loving things,
Each little bird sings in the green shaded valley.

Now Felix Magee puts his pipes to his knee
And with flourish so free sets each couple in motion;
With a cheer and a bound the lads patter the ground—
The maids move around, just like swans on the ocean.

Poor Pat feels his heart, as he gazes, depart,
Subdued by the smart of such painful yet sweet love.
The sight leaves his eye, as he cries with a sigh:
"Dance light, for my heart it lies under your feet, love!" [15]

The last verse is marked "rallentando e con espressione" to ensure a slow, languishing finish. The references to the beauties of the Old World setting are all that link this song to the Polish item cited above. The text has a strong Victorian quality, and its cuteness cloys today.

Compare, for example, one stanza from a parallel folksong, "Barney McCoy," which is rather more straightforward in its diction:

I am going far away, Nora darling;
I'll be leaving such an angel far behind.
It will break my heart in two, which I'd fondly give to you,
And no other is so loving, kind and true.[16]

Songs of Accommodation. Early specimens of ethnic nostalgia such as "Kitty Neil" served as the foundation for an emerging genre of homesickness songs that flooded the American market for generations. By the late nineteenth century, the foreign and the American rural immigrant were fused as the nostalgia genre branched out. We find standardized "back home" ditties sung about small-town America by Jewish entertainers from 1910 on, such as Al Jolson's "Just Try to Picture Me Back Home in Tennessee" (1915) and Sophie Tucker's "Don't Be Afraid to Come Home" (1925). While the Jolson song still relies on the blackface image as the all-American cover for a variety of sentiments, the Tucker song introduces a more apparently realistic setting. The sheet music cover illustration shows the singer on Broadway, dreaming of her sad old parents on the veranda. The picture hardly tallies with Tucker's actual parents, who ran a delicatessen in Hartford.

So the ethnics' own concern for preserving memories of a past life elsewhere can be accommodated to a popular genre founded on the feeling of being uprooted, a strong emotion common to great masses of nineteenth-century Euro-Americans, natives and newcomers alike. At the same time, the ethnics were subject to a barrage of public caricature and stereotyping which tended to cut them off from such shared feelings. Here accommodation can have a darker side: the acceptance of the stereotype by the group being satirized. Indeed, the group may take the mask proffered by the mainstream, decorate it, and sell it back to the majority audience in an improved version. Such self-parody for profit is found among entertainers of various ethnic groups, including the Jews. Many of their songs can now be read only with an acute sense of embarrassment. In a way, the acceptance of a stereotype is akin to the false identity foisted upon, and taken up by, victims of colonialism, as documented for Africa and common in discussion of the effects of slavery on black Americans. Yet the possibility exists that ethnic Euro-Americans could both celebrate and ignore the mainstream image of their culture. As Richard Gambino has noted for working-class Italians, "In effect they neutralize the degrading picture society paints of them by accepting it as true but at the same time holding it at arm's length from their real self-esteem."[17]

One way of "neutralizing the image" is to create positive stereotypes. Alongside the drunken, brawling Mick, Irish-American songwriters painted a portrait of the mother-loving Hibernian. Like nostalgia, mother love was a matter of universal interest to turn-of-the-century Americans. The genre branched out in all directions: orphan songs (loss of mother), disaster songs (orphan-creating), and temperance songs (abandonment or abuse of mother) are but three of the main song types of the period that fed off devotion to Mom. In part, this success was anchored in the same feeling of isolation from home and tradition that characterizes the emigrant/immigrant genre. In popular song the mother left behind is mentioned as often as the abandoned sweetheart. (Folksong seems more neutral on the subject.) The handsome Irish tenor, a matinee idol who was able to cross the ethnic boundary and achieve national prominence, used this theme of filial piety common to both in-group and general audiences. The title of "Ireland Must Be Heaven, for My Mother Came from There" epitomizes the association of heritage with mother. "Mother Machree," sung by the two leading Irish tenors, Olcott and McCormack, can well summarize the pull of Mom at the time of its writing in 1910:

There's a spot in me heart which no coleen may own;
There's a depth in me soul never sounded or known.
There's a place in my mem'ry, my life, that you fill,
No other can take it, no one ever will.[18]

Jewish-American entertainers were quick to pick up on the Irish tenor's effective use of the mother song. Al Jolson built a career singing "Mammy," and he wrote "Mother of Mine," straight out of the Olcott-McCormack tradition, for the film *The Jazz Singer*.

All of this indicates how the ethnic group can accommodate itself to mainstream music and values through its representatives, the entertainers; yet it tells us very little about how such posturing affected the internal cultural balance of an immigrant community. To understand that question, we must compare the inside song world of an ethnic group to the sphere that overlaps the mainstream. Ethnic caricature, for example, can be seen in a somewhat different light when displayed for an in-group audience. Edward Harrigan, architect of the most visible and viable ethnic theater tradition of the 1870s and 1880s, knew how to soften the edges of the stiff stereotypes of Irish-Americans. Writing for an Irish audience, he could turn out a song like "John Riley's Always Dry," about the prototypical hard-drinking Hibernian, and still manage to pull back from the brink of caricature by saying John Riley, "an old companion," has a heart "like a mountain," and that "his honor ye can't buy." [19] In one of his plays, Harrigan even has a black character remark that "if the Irish in New York thought home rule was such a great thing, why didn't they all go back to Ireland and rule there?" [20] It is within the confines of an ethnic group that stereotyping is usually most true to life, as well as least resented, for the softened self-caricature stands out clearly from the more common use of stock figures to make fun of someone else. Thus in Harrigan's plays the benignly comic Irishman, exposed with all his foibles, serves as foil for the much more broadly caricatured Italians, Germans, and blacks. After all, when your ethnic group runs New York, you can afford to laugh at yourself. Harrigan has one of his Irish politicians say, "My district is the town of Babel, and the Irish flag floats from the top." [21] Even for less powerful groups like the Jews, it was easier to absorb self-criticism when it was diluted with large doses of ridicule for others; later we shall see that this trend pops up in Yiddish vaudeville.

We have eloquent testimony on the Jewish view of self-caricature from an expert, Fanny Brice. Rising rapidly from obscurity to Ziegfield Follies stardom, Brice excelled in both Jewish stereotype numbers and in sophisticated French cabaret songs. She represents the ambivalence of ethnic entertainers who join the mainstream late in the immigrant era. Her quintessential Jewish monologues and songs ("Second-Hand Rose from Second Avenue," "Mrs. Cohen at the Beach") were widely copied. How did Brice herself feel about this side of her stage persona?

> I never did a Jewish song that would offend the race because it depended on the race for laughs. In anything Jewish I ever did, I wasn't standing apart, making fun of the race. I *was* the race, and what happened to me on the stage is what could happen to them. They identified with me, and then it was all right to get a laugh, because they were laughing at me as much as at themselves. It is the same with any race, and it is something I always knew from instinct. . . . It is okay for one Irishman to call another Irishman anything, any kind of name. But if you are not an Irishman, keep the mouth shut. The same with all people.[22]

Harrigan would certainly have agreed. And so did the mainstream, which applauded displays of ethnic stereotyping. Here is Brooks Atkinson, powerful drama critic of the *New York Times*, responding to a revue pairing Brice with eminent the black self-caricaturist Willie Howard: "Something constructive has been accomplished toward the welfare of nations. . . . Fanny Brice and Willie Howard are well met in the theatre—both racial in style, both given to the rolling, roguish eye and both mighty good company." [23]

Fanny Brice could serve as a source for Molly Picon in the Yiddish theater of the mid-1920s, or for Barbra Streisand ("Funny Girl") in the Broadway and Hollywood of the 1960s. Yet during the peak decades of immigration, the Lower East Side was still acting out its adjustment to the New World in ways that related to older patterns.

We have seen how a popular music tradition was born amid the tumult and terror of Eastern European Jewish life, based on an age-old experiment in eclecticism. We have also toured the frenetic frontiers of American showmanship, improvised in a turbulent, industrializing land of uprooted natives and immigrants. Now we can focus on the core area of the present study: the Lower East Side of New York in the peak years of immigration. We will continue to view popular culture as a source of ethnic strength, questioning and explaining the immigrant predicament to a community seeking solutions to the problems posed by America. After all, popular entertainment is essentially conservative, traveling the middle of the road to satisfy, as well as to define, the mainstream of its audience. In our case, this broad avenue parallels the main thoroughfares of the ghetto, with music stores, low vaudeville halls, and pretentious legitimate theaters; the streets are peopled by organ-grinders, hawkers of sheet music, and outdoor musicians. Two chapters will detail this dense urban environment before we move in still closer to examine the main material legacy of the period, the sheet music itself.

NOTES

1. Lines from a parody of the Irish song "The Widown Dunn," which became "The Widow Rosenbaum." Quoted in Douglas Gilbert, *American Vaudeville: Its Life and Times* (New York: Whittlesey House, 1940), p. 73.
2. The following description is adapted from ibid., pp. 114–20.
3. *The Universal Songster, or Museum of Mirth* (London: Jones & Co., 1826), II.
4. E. R. Page, ed., *Metamora and Other Plays*, in *America's Lost Plays* (Princeton: Princeton University Press, 1941), XIV, 4.
5. For a survey of the Yankee on stage, see Francis Hodge, *Yankee Theatre: The Image of America on the Stage, 1825–1850* (Austin: University of Texas Press, 1964). For a concise survey of ethnic stereotyping on the American stage, see Carl Wittke, "The Immigrant Theme on the American Stage," *Mississippi Valley Historical Review* 39 (Sept. 1952): 211–32.

6. The Wehman series tends to be undated, but the books seem to antedate 1920.
7. *The Treasury of Song*, ed. Prof. D. H. Morrison (Philadelphia: Hubbard, 1882), is also useful for its "appended brief biographies of eminent composers, performers, and singers."
8. *Heart Songs* (Boston: Chapple, 1909).
9. The song, published by Berlin, Waterson, and Snyder, features a cover illustration of an ethnically ambiguous, lantern-jawed doughboy against a silhouetted line of soldiers. The basic colors are red, white, and blue.
10. The song has been reissued on New World Records NW233, *Come Josephine in My Flying Machine: Inventions and Topics in Popular Song, 1900–1929.*
11. Israel Zangwill, *The Melting Pot*, rev. ed. (New York: Macmillan, 1930).
12. N. Glazer and D. Moynihan, *Beyond the Melting Pot* (Cambridge: MIT Press, 1969).
13. The pioneering book on the subject is Frederik Barth, *Ethnic Groups and Boundaries* (Boston: Little, Brown, 1969).
14. The song can be heard on Library of Congress LBC6, *Folk Music in America, vol. 6: Songs of Migration and Immigration*, from which the cited text is taken.
15. "Kitty Neil" was published by Wm. Hall & Son, New York. For a thorough discussion of the sentimental Irish song in America, see Charles Hamm, *Yesterdays* (New York: Norton, 1979).
16. "Barney McCoy" is taken from the Library of Congress LBC6, cited in note 14.
17. Richard Gambino, *Blood of My Blood: The Dilemma of the Italian Americans* (New York: Doubleday, 1974).
18. The song, by Chauncey Olcott and E. R. Ball, was published by Witmark, New York.
19. The entire song, as well as other Harrigan favorites, can be found on New World Records NW 265, *Don't Give the Name a Bad Place: Types and Stereotypes in American Musical Theater, 1870–1900.*
20. E. J. Kahn, *The Merry Partners: The Age and Stage of Harrigan and Hart* (New York: Random House, 1955), p. 70.
21. Ibid., p. 64.
22. Quotes in Norman Katkov, *The Fabulous Fanny* (New York: Alfred A. Knopf, 1953), p. 205.
23. Ibid., p. 236.

PART II

ENTERTAINMENT
IN THE GHETTO

"I like melodrama,
nisht keyn filosofie
(none of that philosophy)"

—old Jewish man;
last line in the Woody Allen film
Stardust Memories (1980)

CHAPTER 4

MAKING
A MUSIC CULTURE:
THE AVENUE AND
THE HIGH ROAD

"CONCERT"

He has a piano for the girl
And a guitar for the boy,
But don't envy him!
He has sorrow from both.

They brought the instruments in
On credit;
He pays installments on them—
He has a mountain of worries.

And only rarely can he hear
The sound of music,
Since both children toil
Daytimes in the factory.

They have deep feelings,
But limited possibilities;
They have no time to play—
They suffer in the shop.

And he's preoccupied too
All day at the machine.
He hears the wheels roar
And whir without meaning.

At night, life comes
Though all is black around;
The sweet tones hover
And fill the heart.

The dad sits, pale;
The children give a concert.
His gaze grows damp, and damper—
He sits and coughs, and listens.

Morris Rosenfeld was the Yiddish poet laureate of the first generation of immigrants. In "Concert" he captures the improvisatory quality of the early years of Jewish-American music.[1] Primal needs for work, food, and shelter left few gaps for diversion in the twelve- to sixteen-hour day. Yet what leaps out from the memoirs, poems, sketches, and outsiders' descriptions of Lower East Side life is a thirst for entertainment almost as strong as the hunger for upward social mobility. The sheer drive of the worker in "Concert," who adds to his health and earning worries by taking on installment payments for a piano and guitar, is extraordinary. It is usually the self-sacrifice necessary for the children to receive an American education that is stressed in the literature on this period of immigrant life. These senses of accomplishment inherent in mastery of both American history and the piano are merely two aspects of the same quest for positive acculturation, the process that caused the group to rise rapidly in the tumultuous conditions of turn-of-the-century American life.

To date very little has been written, or even gathered, about the musical life of what was usually called "the Ghetto," though we have admirable contemporary and present-day accounts and histories of the Yiddish theater. In this chapter we will traverse the broad avenue of the music culture—its public events—and then take a stroll on the "high road," the path of the Yiddish theater, to see how music fit into drama, before turning to the "low road" of vaudeville and street songs.

For the earliest period (ca. 1881–96), information on music is quite fragmentary. There is little regular Yiddish press, and the institutional musical life of the Ghetto is as yet weak. In 1897 the crucial newspaper, the *Forverts*, is founded, and the in-group sheet music industry gets on its feet. Increased social activism and organizational activity of all sorts lead to focused entertainments whose structure and goals clarify the role of music.

We begin our survey in the streets and courtyards. Even today there

are older singers who remember learning songs from blind street musicians, some of whom camped outside Yiddish theaters and hawked
broadsides of the latest hit songs. A child could pick up songs by
listening to these mendicant musicians repeat a tune tirelessly, and
then run home and teach it to his whole family. Exactly the same
process is described by folk singers for European cities and towns. As
usual, it was not just in-group music that was spread through these
channels, but a variety of styles that allowed the creation of a highly
eclectic Jewish repertoire. Though many of the songs thus transmitted
were of the low repertoire, street singers could apparently rise to heights
as well. We turn again to Morris Rosenfeld for a vivid portrayal of the
impact of courtyard musicians on an observer in those early years. In a
sketch entitled "A Cantor Without an Altar," he contrasts the normal
run of minstrels with a striking old Jew who has decided to act as cantor
for the neighborhood at the time of the High Holidays:

> . . . I had already seen and heard various poor folk in our
> courtyard, who played out their poverty and misery on all sorts
> of instruments: fiddles, barrel organs, accordions, and flutes.
> But I had never seen a silver-bearded blind Jew in a Jewish
> courtyard, never heard—moaningly—the holy prayers of the
> High Holidays.
> This was the newest innovation of poverty.
> I had already seen how necessity taught bare feet to rhapso-
> dize on a cimbalom. I had seen a graybeard Negro sing of his
> former slavery and present misery with pale lips, beating on a
> drum. . . . I had seen two blossoming Gypsies sending out
> sparks from their fiery, hellish eyes and shining with their
> white, seductive teeth, waiting to be thrown a penny. I had
> seen a skinny old Irishwoman rejoicing in her Ireland on the
> fiddle with both hands, singing the pathetic song of Ireland's
> beloved flower, the shamrock, in a strong accent. I had seen
> Goldfadn's song "Shabes, yomtov un rosh khodesh" poured
> into the old fiddle of a fainting street musician in the hubub of
> the tailors' courtyard.
> Oh, I had seen and heard a lot, but never had I heard and
> seen an old man fixing his extinguished eyes on Rosh Hasha-
> nah prayers in the damp cavity of a New York tenement.[2]

The Goldfadn song, written by the founder of the Yiddish theater, is
from the very popular opera *Shulamis*. We see here how so-called

popular songs were folklorized in America, much as they would have been in Europe. Rosenfeld knows that the song is by Goldfadn, but kids in the courtyard might not, and their children need have no knowledge of the source. A discussion of the generation gap in music and culture arises in the succeeding passages of "A Cantor Without an Altar," well worth quoting at length for the atmosphere evoked:

> We were all sitting comfortably at the table eating lunch when suddenly our hands, with the silverware, stood still on the tablecloth, or in the air. We thought a weeping High Holiday tune could be heard from the window that leads to the courtyard, and everything fell silent. . . .
>
> An old, hoarse voice fluttered, shot through with a sweet, thin, silky little child's voice from time to time. . . . "Haneshoma lekha" resounded with penetrating Jewish sorrow, and grasped all of us in the house. "V haguf shelekha," he moaned further. . . . The old man sobbed, and with him the whole audience. . . .
>
> An old man, with white hair like milk, with a respectable, snow-white beard, tall and slender, stood leaning on a staff. Holding his quick eyes aloft, he was rapt in recitatives, which a small pale boy supported with resonant accompaniment.
>
> His sad, minor recitation did not speak to everyone. Young Jewish-American children looked at him with a smile. . . . A rascal threw a piece of orange peel down on the old man, but the blind cantor didn't stop his pitiful singing, which bounced off the cold stone walls.
>
> When he began to recite "Unsane toykef" they began to throw coins from all sides, which the little choirboy picked up. However, the old man didn't listen to the cold clink of earthly metal, and did his part. It appeared that the alms were accepted only by his poverty; he himself prayed gratis. . . .
>
> Older women shook their heads and wiped away the tears, but the young folk, who came from the factories and shops to gulp their lunch, had no interest in this scene of exile. They ran to the windows but soon disappeared. . . . They don't understand loshn koydesh [sacred texts], don't know the Jew, and find his prayers foreign.
>
> But I stood at the window and looked. My ears soaked up the sorrow of the holy melodies, and my gaze wandered from the blind eyes to the white beard and the black staff.

I thought of the whole Jewish people, which is a cantor without an altar. . . .

Rosenfeld's conclusion, like his description of the "young Jewish-Americans," reveals the distance between his generation and the next. The young folks who would flock to the American dancing schools and music halls to soak up mainstream culture would have had little sympathy indeed for the depiction of "the whole Jewish people" as "a cantor without an altar."

One of the most trenchant accounts of entertainment among the first American-born generation comes from the pen of one Charlotte Kimball Patten, a social worker.[3] Like so many other turn-of-the-century observers of the Ghetto, Mrs. Patten offers a combination of bemusement, hard fact, and sympathetic commentary. The generation gap is a special target of her description of Philadelphia Jewish life. The relatively smaller size of the Philadelphia community, as opposed to the gargantuan nature of New York Jewry, allows for more concise and comprehensive coverage of the question of music and entertainment. Mrs. Patten opens with a flat statement: "Sharply contrasted with the middle aged, transplanted Russian Jews who accept even their pleasures sadly, are the young immigrants, pioneers rather than refugees, and the native born, who seize eagerly on every social outlet offered by a niggardly environment. Unworn enthusiasms hurry them to tawdry American amusements while their fathers stand steadfastly by their old world observances." Warming to her topic, she sums up the older generation: ". . . of amusement pure and simple, of seeking pleasure and jollity for their own sweet sake, without the base of a ramifying religious impulse, the Russian Jew of the passing generation has never learned. Body and mind have hungered and thirsted under conditions so wearisome that when ease comes he acquiesces to its circumstantial pleasures as an old person whose senses tire and dull. . . ." Here Patten could be describing Rosenfeld's image of the father slumped pale-faced in the easy chair as the children play on the rented piano and guitar. What she misses, though, is the father's willingness to pay the monthly installment: the usefulness of "frivolity" has not entirely faded from his work-worn mind.

As to the amusements of the young folks, Patten neatly summarizes the possibilities for Philadelphia, third-largest Jewish-American city:

First in its formative influence is the theatre, after which comes that distinct class of pleasures clustering about the desolate dance hall: the Pleasure Social, the Hall Wedding, the

Dancing Class, the Ball or Masquerade Dance for Charity, and the Literary Concert and Ball of the political and industrial bodies. About the last group are found debating, literary, and dramatic societies, dancing and social clubs, and Sunday school and philanthropic entertainments conducted by Jews of an up-town district.

This is no mean listing of entertainments; it is a veritable smorgasbord of amusements. The division of the community into "uptown" and "downtown" sectors is hinted at, and the great variety of communal organizations—religious or political—is also implied. We will detail their patterning and activities below.

Beginning with theater, it is well worth citing Patten's breakdown of the types available to the Philadelphia Jews. We start with the Yiddish theater:

> There were three play houses patronized by Russian Jews. . . .
> The least successful of the three was the theatre on Arch
> Street, which was conducted as a Yiddish play house. . . .
> Many young men and women whose weekly evening at the
> theatre is as regular a function as their wage payments, ex-
> pressed surprise and amusement when told that systematic
> visits had been paid to the Arch Street Theatre. . . . "Why ain't
> it a rank play? Something about Siberia, ain't it? Now you
> ought to see 'The Electrician.' There's a great coon song in it;
> it goes this way. . . ."

The situation of Yiddish theater was not quite so desperate; in a footnote, Patten points out that "the Academy of Music is now used occasionally for a Yiddish performance. There is also an up-town Yiddish theatre of a lower grade." Yet even these cheering references corroborate the laments of Boris Thomashefsky, matinee idol and businessman par excellence, on the eternal struggle to find a home and an audience for Yiddish theater. In the above quote's mention of admiration for a coon song we dimly sense the onset of a desire to join the mainstream. Mrs. Patten's book was published in 1905, only one year before an obscure immigrant named Jolson makes his mark in post-earthquake San Francisco—in blackface.

The second theater is the Standard, where "eighteen hundred people daily run the gamut of human emotions and are molded by the deportment of the players." Clearly, Patten has a bone to pick with the muckrakers who hold a universally dismal view of the Ghetto:

> Ask the cynic and the doubter . . . who has been saddened by
> the photographs of the seamy side of life shown by our first-
> rate theatres to . . . buy a ten-cent seat beside the gallery loaf-
> ers and unskilled working-boys. He will look down upon the
> floor crowded with young men and women, trouping in from
> nearby shops, markets, and factories; clerks and garment-
> workers of the upper class of industry, who can pay thirty
> cents for an orchestra seat and an additional dime for the
> wares of refreshment vendors. He will note that the majority of
> the audience are Judeo-Americans of the first generation. . . .

As for the repertoire of the stock company, it includes "old popular plays
of five acts, supplemented by long entre-acte vaudeville turns, [which]
often extend the matinee from two until six o'clock." Examples include
" 'The Two Orphans,' 'The Three Musketeers' and the greatest 'char-
mer' of them all, 'The Black Flag' . . . given yearly to large audiences
which can anticipate the details of every act. More recently, melodramas of American life [such as] 'Hero, the Warm Spring Indian Chief' . . .
have been added." The works mentioned are part of the great backbone
of American popular entertainment, as we have seen. Yet we need not
view the immigrants as passive recipients of an aggressive American
popular culture; at this time native American writers were already
crafting their entertainments to suit the newcomers' taste. Writing
about his own technique, the highly successful melodramatist and
playwright Owen Davis notes:

> One of the first tricks I learned was that my plays must be
> written for an audience who, owing to the huge uncarpeted
> noisy theaters, couldn't always hear the words and who, a
> large percentage of them having only recently landed in Amer-
> ica, couldn't have understood them in any case. I therefore
> wrote for the eye rather than for the ear and played out each
> emotion in action, depending on my dialogue only for the no-
> ble sentiments so dear to audiences of that class.[4]

Davis does not mention that music, written "for the ear," was another
good way to get a message across to an immigrant audience.

Just as America had a common impact on all the ethnic theaters
described earlier, we must also admit that all the immigrants left a
certain identifiable stamp on American drama. The impulse toward
pictorial rather than spoken drama led inexorably toward the development of and popularity of the silent film. While this trend has been well

described in histories of drama, the immigrants' role in shaping style has rarely been the subject of comment.

Returning to Philadelphia, we find Charlotte Kimball Patten describing the third type of theater, the National, which

> attracts a different patronage. . . . The plays are given by second rate and third rate road companies . . . [and] an abundance of the heavily tragic [is] relieved by a series of the lightly comic. A large share of its patronage is drawn from the downtown shop-keepers whose social aspirations point northward, warning them not to mingle with the democratic throngs at the Standard; from grammar and high school pupils; from the higher ranks of labor—the men who belong to unions and read the literature of their craft; and from the over-running swarms of boys who know every coign of fun from Kensington to Point Breeze.[5]

Patten mentions that *Zorah*, a play on a Jewish topic, was performed at the National and evoked an immediate, strong response. It is an approach roughly analogous to a situation described earlier: the German circus in Dvinsk putting on a Yiddish opera to attract the Jewish audience. The ways of enticing the public vary little from Old to New World.

Patten's astute commentary makes it very clear that, along with the generational split among audiences, socioeconomic factors are of considerable importance to a full understanding of immigrant music and entertainment. There are clearly times when younger and older uptowners may show solidarity in their tastes, as opposed to downtowners of whatever age.

While her depictions of the theatrical scene are interesting, Patten's account of 1900-vintage Philadelphia Jewish entertainment broadens out and gains in value as she painstakingly outlines the organized social entertainments, of which there seem to have been countless varieties. We will touch upon only a few salient points here.

Our first category includes the three types of "socials," the pleasure social, business social, and chartered social: "The first, as the name implies, is a friendly group of a dozen or more young men combined for pleasure with the sub-motive of pecuniary profit; the second is a business association of three or more men giving dances under club names for profit alone; and lastly the 'chartered social,' a gambling concern masquerading as 'The Early Rose,' 'The Jolly Fifteen,' 'The Jolly Bunch,' or 'The Ad Libitum.' " These outfits, which almost seem more likely among Dickens's clerks than in Jewish Philadelphia, advertise their events by signs in shop windows. Patten gives a sample:

ROUDIOS SOCIAL

December 2d

Kilgallon, America's White Champion CAKE WALKER
Last Chance to see him prior to him going to NEW YORK
PRIZE WALTZ for up-towners and down-towners
GREAT SPORT
Ad. 15 cents   Pennsylvania Hall

The high point of the pleasure social is reached around midnight, at the time of the Grand Prize Cake Walk. The acculturation implied by the appearance of a visiting artist like Kilgallon the Champion is intensified by the fact that the local dancers are involved purely in American dance steps. The event is brought to a climax through the outward symbolization (costumes) of America and, indeed, by the participation of outside ethnic groups:

> They are fantastically and hideously dressed, the little girls in short fluffy skirts, soiled fancy shoes and stockings, hair floating or strangely coiffured, necks and arms bare, and prize medals won at cake walks of other socials proudly decorating their little chests. The young men appear as darkies, Uncle Sam, or vaudeville tramps. . . . Many couples are, in fact, semiprofessional walkers who go from one hall to another, competing for prizes. Such rounds are more frequently made by Italians and "Americans" than by Jews.

We begin to detect what has been called, in a different context, "rites of modernization." James L. Peacock, describing Javanse popular theater of the 1960s, carefully analyzes the street-drama forms and costumes to indicate how a culture mediates social and cultural change via entertainment.[6] Here in 1900 Philadelphia we see the concatenation of passive theater-going and active mumming-and-dancing events which mirror each other as Jews, Italians, and even "Americans" watch the same melodrama and transmute the stage action into body paint, circulating at each other's entertainments. The appearance of brazen prostitutes at such events shows how close the parallel "high" and "low" roads come to intersecting. Patten notes sharply: "This is but one of many indications that the younger American generation of Jews has neither the social desire nor the religious scruple to keep itself to itself which has been the basic principle with its Russian born parents." [7]

Perhaps the high point of entertainment's role as acculturator was reached in the dancing schools, the foundation of the innumerable socials and dance parties:

> The "Dancing Class" usually meets in a second story room over a shop or in a tenement. . . . In the course of time partners develop specialties of their own which, when carried to a certain degree of perfection, promote them as prize waltzers at public balls or to the rank of cake walkers. The class may be mixed in its nationalities. Jews, Italians, Irish and "Americans" meet amiably, waiving all differences of race and religion but clinging to personal differences in step and bearing.

The shape of such events is not unlike the Brooklyn scene pictured in the film *Saturday Night Fever*, where different ethnic dancers competed for public honors. Yet the greater hostility evinced by the Italians toward the Hispanic winners indicates that entertainment as ethnic battleground has intensified, rather than diminished, in the years since Patten's description.

Within the Jewish community the dance hall was widely regarded as a place of real danger to young women, because pimps would try to pick up charges there. Countermeasures came late; only in 1917 could the Workmen's Circle note with satisfaction that the interests of female workers were being protected by dance classes sponsored by their fraternal organization.[8] We are not well informed on the extent to which "high road" activities like the Workmen's Circle endeavor arose in direct response to the lure of the low.

To round out the calendar of social events, one must add the standardized catered-hall wedding, the repeated focus of satire of the Jewish establishment in 1960s novels and films. That Italian-theme pop culture also deals with the bourgeois wedding again underlines the similarities in American ethnicity. Somewhat less prominent today, but of great importance early in the century, was the plethora of organizationally sponsored entertainment events to which we will now turn. These were backed by three basic types of groups: unions, *landsmanshaftn* (benevolent societies organized by European town of origin), and political groups (social democrats, anarchists, etc.). A host of ad hoc events for worthy causes were also sponsored by temporary groups.

We shall examine closely the range of events available in New York in 1905, since that fateful year of revolution in Russia evoked a strong response in the American Jewish community. Stung by the wave of repression and pogroms and buoyed by hopes for the czar's downfall, the largest Jewish city in the world organized an unprecedented panoply of solidarity demonstrations. We begin with the roster of events advertised in the *Forverts* for December 31, 1904. Following American custom, New Year's, not a particularly Jewish festive date, was picked as an appropriate occasion for balls and parties. No fewer than eleven main attractions were scheduled for this period; together they give a full picture of the range of purposeful public entertainments that New York could muster. They can be conveniently ordered by type of sponsorship.

A. *Landsmanshaftn*
   1. Full Dress and Civic Ball of the Independent Lekhvits Young Men's Benevolent Association.
   2. Theater & Ball of the Odessa Mutual Aid Association. Profits to go to unfortunate victims of pogroms. A play will be performed: "The Odessa Pogrom, or the Unfortunate Family," with a first-act ballet by Prof. Levine's Dancing School. Jacob Adler and other Yiddish theater stars to perform. A ball will follow.
   3. Bialostok Branch of the Workmen's Circle. "Bialostokers! don't forget the grand concert and ball!"
   4. Entertainment (spelled out in Yiddish) and Ball of the United Austrian Hebrew Charities Association for the goal of establishing a hospital for incurable patients. "Significant artists will appear, and the musical numbers of this evening will be among the finest," including Joe Fuchs, "the talented boy musician." Prominent personalities of the City of New York will open the ball.

The third event shows the combination of union/fraternal organization that strengthened the structure of both. The "talented boy musician Joe Fuchs" may well be Joseph Fuchs, well-known American concert artist.

B. Unions
   5. International Furriers' Union Masquerade Ball. Prof. Shpilberg's orchestra will perform.

Unions are somewhat surprisingly underrepresented in our listing. By the following decade, a comparable roster of events shows three union balls for a single day's advertisements at the same season (January 18, 1914), those of the Waist and Dressmakers' Union, the Furniture

Varnishers and Polishers' Union, and the Wrapper, Kimono, and Housedress-Makers' Union.

    C. Ad hoc events
        6. Grand Memorial Concert in Cooper Union by the Russian Artists of New York. Profit to the Self-Defense Fund of the Bund. Included: performances by the Trio of the Russian Symphony and the Halevi Singing Society, featuring magnificent memorial songs [underlined words in English].

The existence of a Russian Symphony made up of emigre musicians rings disturbingly familiar in our own day, when such an orchestra was assembled in New York to accommodate the new wave of performing artists. In July, 1979, an entire festival of emigre musicians was held at Carnegie Hall. The Self-Defense Fund of the Bund, however, is strictly a 1905 phenomenon. The Bund was a major political organization; its effort to arm the Russian Jews against czarist repression was the subject of considerable tumult and heated debate among American Jews, provoking a controversy that even included members of the German-Jewish establishment uptown.[9]

    D. Politically sponsored events
        7. Anarchists' Party [*vetsherinka*, a Russian word] and Ball.
        8. Socialist-revolutionaries' Ball. The violinist Nitke will perform.
        9. Russian Social Democrat Society Ball. The ad for this, the sixteenth annual ball, is completely in Russian.
     10. The annual masquerade ball of the *Forverts* itself, to be held in Madison Square Garden, with $500 in prizes for costumes. This sumptuous event was one of the high points of the Ghetto's social calendar, and remained so into the 1920s.
     11. The Bund's Concert and Ball. For this event we have a detailed listing of the program, worth giving in full: 1) Mr. Hill Vikhnin, a *Forverts* staff member and very famous opera *Heldentenor*, along with the famous basso Mr. Louie Lefkowitz, accompanied by the famous pianist Miss Helen Gottlieb, will sing a duet of Anton Rubinstein, "Sang das Vögelein," and Donizetti's "Adieu"; 2) Max Margolis, graduate of the Berlin Conservatory, famous violinist known in Königsberg, Vienna, and Berlin, accompanied by the well-known pianist Hyman, will play Tchaikovsky arias;

3) Comrade Rubin, who needs no advertisement, will doubtless declaim; 4) Mr. Gerson, the famous declaimer, will do "The Worker's Woes" and "The Unfortunate Worker"; 5) Comrade Rubin will do his best Russian declamations. A ball will follow, led by the famous and well-known dancer, Comrade Shtamler, accompanied by a double union orchestra under Prof. Shpilberg until 5 A.M. [If Prof. Shpilberg sounds familiar, see #5 above.]

What an abundance of eclecticism is displayed in this generous listing of events! Throughout, there is a striving for "high-class" entertainment, which means an association with classical music. We are barraged by boy-wonder violinists and accomplished pianists, and even by a *Forverts* staff member who doubles as heroic tenor. Among the selections cited, the Russian composers (Rubinstein, Tchaikovsky) stand out. We can even see the aspiration of the dancing-school master, "Prof." Levine, to have his pupils appear on stage at the Yiddish theater with the great Jacob Adler. This upward push is clearly matched by the mention of "prominent personalities of the City of New York" being invited to open the ball benefiting a new hospital project. The social pretentions of the *Forverts* are underlined by the vast sum—$500— available in prize money; compare the anarchists' 25¢ for a ticket and hat check. This combination of grandeur and classical music was to climax in a single magnificent event sponsored by the *Forverts* in 1914. On February 28 a full-page ad announced that tickets were available for a week-long music festival to be held at Madison Square Garden. Jointly sponsored by the Wage-Earners League, the event would feature top international artists; e.g., the great violinist Eugene Ysaye and several Metropolitan Opera stars. As a special event, a concert with the Russian Symphony Orchestra would be held for 1,500 children.

Returning to 1905, our New Year's listing is not yet complete. No fewer than seven theaters publicized ongoing shows, along with numerous benefit performances for various societies to "aid the Russian Revolution." These seven were the Columbia, Thalia, People's, Adler's, and Kalich theaters, along with the Academy of Music and the Irving Music Hall. Some of these were "legitimate" Yiddish theater houses, while others were music halls with variety billings.

Before leaving the bounty of New Year's 1905, we must linger on the word "declamation" (*deklamatsiye*). The idea of delivering a stirring oral presentation on a particular topic, or a comic monologue, was part and parcel of Euro-American culture in the nineteenth and early twentieth centuries. Hundreds of books in both Russia and America taught young people how to stand straight and deliver short speeches—as well as yards and yards of poetry—from Pushkin to Longfellow. The Eastern European Jews had their own internal traditions of oral presentation, based on very early childhood training of males to tell parables and to undergo rigorous examination in oral exegesis of sacred texts. The *magid*, an itinerant preacher, even filled an occupational slot as professional orator. Declamation in Yiddish culture lay somewhere between speech and song. Formal intonation and gesture patterns were stressed, almost to the point of assuming a dance-like quality. Even Yiddish literature had an oral tradition: in his will, Sholom Aleichem asked that his works be read aloud each year on the anniversary of his death, as they regularly were during his lifetime.

With this background, it is hardly surprising that declamation was a valued skill, fit to rank with music as part of an evening's entertainment. It is a concept which fit in with America as easily as it suited a European way of life. The distinguished and influential tradition of Jewish-American professional comedy must owe at least some of its heritage to the old tradition of public oral performance. A gem of a book called *Der Idish-Amerikaner Redner* ("The Jewish-American Orator"), published in 1907 and reprinted at least until 1916, gives a comprehensive picture of the sorts of occasions and materials associated with declamation in the immigrant period. The topics range from the stages of the life cycle (circumcision, bar mitzvah, golden anniversary, funeral) to civic occasions (opening a library), religious events (dedicating a new set of Torah scrolls in a synagogue), and special events (for an evening of music). The last-named prepackaged speech is worth quoting for both style and content; its stiff and formal prose style is as awkward in the original as in the translation:

Dear Friends!

I have been asked to speak in honor of this evening. They have told me to say something about music.

Music, my friends, is angel's speech and I, a mere mortal, can say little about it. So I will attempt, with my limited understanding, to share some of what I felt this evening as the musical tones poured through the hall.

Music is the language of the soul, and the soul does not speak French, Japanese, Arabic, or Chaldean. It has one soul for all peoples, for all nations, and anyone who has feelings can understand this language.

I'll offer you two legends from olden times about the concept of music.

The Greeks tell of how at the battle for Troy, the hero Arthur lay stabbed, wounded, thirsty and hungry. He was about to expire, to give up the ghost, when the fairies, a kind of goddess, had pity on him. However, the fairies did not dare bring him food, drink or medicine. All they could do was to play on their harps. As they began to play, his soul held back. As they played on, his wounds stopped bleeding. His hunger and thirst disappeared; the music gave him new life. Standing up, he found new strength and with the accompaniment of the goddesses he found his camp and was saved from death.

Now comes a second legend, about Moses. The Angel of Death had no power over him. But since man must die, God opened the heavens and Moses heard how the angels sing songs. The sweet heavenly musical tones lulled him to sleep and his soul went hence to where the angelic music resounded harmoniously over the heavenly realm.

That's music. It can revive one who is dying or tear out the soul and the life from one who is living.

In the history of crime it is well known that great, terrible criminals have become good, honest people when they begin to understand the sweetness of music. Mentally ill people are cured through music. Those who have suffered the deepest melancholy have become healthy through music.

My friends! This musical evening has made at least me a much better person than I was several hours ago. The tones of the instruments have permeated my soul; the sound of the voices penetrated deep into my heart, and now I feel like the hero Arthur when he sensed the harp-playing of the fairies, like Moses when he heard the angels' song.

Music, my friends, is one of the most holy inspirations of the human soul. Continue to cultivate a taste for music, and the effect on you will be heavenly! [10]

This monologue-declamation "For a Musical Evening" is a remarkable blend of old and new, European and American, all filtered through an obviously awkward immigrant sensibility. The biblical reference is not completely incompatible with legends about King Arthur, the latter having circulated in Yiddish versions in Renaissance times. The confusions of Arthur and Troy, of fairies and goddesses are perhaps not unusual in the sense of unfamiliarity with classical and Christian themes. The appeal to science through the mention of music therapy shows a modernizing bent, and the stress on the value of instrumental music would seem to go against tradition. Yet we have seen that the *klezmer* in Europe was felt to penetrate to the soul of the occasion at weddings, and in a Yiddish play (to be examined below) it will appear that "the magic power of music" (the play's subtitle)—even secular music—was admissible by 1900. That the declamation appears in a book consciously entitled "Jewish-American Orator" indicates that such speeches were felt to belong to the New World as well as to the Old, though there are no specific American references. We return again to one of our recurring themes: to locate the nature of a particularly American immigrant experience, we must first understand all those experiences that are common to the general Euro-American world of the late nineteenth and early twentieth centuries. Against this background of Western culture, the distinctively Jewish-American styles, repertoires, and contexts will stand out all the more clearly.

In 1905 there occurred one particularly fine example of a Jewish-American event. During December, the same month which saw the host of balls and entertainments we have examined, the Lower East Side staged and witnessed its largest single demonstration, a massive march and rally that involved somewhere between 100,000 and 200,000 people, with many more as audience.[11] Significantly, events in Europe, not in America, triggered the outpouring. Called simply "The March" by the *Forverts*, which cosponsored the rally with the Bund, this event was called to protest the brutal excesses of the czarist regime. The *Forverts* explicitly stated the hope that such a demonstration would help arouse dormant government and public opinion in America to intervene on behalf of the Jews. Thus in some ways the 1905 march was a direct ancestor of the many solidarity parades for Russian Jewry held in New York in the 1970s.

The march was efficiently organized and faultlessly executed. It began on East Broadway, snaked through the entire Jewish quarter, and finally spilled into Union Square. A series of post-march oratory-cum-theater events was scheduled for all the available theater houses, led by the most prominent citizens of the Ghetto. The parade had eight divisions; of considerable significance for our interests is the fact that Division I was made up largely of the entertainers' organizations: the Musical Club (the Jewish Musicians' Union had not yet been founded), Choral Union, Boys' Synagogue Singers (in America even the choirboys were organized), Hebrew Actors' Union (the oldest actors' union in the world), Variety Actors' Union, Bill Pasters' and Ushers' Union, Variety Stage Carpenters' Union, and the Theatrical Tailors & Dressmakers' Union. This division also had the principal musical unit, a band, which played a funeral march subsequently published as "Der yidisher troyer-marsh" ("The Jewish Funeral March"). True to its theatrical placement and performers, this tune comes from a 1903 operetta by Perlmutter and Wohl, leading theater composers, on the Kishinev pogrom. A revival performance was given at the post-march theatricals. All observers agreed as to the force of the music at the event. The *Forverts* noted that "there was not a great deal of band music, but it was so quiet that the sad tones of the couple of orchestras virtually filled every corner of the district." The pastor of Grace Church at Broadway and Tenth had his church bells toll and stood bareheaded on the steps throughout the entire parade. This indicates that the hope for Christian response was not entirely in vain.

The foregoing survey of the musical life of the Ghetto is only a first step in our appreciation of that complex and culturally dense music culture; it will take years and many researchers to arrive at a full understanding of music's role in those early decades. The centrality of the Yiddish theater to many of the events described requires that we turn our attention to the role music played in that dominant expressive form, in which the hopes and fears of the immigrants were literally acted out. The Yiddish theater represented an attempt at a serious, almost high-culture institution, as opposed to the raw street culture we will examine later. Such a point of view has rarely occurred to some recent describers of Lower East Side life—Irving Howe, for example, tends to view the early Yiddish theater as faintly comical. Contemporary descriptions such as those of Corbin and Hapgood were much quicker to point out the artistic and social value of the Yiddish theater, which they see as a quintessential expression of the artistic strivings of the immigrants: "In all the artistic output of the Ghetto there is the same correspondence between the life and history of the people and their art that is evident in the theatres. . . . The arts of the Ghetto, as is usually the case when arts spring from the masses, are imbuing their patrons with a sense of the community of their life and interests. In the truest sense of the word, they are national arts." [12] Here Corbin, writing in 1898, touches on the centrality of the theater. Though he has the prescience to realize that "in a generation or two the native color of Yiddish life will fade, and the theatres with them," he can't help wondering if the trade-off for Americanization will bring the Jews equivalent aesthetic satisfaction: "In a democratic community the genius for artistic creation is most likely to be manifested when the community falls heir to aspirations above its worldly condition—as occurred when these Yiddish people reached our shores. If in the course of years our souls should cease to fulfil their largest hopes in out-of-door sports and porcelain baths, is it more than reasonable to suppose that the longing for ampler life can be satisfied only by something very beautiful?"

As eloquently as Corbin addresses the Yiddish theater, he might just as well have addressed his remarks to a variety of other ethnic-dramatic situations in America. Certainly the East Side Jews were passionate in their attachment to theater, but theirs was a mania shared at least in part by members of other ethnic groups. The Yiddish theater has its own striking characteristics, but it cannot be fully appreciated as a phenomenon unless we have a general sense of the parallel ethnic and mainstream dramatic traditions of the period. It has been all too easy to think of the Yiddish theater, like everything else Jewish, as "a special case." It is insufficient to say, as Irving Howe has done, that "Jewish audiences relished the details . . . shouted denunciations of villains, and showed no displeasure with the mixture of tragedy and vaudeville, pageant and farce," or to note that "it is characteristic of the Yiddish theatre during these years [1880s and 1890s] that together with *shund* [trash] it should turn to productions of Shakespeare, Schiller, and Goethe" [13] without attempting to ascertain whether this sort of behavior was typical only of Jews, or whether it formed a part of the general theatrical world. Nahma Sandrow, in her excellent history of the Yiddish theater, is closer to the mark when she says that "*shund* is the sort of art that most cultures and most peoples like best." [14]

The American theatrical scene of the late nineteenth century was dynamic, even spectacular, on the one hand and completely routine on the other. Extravagance was displayed in fantastic scenery and special effects (train crashes, avalanches, waterfalls) which foreshadowed the development of motion pictures. The mundane nature of popular theater lay in the endless recycling of familiar plots and plays and the evolution of touring networks of stock companies that insured continuity and homogeneity of repertoire across the United States. As the century progressed, more and more entertainment forms were added, as entrepeneurs like P. T. Barnum dreamed up new formats and marketing ideas. The staple item was the melodrama, in which virtuous heroines were rescued by strong (but not too bright) heroes from the clutches of thoroughly evil villains. Owen Davis, a highly successful concoctor of plays, concisely summarized his craft:

> In the days of which I am writing, the characters of our popular-priced plays were as sturdily founded upon a conventional mold as the most dogmatic creed of the most narrow-minded religious fanatics of the day, and any stepping aside upon a more flowery path was sternly frowned upon. The good play

maker of the popular-priced theater was supposed to know
what a proper list of characters for a play must be and any departure from that accepted list was taken as a sign of the bad
workman. [15]

Scenically, these plays of ours were very elaborate . . . the
mechanical dexterity demanded in writing a play of this kind
was very important and an extremely difficult trick to acquire.
. . . The expert workman let his front scenes run the exact
time it took the stage carpenters to set the next scene back of
it and not a moment longer. [16]

In many respects, immigrant theater in America simply emulated the
amazing success of melodrama, the dominant genre of Western entertainment. Melodrama offers exactly those characteristics cited by Howe
as being typical of Jewish theatrical fare. To quote a historian of the
melodrama: "Farcical scenes and scenes of violence and pathos follow
each other in rapid alternation, this sequence being one of the
trademarks of melodrama. . . . Indeed, melodrama is eclectic in content: tragedy, comedy, violence, sensation, pathos, love—a bit of everything to everybody's taste." [17]

In addition, the Yiddish theater's thirst for musical commentary and
distraction was simply part of the general scheme. As early as 1814 a
keen observer of popular drama noted that: "its music is not more
remote from nature than the blank verse of the rhymes of tragedy . . . in
fact, the music supplies the place of language." An observer in 1880
remarked: "Nearly all the performers had a bar of music to bring them
on each time, and another to take them off; a bar when they sat down,
and a bar when they got up again; while it took a small overture to get
them across the stage. As for the leading lady, every mortal thing she did
or said, from remarking that the snow was cold, in the first act, to
fancying she saw her mother and then dying, in the last, was preceded
by a regular concert." As for the "hack" quality of early Yiddish theater,
discussed below, it turns out to be the rule rather than the exception:
"To make any sort of living from the stage . . . one had to write and adapt
with great speed, and it is no wonder that authors stuck to the tried
formulas of melodrama; there was no time for experiment. . . . It was
common for a dramatist to have well over a hundred plays to his credit.
. . . The melodramatist was therefore naturally inclined to borrow a
story rather than invent one."

The prominence of comedy, as well as of ethnic stereotypes, was as
crucial to melodrama as were the violence and stage effects. As Owen
Davis flatly states, the comedian had to be "either Irish, Jew, or Ger-

man." He was "the most important member of the company in the old days and the one who drew the largest salary. We might, and as a matter of fact we frequently did, get away with a terrible leading man, but the comedian had to be good." [18] Michael Booth points out, regarding comic figures, that "their comedy is low comedy, as consistently exaggerated in its way as the scenes of violence and pathos in theirs. The comic sub-plot of a melodrama is not entirely separate from the main story." [19]

The worldview presented by Western popular drama in the period under discussion is as simple as the characterization and the mechanics: support for the status quo. This meant unflinching belief in the victory of virtue over vice, and of the prevalent morals of the middle class. Any woman who strayed from the straight and narrow was doomed: "Our heroine must be pure at any cost, or else she must die," says Davis.[20] The particular genius of the melodrama is its combination of the fantasy world—triumph of virtue, spectacular staging—with a base in solid, everyday reality of the sort familiar to a lower-class audience. Only this mixture of the real and the unreal could effectively charm the spectators. As Booth notes, "reality and ideality are curiously blended; the dream is more real and therefore more powerful because its framework is familiar." [21] Here again, commentators like Howe over-specialize the Jewish case when they say "the writers and actors of this early Yiddish theatre understood instinctively that their audiences, seemingly lost forever in the darkness of the sweatshop, wanted most of all the consolations of glamour. . . . Realism seldom attracts uncultivated audiences: it is a sophisticated genre resting on the idea that a controlled exposure to a drab reality will yield pleasure." [22] The contrast between "drab reality" and streamlined fantasy is what makes popular drama work. In addition, one does not do justice to the immigrant theater—whether Jewish, Irish, or Swedish—to speak of "instinctive" creation of forms and style. Just as the musicians with whom we became acquainted earlier founded their American efforts on abundant experience with European audiences, so the playwrights and actors must be seen as thoroughly competent professionals, rather than as intuitive amateurs.[23]

Above all, the musical drama of the Jewish immigrants needs to be seen as merely one of a number of such theatrical enterprises among the ethnic groups of the late nineteenth century. Though the scripts and records of many of those ephemeral stage traditions lie untouched in archives around the country, the glimpses available now allow us to see a certain consistency in all the ethnic attempts to create internal worlds of drama. Be it the New York German theater of the 1860s, the Irish stage of Harrigan in the '70s, or the Swedish theater in Chicago of the '80s, certain structural characteristics indicate a common approach, and all these traits are shared with the Yiddish theater. A quick rundown of three salient features will pave the way for our discussion of the Jewish case.

Common stock of repertoire. Ethnic theaters all featured several basic sources for plays: 1) European melodrama, largely French and German, also a prime source for the mainstream American stage; 2) Shakespeare, or parodies thereof, another staple of the Western world shared by minority and majority theaters; 3) plays on the process of immigration and acculturation, taking various forms but being nearly identical in certain features, such as the mockery of the "greenhorn" newcomer; 4) plays stressing nostalgia for the homeland, a theme paralleled by (and featuring) the popular song traditions we have examined; and 5) plays on crises of the ethnic group, usually involving a response to wars or disasters "back home" in Europe.

Struggle and transience. Every account of an immigrant theater relates the difficulties of finding adequate performance space, actors, and audiences. The size of the internal audience oscillated as immigration fluctuated year by year and decade by decade. A new infusion of greenhorns was always necessary to offset those Americanized ethnics who no longer wanted to hear songs or see dramas in the Old World languages.

Common worldview and principles of stagecraft. As already noted, American ethnic theater was simply part of the general Euro-American tradition which centered on melodrama. One reads accounts of how the great Mogulesco imitated some street person down to the last detail of dress and speech, as if copying were a special talent of this Jewish genius. Yet Edward Harrigan, the mainstay of late nineteenth century Irish-American theater, was famous for exactly the same reason: he possessed a gift for perfect mimicry of ordinary life. Nor is such a strategy purely American. There is a poignant scene in the classic French film *Les Enfants du paradis*, a work about the French nineteenth-century melodrama, in which a ragpicker storms backstage to protest being so scrupulously caricatured onstage. He regarded the act as an insult, but the audience thought of it as basic to their evening's entertainment. Such techniques were essential to create the reality that then blended with fantasy.

Another commonly held principle was the primacy of the happy ending and the triumph of virtue, which were nearly universal in ethnic theater. The exceptions—perhaps most notable among the Jews—occurred in those plays that dealt with the history or present crises of the ethnic group, in which the outcome may have been unhappy or in doubt. In the few such plays, the ethnic group deviates sharply from the mainstream. The latter tends to avoid protest over the results of battles, wars, or persecution in favor of popular entertainment's main task: to gloss over, rather than to stress, the diversity and the origin of its audience.

Now we are ready to examine the Yiddish theater on its own terms. This can perhaps best be done by a close reading of a single typical work. Our case study, a play about a musician, allows us both to examine the stage image of the entertainer and to see how music is integrated into the structure of the standard *shund* melodrama of the early immigrant era. Along the way we will note ways in which our chosen work fits into the general context of American theater.

Dovids fidele ("David's Violin") by Joseph Lateiner, premiered in 1897. The title itself contains the seeds of the dramatic tension, which centers on the musician's role. *Fidele* ought to translate as "fiddle," but the sheet music for the play translates the word as "violin," introducing the conflict between older and newer views of the musician as presented in the play. The subtitle, "Or, the Magic Power of Music," again indicates a definite cultural perspective on music's role.

According to Sholem Perlmutter, the eminent theater historian, *David's Violin* was one of Lateiner's ten most popular plays.[24] Considering that Lateiner's output is generally estimated at two hundred dramas, this is no mean ranking. The play was particularly popular in Europe, being performed at least through World War I. It was still produced at the Detroit Yiddish theater in the mid-1920s, used for a one-night stand in a provincial playhouse. It is clear that we are dealing with a work that is standard, in the best sense of the word. Reinforcing an impression of durability is the fact that one of Mogulesco's songs for the show was not only recorded on a Columbia record, but was still listed in the 1916 catalogue, a generation after the premiere.

David's Violin takes place in Europe, which tends to mark it as a product of the first generation, when both playwrights and audiences could readily identify with life in the Old World. It is written in *daytshmerish*, the highfalutin stage language evolved by that generation. (Excerpts cited below are from a 1976 performing version, in which the English reflects little of the original fustiness.) Even more archaic than the language is the plot. According to Zilbertsvayg,[25] Lateiner took the story from an older German play called *Der Geiger* ("The Violinist"). The theme of the play might well relate to the German provincial stage of two generations before Lateiner.[26] Such backwater European sources feature prominently in the work of prolific playwrights like Lateiner and his archrival, "Prof." Hurwitz.

The story centers around two brothers, David and Tevya. The latter is referred to as the *gevir* (local rich man, translated here as "nabob," the equivalent given in Harkavy's contemporary Yiddish-English dictionary) of the town, who has worked his way up to become a pillar of society. Tevya has a son, Yankele; a drunken servant, Noah; and a gold-digging niece, Evie (Khavele in the original). Tevya wants to keep Yankele from marrying David's daughter, Tabele; at the same time he covets the twenty-year-old Evie for himself. This is a good Yiddish theater plot already, because 1) it involves domestic dissension and intrigue, and 2) it allows for various engagement and wedding scenes, often the heart and usually the climax of a period play. One more character rounds out this side of the dramatic action: Solomon, a student who is madly in love with Evie, and whose jealousy becomes a threat.

A second platoon of characters, all comic types, serve both as clowns—so essential to popular drama—and as two-faced friends to Tevya. Keyla Beyla is a widow with a foolish son; Itsele is a widower with a nitwit daughter. Their capers and pretentions provide comic relief, along with the servant Noah's drunken antics, and end up conveying part of the play's moral message: when Solomon, crazed by jealousy, steals Tevya's hard-won fortune, Keyla Beyla and Itsele have not a nickel to lend their old benefactor in order to save him from ruin.

What has this to do with David and his violin? A second level of plot, overlaid on this melodramatic matrix, involves David's struggle to convince Tevya to allow the marriage of the two brothers' children, Tabele and Yankele. Out of that conflict comes the chief message of the play, relating to "the magic power of music." When the play opens, David has been absent from town for fifteen years. He had insisted on pursuing a musical vocation, much to the grief of his (and Tevya's) parents; after his young wife died, he left the area. He has returned dressed as a poor street musician. In a towering rage, Tevya throws him out. Here is how Tevya describes his brother's career to Yankele:

> He was as lazy as I was industrious. He had only one obsession, and it stuck with him his whole life: his fiddle. He did nothing day and night but scrape on that fiddle. As hard as our blessed father tried to dissuade him from becoming a fiddler, a gypsy, he stood fast and unrepentant. Well, he found some sort of poor girl to marry, and you can believe that none of us

attended the wedding. Our parents were so deeply hurt by his behavior that they died before their time. He went on fiddling. He had a child, but that made no difference. Poor and impoverished he became. He fiddled on. Then his wife died. His child is that Tabele, whom he left in strangers' hands when he went off into the wide world. How can you even consider marrying a girl whose father sacrificed everything and everyone for the sake of a stupid fiddle? [27]

Tevya's position is an almost classic statement of the respectable townsman's view of the *klezmer*, the itinerant instrumentalist; even the pejorative word "gypsy" is used in his tirade. David's response indicates a radically different, more modern sensibility:

So, I brought my parents to the grave? I let my wife starve? What tales these people tell of me! You would think I was the devil incarnate to hear them talk. I tell you, it is this Mr. Itsele with his bulging belly, he and villains like him, who set my father against me. Yes, these overfed, uneducated fools, they are the ones who hate the arts. And my own brother! To turn me away with curses! If only he realized that by cursing my gift he is cursing the Lord who gave it to me. Ah, for treating me so, it is sure God will visit upon him tribulations and troubles. But it is not in my heart to wish my brother harm—even if he does turn me from his door.

So philistinism, and not conventional melodramatic evil, is the source of Tevya's misfortunes: the proposed misalliance with a niece one-third his age, his trusting of deceitful friends, his blocking of Yankele's love for Tabele. One can indeed imagine an earlier origin for the play's plot, since the value of Art had long since been introduced as a dramatic theme in Western Europe. At the same time, we see a divergence from the standard pattern of melodrama that reigned supreme in Euro-American culture. After all, Tevya is not the usual black-hearted villain; he is scrupulously honest, charitable, and upstanding, and his fortune is built on hard work, not swindle. David, too, is not the usual melodramatic hero, who should be a not-too-bright but earnest and brave young man. And where is the innocent heroine whose virtue is threatened? In short, we are dealing with what Lateiner calls a *lebnsbild*, a picture from life, of a particularly Jewish variety.

Tevya's view of Art as fiddle-scraping cannot compete with David's almost Byronic musings on the same subject. Here is the exchange

between daughter and father before David reveals his identity to
Tabele:

> DAVID. I am many men, and no man. I am much, and I am
> nothing. The sun, moon and stars move from their courses as I
> play, yet men pass me by with blank faces. I am master of the
> world, its mountains, forests, plains, fires, and floods, and yet I
> must beg for a night's lodgings. I am at once Prince and
> pauper.
> TABELE. These are the riddles of a poet; they are beyond my
> understanding.
> DAVID. Ah, my beautiful child, then let me speak to your
> heart. (*He plays his violin; Tabele weeps.*)

Only when he has seen how music affects his daughter does David
proclaim himself to be her father. She even offers extra evidence of her
heritage by saying she would gladly become a street singer to support
her father, whom she presumes to be old and infirm. One more sign of
musical solidarity: David left his daughter with the local cantor when he
wandered off to play his violin.

The first major turn of the plot comes in a well-orchestrated surprise
ending for Act II. In a renewed, high-tension confrontation between the
brothers, Tevya uses the Protestant ethic as part of his ammunition
against David:

> Am I not famed for my industriousness, my honesty? Am I not
> renowned as a public benefactor and honored pillar of respect-
> able society? While you, what have you got to boast of? Gypsy,
> beggar! Scum! Look upon me—blessed by the good Lord for a
> life of rectitude and honest toil. . . . You left as a beggar, and
> you return as a beggar.

David's retort comes as a total shock:

> He who accumulates the greatest riches is considered the best
> of men in this town. Very well: who is the best now? (*pours
> gold onto the floor*) I wear these rags to test you. In truth, I
> have more money than you can dream of. How can this be,
> you ask in your ignorance? I will tell you. Because I am
> famous in every capital of Europe. Because I am feted by
> Princes and worshipped by Kings. Wherever music is loved,
> the name of David Violin is honored. I am world-famous. Look
> at these (*strips off rags to reveal medals*)—bestowed upon me

by Emperors. Down on your knees, nabob, brother, foolish, ignorant man!

Curtain.

No better vindication of the arts could be imagined—at least for someone like Tevya. But where is the poetry, the magic power of music? For that we must wait until the play's final scene. Tevya has refused to give in to David just because he is rich and famous; he spurns David's money in his hour of need, and is shown on the point of hanging himself. Fortunately, he has an inkling of grace through music: he asks David to play a lament for him. David invokes the shades of their parents to inspire him, and he plays (and sings) the show's final number, "Dor holekh, ve dor bo." This almost shamanistic exercise of music's power immediately exorcises Tevya's demons of pride and philistinism:

> TEVYA. As King Saul was saved by the music of David, so am I saved! O godly man! Let us live in peace and love together. O my dearest brother!

The juxtaposition of King David's therapeutic music and the name of our hero now becomes abundantly evident. The pairing of David and the violin seems to have been commonplace among Jews of the time, for a song of the period called "Di yidishe hofnung" ("The Jewish Hope") tells us that in some future realm the entertainment will be appropriately glorious: "David will play on his violin." The suggestion of music therapy makes the earlier declamation on music's power seem more plausible as well. One is also reminded of a folk riddle about the violin: "What grows in the forest, hangs in the shop, and when you give it a push, it sings?" This organic sense of the fiddle-to-be almost recalls the Siberian shaman's careful selection of a tree suitable for his spirit-enlivening drum. And an animate quality is ascribed to the fiddle in the phrase "give it a push, and it sings."

Returning to *David's Violin*, the power of David's artistry is compounded as Solomon jumps from his hiding place to return Tevya's money, saying that music has cured him of his sick jealousy. Suitably (and almost comically), David gives Solomon a scholarship to music school as a means of rehabilitation. The young couple can now marry, the old comic fools are exposed, and all ends well.

Although the general theme of *David's Violin* is behind the times from a European point of view, in its specific underscoring of a socio-musical process it is very up-to-date in Jewish terms. Around the turn of the century the famous Jewish dynasty of violin virtuosos was established in the cosmopolitan port city of Odessa. Coming mainly from *klezmer* families, the little Elmans, Heifetzs, Gingolds, and Zimbalists poured out of Russia. The use of entertainment (in this case, classical music) to achieve upward social mobility is already familiar from our analysis of the immigrant decades, and it is noteworthy that a durable work of the early Yiddish theater takes up the same topic. The theme is cloaked in the new tenet of the musical belief system—that art can be Art, a praiseworthy value—and is wrapped in the familiar packaging of domestic intrigue.

This overlay of a second plot component has been severely criticized by Yiddish drama critics. B. Gorin, the author of an authoritative history of the Yiddish theater, cites Lateiner's lack of consistency in following up a single narrative thread as proof of the playwright's incompetence.[28] Gorin is similarly appalled at the mixture of drama, comedy, and music that characterizes the early Yiddish stage. True, Ibsen and Strindberg would have disapproved; and later Yiddish dramatists were to reject the Lateiner formula, instead favoring Western European naturalist models. Yet Gorin misses the point. *David's Violin*, like all of Lateiner's work, is devoted to satisfying an audience for *popular* drama, as defined earlier in the present chapter, not *art* drama.

Having examined the issue in terms of drama, we can now take a second look at the play based on the musical principles of popular theater. We have seen that the Jewish public made no musical distinction between folk, popular, and classical styles; their major musical heroes, whose voices were equated, were Rosenblatt the cantor and Caruso the opera singer, both of whom drew on art music models. Yet although the virtues of art music and the lonely (if success-strewn) path of the classical performer were extolled in *David's Violin*, the audience that responded to this anti-philistine stance was ready to accept neither an art drama nor a drama based on art music. Nor were the composers of the Yiddish theater prepared, until well into the 'teens, to consider themselves writers of "serious" music. The contrast here is apparent between the New York musicians and a composer such as Shlossberg of Warsaw. The latter steadfastly declined to come to America to work in Yiddish theater because the pace and quality of "made to order" theater music left him cold. He attempted occasional "serious" pieces for Yiddish dramas; for example, he produced a prologue for chorus and orchestra for Gordin's *God, Man, and Devil*. The manuscript of this work, praised by theater critics, is in the Perlmutter Theater Archives at YIVO. Even a cursory glance at this meticulously copied full score, compared to the scrawled "lead sheets" (tune only) of the New York composers, is instructive. The music shows Shlossberg to be a talented writer with musical aims far removed from those of the choirboys.

Thus it is not in terms of "quality" that we must seek to appreciate the music of the early Yiddish theater. If we take seriously the criticism which states that music was merely so much razzle-dazzle intended to distract the public from the deficiencies of the script, we must analyze the placement and style of musical numbers in a play like *David's Violin*. Is music in fact mere extraneous matter designed to tickle the ear? The text of *David's Violin* (in the pirated Warsaw edition of 1914) indicates fifteen musical moments. This is a generous number, even if not up to the twenty-five required for Goldfadn's more ambitious dramas. The songs can be grouped under four headings, each of which makes a particular type of contribution to the overall shape of the play. Music does indeed contribute heavily to the coherence and cultural import of *David's Violin*.

Entertainment. This category, which Gorin would say included all the music, really fits only two items: an indication of dances and merriment at David's party for the lovers Tabele and Yankele, and a comic item called "The Four Hasidim [Wedding Guests]" in the published sheet music for the play. While there are three engagement parties, there are no real weddings in the play, so just where to put the Hasidim was a bit problematic in my 1976 reconstruction of *David's Violin*. They were finally placed in the midst of the festivities, since the text has the Hasidim being horrified at the way "secular folk" carry on at their parties. The use of an essentially satirical, anti-Hasidic number goes back to the heart of Jewish Enlightenment cultural politics. The Hasidim were the target of many early Yiddish works of satirical fiction; indeed, some of Goldfadn's earliest sketches for the Yiddish proto-theater of the 1870s were in the same vein. Lateiner's use of this comic-musical motif, then, is an almost ritual one, springing from the notion of early Yiddish theater itself.

Action-underlining music. Five musical items serve to mark specific moments of the play. Two congratulatory choruses (birthday, engagement) help underscore the fact that these recurrent domestic events form the basic underpinning of the play's structure. Twice we find solo fiddle music introduced as David's trademark, underlining and, in a sense, advancing the plot. First, the offstage fiddle breaks into Tevya's birthday party and announces David's existence. It allows him to enter the scene in his street musician's disguise when he is invited to play for the guests. The second time David fiddles for an audience of one: his daughter. As noted earlier, she cannot understand his lofty description of the artist's role, so he offers to play for her—the music alone can convey his sentiments. Her tears move him to disclose his identity. The music raises the level of emotional impact beyond that evoked by the rather routine dialogue of reunion which follows, and was bound to extract the audience's cathartic tears.

One other moment of musical underlining comes right at the center of the play, when David sings the young couple a genial song about romantic love. This song, "Dos krigele" ("The Pitcher"), must have been quite popular, since it was reprinted separately in sheet music form. It is a typical Mogulesco lyric song in a tranquil waltz meter. The melody is very repetitive, and chord changes are few and far between, yielding a folk-like quality. The text revolves around a single metaphor, the pitcher. Here the image is biblical: a boy helps a girl at a well lift a heavy pitcher, inevitably evoking the archetype of Jacob and Rebecca. Mogulesco puts the pitcher to good use by concluding each verse with "the pitcher will always be full," symbolizing eternal love. Naive, ingenuous—yes; but Mogulesco's compositional process is also very effective in its straightforward working out of simple images. Drawing on biblical material is a useful way of linking the audience to the dramatic point at hand, as Goldfadn found out in his enormously successful costume operettas. Even the czar got the point, banning Yiddish theater in Russia after the production of *Bar kochba*, the story of a small band of Jews who revolted against a powerful (Roman) Empire. Through the innocent medium of "Dos krigele," the preeminence of romantic love—by no means a harmless topic in 1897, when Americanization was breaking down the system of arranged marriages—is quietly fostered. The flowing, tranquil song serves as a good centerpiece for the melodramatic action of robbery and betrayal which follow in Act III.

Character portrayal. Seven of the play's fifteen musical moments consist of songs which allow the various characters to be broadly portrayed. The clown Itsele's doltish son babbles two parodies of Yiddish songs to show his idiocy; this performance is balanced by a number in Act III, when the drunken comic servant Noah does a comic patter song about swearing off drink. The lovers Tabele and Yankele sing two songs each (in Act I and Act III, respectively) that allow them to give full vent to their feelings, strengthening audience sympathy for their situation. Tabele's songs are passive female expressions of emotion, while Yankele has active, even aggressive texts. The girl bemoans her fate as an orphan (an extremely popular song genre in both Yiddish and mainstream American music at the time) and then sings a "good night" song (a genre found in various Yiddish plays) in which she implores God to help her. Yankele, on the other hand, first actively expresses his strong feelings for Tabele, then sings a rebellious song in which he reflects his resentment over his father's high-handed dismissal of romantic love.

Why does Tevya never have a chance to sing? His voice dominates in the dialogue, and the play revolves around his plight. But in melodrama, unlike opera, there is no need for him to throw his weight around still further by singing—he looms large enough as it is. It is David who gets the most impressive musical exposure of the play. The music quite properly helps Lateiner make his point: the philistine lacks music, and so cannot move the audience, while the champions of Art and Love reap most of the musical benefits. David has the last and most important musical item of the play, the only one to fall into our fourth category.

Plot advancement. In Act IV all is quickly resolved. David comes along just as Tevya seeks to hang himself. Unable to dissuade him with speech, David cures him through music. Through the presumed intervention of the parental spirits and aided by his own artistic talent, David is able to restore the balance of family life, that critical goal of so much of Yiddish theater. "Dor holekh, ve dor bo" ("Generations Come and Generations Go") is the only song from the play to be recorded; we cannot doubt that the audience took it seriously. David's quasi-cantorial number reflects on the transience of life and the need for the older generation to allow the young folks to take over. This is a modern concept, much as were romantic love and the preeminence of Art, for traditional Eastern European Jewish culture. In an extraordinary musical gesture, Mogulesco combines cantorial declamation and operatic turns of phrase with a soothing lullaby on the phrase *alters gey shlofn* ("old folks, go to sleep"). In this song the experienced, eclectic choirboy-turned-composer has melded the powerful expressive references of liturgical melody and the appeal of opera with the most charged affective sound of childhood: the "ay-lyu-lyu" ("rock-a-bye") of the Yiddish lullaby. Surely the highly emotional context of the song (attempted suicide), its placement as the climax of the dramatic action in Act IV, and its power to resolve all problems must indicate that critics like Gorin were wrong. Lateiner *did* know where to place his music, and Mogulesco knew exactly how to write it to both entertain and, at times, edify the audience. Music was truly an integral part of the Yiddish theater. Through their skillful shaping of melodrama, the Yiddish thespians showed that they had "paid their dues" as full-fledged members of the international Euro-American fraternity of musical dramatists.

NOTES

1. *Morris Rosenfeld's Selected Works* (New York: Forverts, 1912), I, 39–40. The translation is mine.

2. This and the passage quoted below are my translations from ibid., pp. 45–50.
3. This and the following five passages cited are from Charlotte Kimball Patten, "Amusements and Social Life: Philadelphia," in C. Bernheimer, ed., *The Russian Jew in the United States* (Philadelphia: John C. Winston, 1905), pp. 233–48.
4. Owen Davis, *I'd Like to Do It Again* (New York: Farrar and Rinehart, 1931), pp. 36–37.
5. This and the following three quotations are from Patten, "Amusements."
6. James L. Peacock, *Rites of Modernization* (Chicago: University of Chicago Press, 1968).
7. This and the following quotation are from Patten, "Amusements."
8. *Der fraynd*, May, 1917, p. 9.
9. See Zosa Szajkowski, "The Impact of the Russian Revolution of 1905 on American Jewish Life," *YIVO Annual of Jewish Social Science* 17 (1978): 54–118.
10. Kh. Gottlieb, "Tsu a muzikalishen abend," in G. Zeligovits, ed., *Der idish-amerikaner redner*, 3d ed. (New York: Hebrew Publishing Co., 1916; first ed., 1907), pp. 134–35.
11. The following account of the 1905 march is taken from the *Forverts*, December 4–5.
12. This and the following quotation are from John Corbin, "How the Other Half Laughs," "*Harper's* 98 (Dec. 1898): 30–48, as anthologized in N. Harris, ed., *The Land of Contrasts* (New York: Braziller, 1970), pp. 178–79.
13. Irving Howe, *World of Our Fathers* (New York: Harcourt Brace Jovanovich, 1976), p. 466.
14. Nahma Sandrow, *Vagabond Stars: A World History of the Yiddish Theater* (New York: Harper & Row, 1977), p. 110.
15. Davis, *I'd Like to Do It Again*, pp. 100–101.
16. Ibid., p. 106.
17. This and the following three quotations are from Michael Booth, *English Melodrama* (London: Herbert Jenkins, 1965), pp. 35–38.
18. Davis, *I'd Like to Do It Again*, p. 101.
19. Booth, *English Melodrama*, pp. 35–38.
20. Davis, *I'd Like to Do It Again*, p. 102.
21. Booth, *English Melodrama*, p. 187.
22. Howe, *World of Our Fathers*, p. 460.
23. Materials on ethnic drama remain scattered in the original languages in various archives, save for a few useful studies, e.g., Fritz A. H. Leuchs, *The Early German Theatre in New York, 1840–1872* (New York: AMS Press, 1966, reprint of orig. ed., 1928), and Henriette C. K. Naeseth, *The Swedish Theatre of Chicago, 1868–1950* (Rock Island, Ill.: Augustana Historical Society and Augustana College Library, 1951). A volume now in press, M. Seller, ed., *Ethnic Theater in the United States* (Westport, Conn.: Greenwood Press), may prove valuable.

24. Sholem Perlmutter, *Yidishe dramaturgn un teater-kompozitors* (New York: YKUF-ferlag, 1952), p. 65.
25. Zalmen Zilbertsvayg, "Yosef Lateiner," *Leksikon fun yidishn teatr* (Warsaw, 1934), II, column 978.
26. Carl Schorske, personal communication.
27. Quotations here and below are from the unpublished performing edition copyrighted by Tony Connor and Mark Slobin, 1976.
28. B. Gorin, *Geshikhte fun der yidishn teatr* (New York: Max Meisel, 1923), II, 74–80.

CHAPTER 5

MAKING
A MUSIC CULTURE:
THE LOW ROAD

On the streets of Warsaw, London, and New York, the Jewish peddlers of song sheets carried on musical traditions born in Elizabethan times. Popular tunes of the day; songs of the theater; ballads about murders, fires, and pogroms; comic and sentimental numbers—all these were grist for the printing presses of the Euro-American metropolis. Older folksingers can remember a blind street hawker crying his musical wares just outside the Yiddish theaters, and similar figures haunted the byways of the Jewish quarters in Europe. Meanwhile, makeshift stages in saloons and lofts offered crude entertainments which also appeared on the "legitimate" boards of the Yiddish theater as afterpieces to heavy melodramas like *David's Violin*. At the same time, the early Victrolas cranked out songs of questionable moral content, sometimes placed on the flip sides of national, didactic, or lyric numbers. Taken as a whole, these frankly broad entertainments form the "low road" of the music culture, one which has been neglected even more than the melodramas of Lateiner.

To allow the immigrants a full-bodied world of entertainment is not to demean their accomplishment in America. In addition, there are ties that bind the immigrants' low-life songs both to ancestors in the Old World and to later generations of Jewish-Americans. We will first examine a sample set of broadsides such as were hawked on the Lower East Side, and then scrutinize one longer work of low entertainment, Minikes's *Among the Indians*, a vaudeville playlet of 1895.

Responding to a request from E. and J. Mlotek in the *Forverts*, I. J. Weinrot sent in a set of broadsides which can typify the "low-life" material; a few additional items from other sources round out our survey.[1] Most of these printings are the work of a certain Sani Shapiro, who changed addresses in Manhattan and Brooklyn frequently, and about whom nothing is now known. A couple of sheets from Toronto and London can serve for comparison. Yiddish broadsides are extremely rare, but our sample is so diverse and so lively that it can well stand for the genre in the absence of fuller findings.

Not much of the material is really coarse or vulgar. On the early 78 rpm recordings, low songs are mixed in with didactic, national, and topical material, as well as with pirated versions of Yiddish theater songs previously copyrighted in the expensive "high road" editions. Some items are tied to recording stars and specific commercial disc releases. One point which will emerge from the full discussion of play scripts, broadsides, expensive sheet music, and sound recordings is the considerable extent to which they all overlap; this phenomenon extends through the days of radio and into the post–World War II period.

The Shapiro broadsides indicate the range of the material and its juxtapositions:

A. 1. an earnest song on the workingman's condition, "Dem arbeters trer" ("The Worker's Tears");
   2. a titillating song called "Di khasene nakht" ("The Wedding Night");
   3. an advertisement for a "thought-reader and advice-giver" who takes no fee if the patron isn't satisfied.

B. 1. "Tsurik ken tsion" ("Back to Zion"), a Zionist song;
   2. "Fregt mikh bekherem" ("Don't Ask Me"), a vulgar song flitting from topic to topic about lowlife in America from the immigrant standpoint.

C. 1. "Aher gey, tsar Nikolay" ("Come Here, Czar Nicholas"), "sung and written by Mr. Karp at the Clinton Moving Pictures" (discussed below), a mixed vulgar and topical song;
   2. "Shabes koydesh" ("The Holy Sabbath"), a didactic song about the joys of the Sabbath;
   3. "Hits, hits, hits" ("Heat, Heat, Heat"), a low song about the New York heat wave.

D. This is a multi-sheet package entitled "Dos kleyne lidermagazin" ("The Little Song Magazine"), 5¢, containing the following:
   1. "Di troyer lid fun der groyser milkhome" ("Mourning Song of The Great War"), to be sung to the tune of "A brivele

fun Rusland" ("A Letter from Russia"), a pop song on the same topic;

2. "Dzhindzher" ("Ginger"), a bawdy song, discussed below;

3. "Dos farblondzhete sheyfele" ("The Stray Sheep"), a pop song of the Yiddish theater by Thomashefsky about the wandering of the Jews;

4–6. three parodies of the *kiddush*, the opening benediction of the Sabbath meal;

7. a cartoon of the suffering Jew;

8. "Di yidishe troike," a popular song on faith, hope, and charity as the three horses of the Jewish troika;

9. "Ven men ruft dikh tsurik" ("When You're Called Back"), a didactic, *memento mori* pop song;

10. "Nyu yorker yingele" ("The New York Boy"), sung to a popular tune on the same topic: the evils of America;

11. "Tate mames frayndshaft" ("Mom and Dad's Friendship"), to the tune of a popular orphan song; on filial love;

12. "Mayn kales apetit" ("My Fiancee's Appetite"), a Rabelaisian gastronomic song, discussed below.

E. "Frenks tragedie" ("Frank's Tragedy"), a Toronto broadside on the Leo Frank case of 1915. The song is sandwiched between extensive illustrated ads for a restaurant and a furniture store. This item can be precisely dated, as it speaks of Frank's pardon (June 21), seeing it as evidence of God's intervention on behalf of the slandered Jew, and omits mention of Frank's lynching, which must have occurred after the sale of the song (August 16).

As the foregoing sample indicates, there is no easy way of catergorizing the broadside material, which cuts across generic and topical lines. A bit surprising is the absence of songs parodying American hits of the day, since the writing of parodies was an accepted practice at least as early as the 1890s, when "A Bicycle Built for Two" and "Do, Do, My Huckleberry Do" were published in Yiddish versions.[2] By contrast, the Sani Shapiro sheets are resolutely in-group in reference.

A look at selected song texts will more clearly indicate the direction in which the low road meandered. "Come Here, Czar Nicholas" is a useful point of departure, since its structure is typical of many immigrant-period songs. The song text's tag line returns in the chorus that follows each verse. (The multiple uses of this format will be surveyed in a later chapter.) In "Czar Nicholas," a fairly unskilled song, the first verse essentially says nothing, except that "wherever you go, you hear people say 'come here, come here.'" Verse 2 details the usage of the phrase when a boy sidles up to his girl in the moving picture show (remember the song's performance place: the Clinton Theater). She retorts with the rhyming line "leytr, doling dir" ("later, darling dear"). Verse 3 shifts the scene drastically, to the battlefields of World War I, where the Germans are inviting the swinish, cowardly czar to "come here" and take a well-deserved beating. Fairly coarse language is used. It is this use of language, more than structure or even content, that truly distinguishes the low tradition as opposed to the high road of the theater and the expensive sheet music. Adjectives like *mamzerish* ("bastardly") and *khazerish* ("swinish," particularly insulting in the Jewish tradition) only rarely appear in the "better" editions of immigrant song.

Of two more Shaprio-printed songs that do not appear elsewhere, one is of the crudest variety, while the other shows imaginative use of speech play. First is "Dzhindzher" ("Ginger"):

Verse 1
This song is called ginger; I sing it quickly, with ginger.
It'll give you ginger, since ginger's the best thing.
It's very hard to live without ginger; whoever doesn't
    have ginger isn't living.
Wherever you go, everywhere you just hear:

Chorus
Ginger, whoever's got ginger, is somebody today.
Girls who have ginger are all right,
Since boys creep around looking for ginger, a girl with ginger.
With a lot of powder and paint.
At the North Pole full of puffs, a face with ginger, full
    of bluffs
Since ginger's the best thing.

Verse 2
A rich man of fifty, dyes his hair every day;
His face has a toothless mouth, and he can hardly walk.
Although he's old and dead, he marries a young girl.
He gives her money without end, since he's looking for:

Chorus
Ginger, a drop of ginger.
He calls her darling dear;
Oy vey! does she give him ginger—he makes way for her.

This old codger gets his walking papers because he doesn't have
   ginger.
He's already old and weak.
And for his money, on the sly, she gets a boy with a lot of ginger
Since ginger's the best thing.

Verse 3
My cousin has a soda stand, fixed up pretty and grand.
She has countless customers that only drink their ginger
   at her place.
All the standkeepers of the street know how to ask for her ginger.
She makes endless money, since everyone runs to her:

  Chorus
For ginger, oy, oy, ginger
They run without end.
Whoever tries her ginger stays her customer,
And my cousin is no greenhorn, she gives everyone ginger
Since she understands the trade.
She knows her business like a hero, gives ginger and takes money,
Since ginger's the best thing.

Like "Czar Nicholas," "Dzhindzher" is obsessed with the catch word,
insisting that "ginger" is all the rage. The boy-girl relationship mentioned in the "Czar" song is pushed even harder. A new element is the
old man/young girl misalliance; this recurs again and again in Jewish-
American vulgar comedy, cropping up in Catskill routines of the 1950s.
That the Borscht Belt takes its pedigree from the street songs of the
immigrant age has not been properly stressed or even basically researched. Yet there can be no question that the links hold in this chain
of low comedy; it is simply that we are largely ignorant about the
biographical facts and networks of diffusion that have allowed the
tradition to thrive for seven or eight decades.

The last stanza of "Dzhindzher" is perhaps the most offensive, since
it touches on the nearly taboo topic of Jewish-American prostitution. Of
all the subjects that have been tacitly declared off limits to public
commentary, this perhaps the most sensitive. Yet we have already seen,
in the case of the dance hall, that it is not possible to discuss immigrant
entertainment without at least mentioning the unmentionable. Michael
Gold's *Jews Without Money* (1930), a description of the Lower East
Side of his youth, parallels the accounts available in memoirs and
fictional sources of his time: "Pimps infested the dance halls. Here they
picked up the romantic factory girls who came after the day's work.

They were smooth story-tellers. They seduced the girls the way a child is helped to fall asleep, with tales of magic happiness. No wonder East Side parents wouldn't let their daughters go to dance halls. But girls need to dance." [3] For Gold, music was an important part of street life. He describes Italian organ-grinders and other readily available entertainment, and he keenly recalls the singing of Masha, the blind prostitute: "Many nights I fell asleep to the melodies of Kiev she sang to her seven-string guitar. We could hear it in our home. She sang between 'customers.' " Masha served as living bridge between the low music of Russia (for many of her romantic tunes must have been songs of the Kiev streets) and the parallel tradition growing in America.

Returning to the Shapiro broadsides, "My Fiancee's Appetite" takes quite a different stance on the question of male-female relationships. The vulgarities of gastronomy substitute for those of sex. This approach pops up now and again in songs and sketches; some of the coarsest of these belong to the late 1940s and serve as the immediate antecedents of the scatalogical-culinary horrors of Philip Roth's *Portnoy's Complaint*, which so shocked American Jewry. In a way, this exploitation of food is merely the comic extreme of the preoccupation with in-group cuisine that has always been strong in American ethnic life. "Foreign" dishes are usually the focus of ethnic display days in American communities, with music and crafts taking second place.

"My Fiancee's Appetite" is only lightly vulgar, due to the whimsy of the text. The lyrics suffer a great deal from translation for two reasons: first, the words rhyme in Yiddish, with each phrase of the two-part line matching up; second, the contrast of Yiddish and English is carefully programmed throughout. This can only be indicated by underlining of those English words that were spelled out in the Yiddish song text:

Just listen, folks, to my curse: I take my fiance out one day,
I want to give her <u>pleasure</u> and take her to Coney Island,
And there, I tell her nicely, "come to the restaurant with me."
O, woe is me when she <u>ordered</u> from the <u>bill of fare!</u>

Chopped liver, sardine <u>delight</u>, duck's eggs with geese feet,
<u>Fried</u> fish with salty <u>cake</u>, stuffed duck with black <u>steak</u>.
14 sausages with <u>green salad</u>, sour pickles with chocolate,
17 <u>sponge cakes</u> did she order, and the waiter brought it
    quick.

Fried <u>peanuts</u> with Swiss cheese, soapy pancakes with a
    stopped nose,
Ironed <u>oysters</u> with <u>apple pie</u>, salty <u>pudding</u> filled with lead,

Plum pudding with <u>corned beef</u>, a glass of brandy six feet
  deep,
Leather blintzes with paprikash, that's what she ordered
  courageously.

Chopped meat, mince meat <u>fricasee</u>, half an ox with two
  calves,
<u>Strawberry</u> <u>short</u> <u>cake</u> <u>fixed</u> with herring, <u>mustard</u> with honey
  with mixed pickles,
A goulash a la <u>Houston Street</u>, a mamaliga with pepper and
  meat,
<u>Potatoes</u> with <u>peaches</u> beautifully cooked, all this the waiter
  brought and she gobbled up.

Oxen eggs with pea soup, <u>fried</u> duck face down,
Chinese beans <u>fried</u> with wind, Spanish <u>potatoes</u> cooked with
  mint,
Italian macaroni with <u>castor</u> <u>oil</u>, Turkish coffee with
  buckwheat flour,
Young <u>toothpicks</u> with a glass of raisins, and all this the waiter
  brought to the table.

A bowl of borscht with a barrel of fabric, a tub of kasha with
  a plate of pilaf,
A <u>box</u> of knishes with a bucket of kraut, a <u>fried</u> Tageblatt
  [Yiddish newspaper] with a <u>union</u> bread,
A bowl of <u>ice</u> <u>cream</u> with hot kreplach, the <u>ice</u> <u>cream</u> cooled
  the sweat from the kreplach,
The Russian czar chopped in three, and the waiter brought it
  quick.

A <u>fried</u> ox with a long tongue, cooked magnesium with stewed
  lungs,
Dried peas with wet tea, roasted rain with cooked snow,
Bitter honey with sweet horseradish, polished shoes with a
  marrow bone,
Until, with God's help, she burst!

Of particular textual interest in this song of a lunch gone mad is the
slow build-up of fantastic elements, which eventually acquire a surreal
character toward the end: "roasted rain with cooked snow"; "bitter
honey with sweet horseradish." No other item in the available broadside
repertoire or in high-priced sheet music equals this parody. But what
does it parody? Surely it extends beyong the typical misogyny of many

folk and popular comic numbers to express a feeling about America in general. Food is indeed an important part of people's self-identification; anthropologists have found that "Cooking is . . . universally a means by which nature is transformed into culture, and categories of cooking are always peculiarly appropriate for use as symbols of social differentiation." [4] What we are dealing with is a comment on the hurly-burly, hodge-podge nature of American life, where strange foods are bolted down indiscriminately, often mixed with Old World specialties. What better symbol of Americanization at its worst than a bowl of ice cream with hot *kreplach* (dumplings)? The mixture of languages in the song has three basic impulses worth enumerating. First, there is the simple urge to create a rhyme. This is not trivial, since it is in search of such means of amusement that popular entertainment changes a language. Second, purely American dishes—such as strawberry short-cake—are called by their proper names. Finally, Yiddish is obscured through the substitution of English words ("fried," "salad") for Yiddish ones. This complexity of motivation reflects the cultural confusion of the situation being described. One of the main arguments of this chapter is that the details of supposedly vulgar entertainments yield new insights into the process of Americanization. Linguistic variety and hyperbole, along with cultural excess, reflect the disarray of immigrant life.

The relationship of boarder to landlady was also of central importance, and was not overlooked by the balladeers. Short stories, plays, letters to the editor (the famous "Bintel Brief" column of the *Forverts*), sheet music, and broadsides all speak to the point. Overcrowding and a surplus of single males led to the widespread practice of renting a room to supplement the meager family income. In the popular stereotype, the male boarder takes advantage of the landlord's absence to further his amorous interests with what is usually described (in the songs, but not in the letters to the editor) as a complaisant housewife. Of course, this plot outline is as old as the institution of the rented room, and it echoes throughout Western literature in one form or another. A typical broadside treatment of the subject can be found in "Motke." The song's narrator exclaims, in every refrain, how he always goes along with whatever his bosom buddy Motke does:

Just listen to how Motke moves in to a missus who has no husband.
Since Motke's living there, right away I take my trunk and move in.
Once it happened that I got up at night,

And what did I see but Motke holding a light in his hand,
   creeping to the missus.
I grab him and shout out loud:
Chorus
Motke, oy it's good, I'm coming,
Take me along, I want to go where you go,
Don't go without me, since I want to go with you . . .

Only in Verse 3 does the narrator change his mind about Motke, when
he is chased by the police for trying to extract a *vatch-en-tsheyn* (watch
and chain) from someone's pocket:

I know they give you lodging and board free in Sing-Sing,
But it's not OK to live with you, dear friend.
Motke, it's not good, this time I'm not coming along;
This time you go alone.

The moral seems to be that adultery is fine, but thievery is not. Like
prostitution, street crime is a topic that has become taboo in the Jewish-
American world, outside of the broadsides and a few sheet music folios.
The existence of networks of gangsters on the Lower East Side has
been largely concealed from public view, save for occasional forays into
memory like *Jews Without Money*. Nevertheless, as the historian
Arthur Goren has pointed out,[5] the Jewish gangster, like his counterpart in Warsaw and Odessa, was at least secretly admired for his
prowess. Men such as Big Jack Zelig were mourned by throngs when
they fell victim to rival forces. Even the official New York Jewish
communal organization noted that deplorable fellows like Zelig had
helped clear the district of Italian competitors.

It is odd to find so few songs about the Jewish gangster in America,
considering that large anthologies were collected in Warsaw in the
'teens. One would think that the low tradition would have embraced the
saga of the unfortunate youth who strayed from the path and ended up
imprisoned (or worse), or that it would have sung the praises of heroes
like the immortal Benya Krik of Isaac Babel's Russian stories of the
Odessa underworld. Perhaps internal censorship began quite early. Or
perhaps the experience of immigration, so richly represented in songs,
simply overshadowed the exploits of the daring gangster.

Having briefly surveyed the landscape along the low road, we can
now turn to a detailed survey of a particular larger work. Our sample is
chosen to speak to the question of Americanization. It is also the only

surviving specimen of a complete Yiddish vaudeville playlet, so commands our attention as a happily preserved rarity. *Tsvishn indianer* ("Among the Indians") by Khanan-Yakov Minikes (1867–1932) was performed for the first—and probably the only—time on April 17, 1895. The playlet has survived for reasons which indicate how such works were presented: the text forms part of the printed program for the evening's entertainment. The main part of the show consisted of a standard Yiddish melodrama starring a leading lady of the day. Minikes's number was an afterpiece, and the evening was designated as a benefit for the author. The custom of benefits for theater personnel has a long and honorable history in America, particularly on the immigrant stage (e.g., Harrigan's Irish company) due to the fluctuations of fortune that characterized ethnic drama. In addition to *Among the Indians*, the April 17 program included a wide variety of ads and a parody (presumably also by Minikes) of a portion of the Passover Haggadah, called *The Peddler's Haggadah*, relating the old ritual heritage to American concerns.

Minikes was a curious figure in the Jewish-American world. A prominent do-gooder for a variety of worthy causes, he was involved in many different ventures. In the Yiddish theater he functioned first as ticket-taker, then as accountant, publicist, and advertising manager. He was responsible for the first major collection of immigrant popular song texts in 1897; *Di yidishe bine* ("The Yiddish Stage") is a gold mine of early Jewish-American popular taste. At his death Minikes was described by the great writer Sholem Asch as a "sexton" in the Jewish community, one who gave up his private life for the public good.

This high estimation of Minikes would seem at odds with our selection of his work as representing the low road. This apparent paradox only underscores the subtle intertwining of cultural activities and entertainment genres during the immigrant period. In 1895 there prevailed a relatively broad definition of what was culturally allowable for a socially active American Jew. *Among the Indians* is not low in the sense of displaying coarse sexuality; indeed, there is not a dirty joke in the whole script. "Low" here means vulgar language and crude caricature, combined with flagrant commercialism. These characteristics put Minikes in tune with the main trends of American popular entertainment.

To properly understand this revealing playlet, we must first concentrate on its levels of language. These are necessarily changed or bypassed in the English translation from which quotations will be excerpted, yet we must delve into the sociolinguistics of the work to see it as ethnic theater. Basically, each character has his/her own level of language, creating a comedy of dialects and accents.

1. Willie, an East Side peddler of dry goods traveling through 1895 Kansas, speaks a low-grade American Yiddish.
2. Harry, a competitor of Willie's, speaks better-quality American Yiddish.
3. Kalomfulo, an Indian chief, speaks a mixture of passable and caricature Yiddish (if one can visualize a Yiddish equivalent to stage Indian talk).
4. Miss Meisel, a "farmer's daughter," speaks German and is essentially a parody of the uptown German Jew.
5. Dixon, Miss Meisel's black fieldhand, speaks broken English.

These five levels have the following two variations:

6. Willie, trying to speak German to Miss Meisel, uses broken German.
7. Miss Meisel, speaking to Dixon, uses broken English.

Some of these linguistic usages may reflect Minikes's own inadequacy as well as the clumsiness ascribed to his characters. When Miss Meisel says "Go to the hell," it is probably the author's error, rather than the character's. Likewise, even Miss Meisel's presumably polished German (as compared to Willie's comic attempts at uptown language) is not very grammatical. Yet Minikes was educated in Germany. We know little of the Jewish-American cultural milieu of 1895, so it is hard to tell exactly what American Yiddish was like, in its variegated forms, before the emerging Yiddish press created standardized usages. The ability of the average theatergoer to handle American English is also not known, nor is it easy to distinguish caricature from misinformation. What is readily apparent from a work such as Minikes's is the power of popular entertainment to play on the complexity of the linguistic, cultural, and musical situation in which the immigrants found themselves.

A somewhat more esoteric question is posed by *Among the Indians*: to what extent is the topic of Indians exotic for an audience on April 17, 1895? At first glance, it might seem very exotic indeed. Yet one encounters references to Indians and Jews in contact in a variety of literal and metaphorical situations. Two citations will suffice to show the range of possibilities; one is an anecdote from the early life of Weber and Fields, the East Side boys who came to have such a strong influence on American vaudeville.[6] As youngsters, they traveled "West" (to places like Kansas) with theater troupes. Part of their job consisted of distributing programs with texts of the show (like the one containing Minikes's playlet), collecting the pamphlets later from those who didn't want to pay for them. Weber and Fields ran into one stony-faced band of Indian spectators who refused either to pay or to hand back the programs. When the boys got too pushy, the Indians silently took out their knives. The programs stayed with the Indians.

The second anecdote comes from *Jews Without Money*. At several points in his autobiographical narrative Michael Gold mentions Jake Wolf, the celebrated Bowery saloonkeeper: "Jake Wolf is standing in front of his saloon. He picks his magnificent gold teeth that every one admires so much and curls his mustache. His white vest sparkles in the sunshine. Jake is a great man. He belongs to Tammany Hall and runs the elections every year." [7] Wolf also impressed the young Boris Thomashefsky and helped support the budding producer's first venture at creating a Yiddish theater in the early 1880s. According to Gold, the neighborhood boys ask Jake Wolf to tell them "about the time you killed that Indian out west." Wolf is "full of fine stories. He spent a year in the west, in Chicago, and saw the Indians. They looked like Jews, he said, but were not as smart or as brave. One Jew could kill a hundred Indians."

The two stories are diametrically opposed: Weber and Fields pale at the sight of Indian knives, while Jake Wolf understands them from the American point of view, as dangerous but basically weak enemies to be inevitably defeated. Weber and Fields's viewpoint is that of the greenhorn, while Wolf's stems from his confidence as a successfully acculturated American, equally at home in the turmoil of the Wild West or of New York politics. As we shall see, Wolf's stance reflects the position of Harry, the successful peddler of *Among the Indians*, while Weber and Fields's fear mirrors Willie's cowardice in the face of savage America. For the moment, the point is that firsthand contact (or at least anecdotal acquaintance) with American Indians was not out of the question for the 1895 Windsor Theatre audience. Behind this web of associations we can glimpse the stage Indian of American melodrama discussed earlier. This 1890s interaction of performing traditions was to prove fertile. The comic side of the Indian-Jewish confrontation is a vein richly worked throughout the history of Jewish-American and mainstream entertainment, down through Hollywood films of the 1970s (*Blazing Saddles, The Frisco Kid*) and television variety-show skits.

The opening scene of *Among the Indians*[8] sets the tone for the playlet:

> Place: a small *kontry* [place] in Kansas. Time: the present. Scene: a forested area. Before the curtain rises we hear savage cries, then singing. The curtain rises. Some Indians carry an idol. Chorus: "Our God is great and strong . . ." etc. They

dance around the idol in a wild Indian dance and dance off the stage. The god remains on the stage. Pause. We hear from off-stage: "You *shlimazl!* Where are you off to?" Willie enters right, with a large pack. He sets it down and sings.

Minikes scatters incongruities like buckshot. The idea of Indians dancing around an idol, ludicrous enough, is set off by the sound of an East Side peddler yelling "*shlimazl!*" after the departing savages. That he immediately launches into a vaudeville song is only appropriate.

Willie's song is on the topic of clothing, which proves to be the leitmotif of the little show. "Adam and Eve were lucky to go around naked," he says, "for now that man has discovered his shame, he uses clothes to put on a false front. All you need to succeed is the right wardrobe these days." However, Willie is not very adept at raking in the profits from this situation:

Here I've been traveling around two whole years, I've already covered half of America with my pack, but it doesn't work even if you break your back. Even the wild Indians have become conoisseurs of our goods, so if you make a little cash already you have to pray you won't get lynched when they look closer later and see you've taken them for a ride. (*sighs*) Yes, yes, it's no good, my business is six feet under and I can't tell whether I'm a shlimazl or my customers are worthless.

Willie's rather crude language is strengthened by his use of Americanisms: for example, "travel" is used for no particular purpose, as there are Yiddish verbs to describe such a process. In these works of popular taste we sense the emerging direction of American Yiddish. The foregoing monologue (of which only a part has been cited) establishes Willie's character. He is a bad businessman, and he wants to blame either himself or his customers for his plight, using the word *shlimazl* again and again for both. What is more interesting is Minikes's insistence on a very odd view of the Indians: first they are seen as idol-worshipers, then as lynchers. The latter is a particularly flagrant slap at convention, since even little Jewish theatergoers would have known (from melodramas and Buffalo Bill dime novels) that Indians invariably dispatch their victims by scalping them or burning them at the stake. But these ventures into the absurd pale in comparison with the basic description of Indians as people who buy suits from itinerant Jewish peddlers, an apparently accepted fact of life in the playlet.

Willie's style of expression and business acumen are further exposed in his dialogue with the Indian idol (the god Hoptsi), whom he takes to be "probably a general or the king's right-hand man." The statue's silence strikes Willie as ominous: "Maybe he's deep in thought, this cannibal; he's probably thinking whether he should have a Jewish peddler for dinner." By alluding to cannibalism, Minikes has carried his savaging of the Indian stereotype one step further. Meanwhile, the salesman's soliloquy is interrupted by the return of the Indians, with Chief Kalomfulo at their head:

> KALOMFULO. Hold, you white devil, how dare you offend our holy god!
> WILLIE. This is really a god?
> KALOMFULO. What? You don't know that?
> WILLIE. Yes, yes, of course I know. (*aside*) He's even a worse *shlimazl* than me.

To avoid being lynched, Willie tells how the great god came to him in a dream. Hoptsi wanted to order a suit: "it's too cold for him to go around naked." Kalomfulo sees through this dodge and recognizes Willie by the shoddy quality of his goods:

> KALOMFULO. White devil! For this you want $25! Do you think our god doesn't understand business? This suit isn't worth more than $5 . . . You're the same peddler from New York who sold me a rotten suit last year. Grrrrr!

Here a central message of the play is foreshadowed: deception won't help if your goods are shoddy. Willie is saved from imminent lynching only by the fortuitous arrival of Harry, his *landsman* and competitor. In true vaudeville style, Harry enters, puts down his pack, and sings, without noticing Willie and the Indians.

Harry's song is considerably more cynical and lower than Willie's. He deals with greed, hypocrisy, and *blof* ("bluff," or deceit), a favorite word in song texts of the period dealing with the social ills caused by immigration. His examples are usually lurid: a man who needs a job sends his cute wife in for an "interview" with the boss, and a mother and daughter travel to a small Coney Island hotel every weekend for shady business. Yet it turns out that Harry is a straightforward businessman; it is his disgust with "bluff" that motivates his song.

Greeted as a long-lost friend by Kalomfulo, Harry manages to win Willie's release. When Willie exclaims once again that he must be a *shlimazl*, Harry corrects him: "you're not a *shlimazl*, just a bad businessman." But before Harry can explain, along comes Miss Meisel, the farmer's daughter/southern belle/uptown German Jewish old maid; she is accompanied by her black fieldhands, led by the idiotic Dixon.

Trying to speak high-class German, Willie trips over his tongue and is betrayed by his lack of education. (She asks him about Goethe and Schiller, whose names he mangles.) A musical moment of extreme piquancy then arrives. In response to Miss Meisel's inquiry regarding his musicality, Willie sings a cantorial number (indicating his Old World unsophistication, one imagines). Stimulated by the sound of music, Dixon and the fieldhands strike up a minstrel show tune, "Johnny Get Your Gun," as counterpoint, before they are muzzled by Miss Meisel's imperious insults. Dixon, who wants "a new suit for Christmas," is every bit as sharp a judge of dry goods as Kalomfulo and the great god Hoptsi. He rejects Willie's "rags" but accepts Harry's far more expensive suit. The Indians also buy great quantities of clothing for their upcoming holiday. Finally, in desperation, Willie implores Harry to explain his success:

> WILLIE. Either you know black magic or I'm not Willie! Where do you get this dark power?
>
> HARRY. You see I'm skinny and frail like all the sons of Israel, just skin and bones.

At last Harry relents and produces the secret of success: an advertising brochure.

> WILLIE. What's this, a book?
>
> HARRY. This is the catalogue of Louis Minsky of 55, 57, and 59 Canal Street in New York. Get a catalogue like this, do you hear? Grrrr!
>
> WILLIE. Looks like you're making fun of me.
>
> HARRY. God forbid! The secret of success lies in this catalogue. Whoever buys dry goods from Louis Minsky must do good business, since the prices are low and the stock brilliant. I've been doing business with this firm for three years, and to date my customers are satisfied, as you've seen yourself.

Minikes has remained true to his calling as advertiser, plugging the house of Minsky, who had a prominent ad in the program. We know not to what extent this surprising conclusion reflects standard practice, but that is not our main concern.[9] What sticks out in the closing scene of *Among the Indians* is a line from Harry's closing speech: "Only fools believe in success; the smart ones believe in themselves." This announcement goes beyond the ad man's call of duty, and prescribes a general policy for the immigrant: follow the straight and narrow path, avoid bluff, work hard, buy your goods from the right merchants, and you'll make a place for yourself in this wild America. Jake Wolf must have heartily approved.

Seen in this light, all the tomfoolery and confused stereotyping of the playlet begin to fall into place. It does not matter whether Indians scalp or lynch. In dealing with America, Minikes implies, you are caught in a struggle for survival, where trickery and savagery of all sorts abound. From the Indians to the blacks to the "farmer's daughter," Minikes internalizes stage stereotypes for his own purposes. The strange inhabitants of this wild New World are no fools: they know shoddy goods when they see them. The almost Horatio Algeresque message of the show stands in sharp contrast to its absurd vulgarity. As is common in Eastern European Jewish culture, every tale turns out to be didactic. What seemed to be the lowest of the low, combining caricature, coarseness, and commercialism, has a message straight off the high road. The moral of the story—that straight dealing leads to success—might easily have emanated from the "high" drama performed before Minikes's afterpiece on April 17. The program's cover illustration shows a bunch of jolly Jewish kids painted up as Indians. Indeed, the message is meant for a younger generation, as witnessed by the high degree of English borrowing and whole lines of English dialogue.

Unfortunately, Minikes's little dramatic foray is the only surviving example of early Yiddish vaudeville. We cannot tell how typical any of its ploys really was, though it probably represented a common run of entertainment. When combined with the evidence of the broadsides and the lower ranges of the sheet music repertoire, two points are reaffirmed regarding the "low road." First, it is a route that remains heavily traveled today. Second, it is a meandering byway of the culture, crossing and recrossing the high road. Both seem essential to the evolution of the music culture and to the history of American Jewry.

NOTES

1. I am grateful to Eleanor Gordon Mlotek for making the Weinrot broadside collection available.
2. These are collected in *Di yidishe bine* (New York: Katzenelenbogen, 1897).
3. This and the following quotation are from Michael Gold, *Jews Without Money* (New York: Liveright, 1930), p. 33.
4. Edmund Leach, *Claude Lévi-Strauss* (New York: Viking, 1970), p. 30.
5. Arthur Goren, personal communication, 1979.

6. Anecdote cited in Felix Isman, *Weber and Fields* (New York: Boni and Liveright, 1926).
7. This and the following quotation are from Gold, *Jews Without Money*, pp. 53–54.
8. For the full script in my translation, see "From Vilna to Vaudeville: Minikes and *Among the Indians*," *The Drama Review* 24, no. 3 (Sept. 1980): 17–26.
9. One strong possibility is a certain influence on Yiddish vaudeville from that thriving American genre, the medicine show, which wrapped entire entertainments around advertisements. See Brooks McNamara, *Step Right Up* (Garden City: Doubleday, 1976), esp. "Indians Shows and Showmen," pp. 105–18.

PART III

THE SHEET MUSIC MICROCOSM

Madame Kaminska . . . gave me some music
from the opera *Shulamis*. It was on
torn scraps of paper, with stains and
erasures. I found it very upsetting.
—RUMSHINSKY

CHAPTER 6

WHAT THE
SONG TEXTS TELL

The tattered folios from the 1897–1920 period constitute an important body of primary source material for understanding the immigrants' adaptation to American life and their maintenance of internal values. Nevertheless, this fascinating material has been badly neglected, and even reviled, in the general denigration of early Jewish-American entertainment. To be sure, the song sheets themselves are not skillfully produced, and the contents may be crude at times. Particularly striking is the haphazard spelling of proper names, song titles, and the song texts themselves. Often the title or composer's name differs on the cover and the inside pages. Since Yiddish is read from right to left, against the flow of music notation, it is necessary to romanize the song text so it can be sung syllable by syllable to the tune. The resulting "English" (as it is often called on the folios) follows no consistent system of transliteration. Small wonder, then, that few have taken this motley set of songs seriously.

Yet these few hundred songs remain our most important musical legacy from the immigrant period. For two or three generations of American Jews, the sheet music served as a valuable song pool— especially in later years, when sound recordings of the same songs were available. Documentary interviews done in the 1970s repeatedly turn up sheet music songs as older singers review their repertoires. In terms of social history, sheet music texts are as valuable as other contemporary materials (newspapers, literature, political and social documentation) in depicting shared values and aspirations. Indeed, since music directly reflects audience interest both in terms of marketability (the folios were expensive, as compared to broadsides) and affective value, in some ways it may be even more significant than other forms of evidence. Linguistically, the sheet music is extremely helpful in shedding light on problems that lie beyond our scope but that are well worth mentioning. In sociolinguistic terms, popular song displays language at its liveliest, ranging from the solemnity of the didactic song through the slangy street talk of the youth-oriented hit tunes. Due to the great popularity of the pop songs, we must assume that the usage presented in the sheet music not only reflected but also influenced the evolution of American Yiddish. Since the music circulated to Europe in print and on records, even Old World Yiddish was affected by the language of the New York popular song.

The Jewish-American commercial repertoire has been badly overlooked and is of central importance to the evolution of immigrant music. Our survey will be extensive, consisting of three sections. This chapter takes up the song texts and topics, while the following one deals exclusively with the language of the cover illustrations—the iconography. A third chapter will consider the strictly musical implications of the transition from Europe to America as represented in the printed sources. But before we can examine this internal world of publications, we must once again try to place the Jewish case in the American context. It might seem that to summarize American sheet music in the 1880–1920 period would be an easy task, yet no history of the industry exists. There are fine anthologies of sheet-music covers (in full color, for the coffee table), and there are detailed descriptions of how to recognize a first-edition copy of "Swanee River." Yet we lack a decent account of how the medium of printed popular music evolved. No one has published statistical data on production and distribution systems, or chronicled the rise and fall of publishing houses. Once again we lack a vantage point from which to survey the Jewish field.

We do know that printed sheet music is as old as America. Its popularity rose steadily throughout the nineteenth century—particularly after the Civil War, when printing techniques made possible the production of large numbers of cheap editions. This trend coincided with the meteoric rise of the parlor piano, discussed earlier. Immigrants thus contributed both to the purchase and to the performance of the new sheet music. They also ended up as a major force in the production and distribution business. As in the case of the parlor piano, then, the spread of sheet music was a cultural/musical process that the immigrants both reacted to and helped shape. In the 1890s the term "Tin Pan Alley" was coined to describe the cluster of publishers' shops which moved progressively uptown from the 'teen streets to the forties along Broadway. The rise of the phonograph, noticeable after 1910, linked music folios to records, creating a mutually reinforcing music industry. When the immigrants had first arrived, sheet music had been *the* dominant medium of American popular entertainment. Virtually the only way to sell a song was to push it ("plug" was the technical term) so hard into public consciousness through live performances that it became a hit. Eventually everyone who wanted to be up with the times had to buy a copy and try it on his (usually her) piano. An industry with such rapid turnover and low production costs had to rely on formula, the basics of which have been succinctly summarized by Sigmund Spaeth. In terms of musical format, he lists the following seven rules:

1. The ideal structure for a popular song is that of a verse and chorus, of which only the chorus really matters;
2. A tune which suggests or definitely imitates one which has already been popular has just that much more chance of success;
3. Waltz time is the perfect expression of sentiment;
4. Putting the verse part in some different rhythmic form will accentuate the delightfulness of the waltz time;
5. A cadence with barber-shop harmony inserted here and there will bring tears to the most hardened eyes;
6. An occasional chance to hang on to a long note, even on an unimportant word like "of," is not to be overlooked;
7. The human mind is incapable of retaining any but the simplest melodic intervals, and the human voice of singing beyond the limits of one octave.[1]

Of these points, only the fifth does not apply to Yiddish sheet music, though some matters of detail and stress may differ. The Rumshinskys, Brodys, and Perlmutters seem to have had little quarrel with the ground rules of the American popular song. (In a later chapter we shall see how distinctive they managed to be within that framework.)

Spaeth also supplies seven commandments for the text component of the popular song:

1. Correctness of English is by no means an asset, and may at times be a positive handicap;
2. Assonance is often to be preferred to rhyme. So long as the vowel sounds are the same, what's the difference?
3. The mispronunciation of words and other evidences of deficient mentality should always be accepted as the height of wit;
4. Correct accenting is a trifling matter as compared with highfalutin artificiality of language;
5. The world is full of wronged women and malevolent villains, and something should be done about it;

6. Death should always be the occasion for a maudlin orgy, increasing in volume according to the extreme youth or extreme age of the victim;
7. Sin is wrong; virtue is most praiseworthy; gold is a highly overrated commodity; marriage may be achieved under almost any circumstances, even on the spur of the moment; and no matter how desperate the situation, evil cannot possibly triumph.

Spaeth could just as well have added the following two items to his list:

8. Mother is sacred, as is the flag;
9. City folk long for the simple life of the country, especially when it is defined as "back home."

Here the Yiddish case overlaps with the general American one, but not quite so strongly. Most of #5 and #7 do not apply; the in-group Yiddish songs have an entirely different set of concerns, as we shall see. Spaeth is merely rehashing the basics of melodrama, and though immigrants loved that genre, they rarely carried its preoccupations into song. The first three points, which outline language use, are only weakly echoed in the Yiddish material. Old World patterns of song-text construction tended to persist. In sum, it appears that while the standard mold of the American pop tune was fairly suitable to the songmakers of the East Side, the cultural content involved a whole other level of decision-making, which is the subject of the present chapter.

Many ethnic groups have produced their own sheet music. Finnish presses in the Midwest turned out religious and workers' music; French-American printers in New England put out lively commentary on life in the United States; Ukrainian firms in New York published regional dances of Eastern Europe . . . the list is too long to even summarize. Yet there has been no survey of the origin, flowering, and impact of printed music, one of the most interesting manifestations of a literate, multi-ethnic society. The formative period of internal Jewish music publishing is as obscure as that of any ethnic group. In 1897 a self-assured home industry springs fully formed from immigrant society; available evidence gives no indication of a European precedent. Given the severe limitations on Jewish publishing in Eastern Europe, this is hardly surprising. The German Jews brought the concept of a Jewish press to the United States, founding publishing houses as early as 1845.[2] The Jewish Publication Society, which began in that year, and Bloch Publishing Company, which entered the field in 1854, are both still in business despite various interruptions. The earliest music publication seems to have been by a certain Katzenelenbogen, first in Brooklyn and later in Manhattan. In *Di yidishe bine* (1897), Minikes's pioneering collection of Yiddish song texts and stage routines, Katzenelenbogen advertised a number of folios for celebrated theater pieces of the day, relying heavily on the Goldfadn repertoire.

An important step forward was taken with the entry of Joseph Werbelowsky, who instigated the formation of the Hebrew American Publishing Company (later simply Hebrew Publishing Company), still a significant producer of religious and reference works. Werbelowsky took over the music catalogue of Katzenelenbogen, and by 1901 his listing of "Jewish music for piano and song" took up 81 pages of the catalogue. Hebrew Publishing Company placed great stress on educating the immigrants, and felt strongly that music was an essential component of ethnicity. As the 1902 catalogue states:

> We, the publishers of "Jewish music," feel fully rewarded in having catered to Jewish taste, Jewish spirit and feeling, and we are getting ready to publish many more popular Jewish operas, which will appear soon; also new operas as they are staged in the Jewish theater.
>
> We hope that Jewish music will occupy a much larger place in the Jewish world than Christian music, since the Jew loves everything that is beautiful and Jewish.

This ingenuous battle cry corresponds with the general worry about losing Jewish youth to mainstream entertainment and language. It is not surprising that Werbelowsky also commissioned Alexander Harkavy, a noted philologist, to compile a Yiddish-English dictionary to help bridge the generational gap. We have already quoted from the firm's "Jewish-American Orator," another didactic venture. This educational urge led Hebrew Publishing to concentrate ever more strongly on cultural/secular, as opposed to religious, publication: "In its 1914 catalogue . . . only 22 pages are taken up by religious items, while literary works, textbooks, dictionaries, and grammars occupy 72 pages, and 19 pages are devoted to music." A trilogy of religion, secular learning, and music seems to have provided a suitable basis for Jewish-American culture in the peak years of immigration. Music's vital role in the catalogue only confirms our thesis that expressive culture was a potent force in immigrant life. The fact that Hebrew Publishing also issued plays in cheap format only underscores the point.

We are now ready to turn to the raw material: the songs themselves. The aim of this chapter, to reconnoiter the bewildering array of topics and means of expression, can best be accomplished by a threefold division of the material. First we will survey songs representing genres shared with mainstream Euro-American popular music. This is in keeping with our general strategy of noticing commonality before turning to ethnic distinctiveness. Next we will closely examine songs stressing the internal identity of the group. Finally we will approach the cultural battleground, where songs confront the external challenge of immigrant life and the attendant internal change. These divisions are merely handy analytic categories; the songs themselves often meander from topic to topic, with a given song perhaps spanning all three headings.

GENRES SHARED WITH THE MAINSTREAM

The Family Tie

America had a passion for songs of home and mother, an obsession that cuts across ethnic lines. A yearning for mother, father, and the innocence of childhood is hardly surprising among immigrants, many of whom were far from home. The most famous Yiddish mother song is in fact about trans-Atlantic separation; it speaks from the viewpoint of a mother in Europe imploring her emigrant child to write home. Entitled "A brivele der mamen" ("A Letter to Mom"), this Small/Smulewitz masterpiece is part of a series of "letter" songs that faithfully follow one of Spaeth's commandments of songwriting: if a topic works, use it repeatedly. Thus we have "A Letter to the Bride" (about a boy away at the front), "A Letter to the Groom," and "A Letter to Dad," among others. It is important to note the context of the sole survivor of this series, "A brivele der mamen," since there has been such overemphasis on the archetypal Jewish Mother in every possible literary and entertainment medium. As maudlin as "A brivele" may be, it is only one of a number of ballads based on family relationships in a community under stress. As the immigration period recedes, sentiment tends to focus on the mother (as opposed to the family) and the Oedipal relationship emerges. In the early decades we find songs such as "Goodbye," which deal with a girl's farewell to both parents upon her marriage, or the companion song "Makhateyneste," which takes up the mother's mixed feelings of pride and loss at her daughter's wedding. Songs recalling childhood as a period of security were also in vogue, e.g., "Es vilt zikh zayn a kind tsurik" ("I'd Like to Be a Child Again"). This genre goes back to European Yiddish folksong sources; it also increases as immigration fades into the past, and the general ethnic topic of nostalgia for the Old World finally begins to emerge among the American Jews. (Unlike the Irish, though, it is quite a while before the Jews can view Europe, scene of pogroms and persecution, through rosy glasses.)

Let us examine one of the songs that make the transition from a general family tie toward sentimentality based solely on the mother. "A brivele der mamen" is interested in the lonely mother across the sea, while the 1925 "My yidishe momme," one of the best known of all Jewish-American songs, centers on the Americanized child's neglect of filial piety: now the abandoned mom is in the "old neighborhood," on the Lower East Side. An intermediate song, written in 1921, stresses the difficulties of motherhood and the child's natural attachment to mom without being overtly didactic. "My Best Friend Is My Mama" ("Mayn libster fraynd iz mayn mamenyu") merely states that sentiment, without saying, as did the Irish song, "Mother Machree," that no "other girl" can ever take her place. The attachment is seen as organic, not erotic:

SONG 1:
"Mayn libster fraynd iz mayn mamenyu"
("My Best Friend Is My Mama")

Di mame farnemt fil yesurim un shmerts
fun dem tog vos dos kind vert geboyrn.
Mit blut vert fargosn ir, nebekh, dos harts
bis zi vert fun der velt farloyrn.
Vos shteyt zikh fun kind nit di mamenyu oys,
ven es pokt, ven es mozlt, ven es hust;
fun tseyndlekh makhn, vi biter, vi groys iz ir tsar.
S'iz ir fintster un vist.
Di mame vet alt un groy far der tsayt
bis dos kind vet a shtikele layt.

Chorus
A mame, a mame, iz der tayerster khaver, mir shaynt.
Bay fraydn, bay leydn iz di mame der trayster fraynd.
In yesurim kholile, ven dem mentsh tut epes vey,
iz zayn ershter geshrey: oy mama, mamenyu, oy mamenyu!

The mama takes on many woes and pains/ from the day the child is born./ Her heart is drenched in blood, poor thing,/ until she is lost to the world./ What doesn't the mother suffer on account of the child/ when there's pox and measles and coughs;/ How bitter, how great is her sorrow at teething./ She's gloomy and desolate./ The mama ages and becomes gray before her time/ until the child's a bit of a person.

Chorus
A mama, a mama is the dearest friend, it seems/ The mama is the truest friend in joy and sorrow/ And when someone is in pain and suffering/ His first outcry is: "Mama, Mama, Mommy!"

The topic of parental love is closely allied to the next genre of songs to be discussed; it is a small step from love of mother to loss of mother.

The Orphan Song

Relatively few Yiddish folksongs on the subject have been collected and published. Yet there are a number of songs of bereaved children in the sheet music repertoire, some of which were also put out on records in the early years. A critical period in Jewish history—the early twentieth century, marked by revolution, riot, and war—here intersects with two kinds of song themes: the European folk plaint of the motherless child, and the strong American stress on songs of disaster and bereavement. Differences between the Old and New World Jewish orphan songs are visible in both structure and content. Structurally, the European songs are in the standard strophic format of the Yiddish folksong. The "American" songs, on the other hand, are subject to the same influence of the popular song's verse-and-chorus format that permeated all Yiddish-language genres. Thus we find refrains of tragic songs set in lilting waltz time, conforming to Spaeth's norms.

In terms of content, the shift from Europe to America is more subtle. European songs stress true folk perspectives on orphanhood. One is the young mother's lament from the grave, worrying about her child. (This theme does not appear in America.) Another is the realistic image of the wandering, helpless child, too young to cope with the adult world:

Zind ikh bin ayn yesoymele gebliben
azoy hob ikh gekrogn farshtand, oy farshtand.
M'hot shoy far mir dem takhles gefunen
tsu gebn di mlokhe in der hand, in der hand.

Di mlokhe iz far mir tsu shver
Un ikh bin tsu kleyn, oy tsu kleyn,

Un haynt bin ikh ayn bitere yesoymele,
Dertsu nokh elend vi a shteyn, vi ayn shteyn.

Since I became an orphan/ I gained understanding, oy, understanding./ They found something useful for me to do/ And put
me to work at a trade, at a trade. The trade is too hard for me/
And I'm too small, oy, too small/ And today I'm a bitter orphan/
And lonely as a stone, as a stone.

The realistic imagery of this Old World song would seem logical for
immigrant America, with its rich documentation of orphans' miseries
and the plight of homeless children, so richly described in the works of
Jacob Riis. Yet the Jewish-American songs are more genteel. Victorian-
isms knew no ethnic boundaries:

SONG 2:
"Leybedig yesoymele" ("The Living Orphan")

Oy lebedig yesoymele,
du opgerisn boymele.
Du host keyn heym hit un keyn ru
ven dayn mame iz nito.
S'iz nito ver zol fleygn dikh,
mit tsertlikhkayt shlofn leygn dikh
Un beten got far dayn gezind:
mame, mame, vi bistu atsind.

O living orphan/ You uprooted tree./ You have no home, no
rest/ Since your mother's not there. There's no one to take care
of you/ And tenderly put you to sleep/ And pray to God for your
help:/ Mama, mama, where are you now?

The foregoing Rumshinsky song (1914) is quite similar to other American songs of the period:

Lone and weary thro' the streets we wander
For we have no place to lay our heads.
Not a friend on earth is left to shelter us
For both our parents now are dead.[3]

Yet there are differences between the Jewish and American styles, even
given a basically similar approach. The Yiddish songs never really cloy
like such American standbys as "Why Did They Dig Ma's Grave So
Deep" or "Two Little Children":

"Mama got sick. Angels took her away,"
she said, "to a home warm and bright.
She said she would come for her darlings some day;
Perhaps she is coming tonight." [4]

While the Yiddish songs maintain some distance from their American models, they also retain a bit of Old World flavor through epithets and tag lines. The phrase *elend vi a shteyn* ("lonely as a stone"), the closing line of the folksong quoted above, is echoed in a number of the commercial Jewish-American folios.

This short look at a single genre, the orphan song, encapsulates our survey of the sheet music songs. Symbolic crossovers from Europe mix with Americanisms, often in a single song, to create an alliance which may now seem uneasy but which must have been natural for the composers and parlor pianists of the day.

The Sexes: Love, Conflict, and the Wedding

Though many songs on the battle of the sexes are distinctly American, one feature of the Yiddish repertoire stands out: it displays a very weak interest in romantic love. The favored topic of Tin Pan Alley and still the all-consuming interest of the popular song, the boy-girl relationship was not prominent in sheet music. One could argue that, for those modern Jewish children immersed in romance, the American songs would have been much more appealing than any possible Yiddish texts on the subject. Nevertheless, the tireless Rumshinsky pioneered in bringing the matter to the Yiddish stage. His 1911 operetta *Shir hashirim* ("Song of Songs," a typically in-group allusion to passion) has been described as the first stage musical about love. The hit song "Dos lid der libe" ("The Song of Love") shows an extraordinary adaptation of non-Jewish sensibilities:

SONG 3:
"Dos lid der libe" ("The Song of Love")

A libeslid zing ikh far dir.
Akh, vi es glit in hartsn bay mir.
O, mayn amor!
Dir din ikh nor.
Mayn apolon!
Her tsu mayn ton.
Her mayn gezang

un harfenklang
der libes trank.

Chorus
Lib mikh nor fil,
lib in der shtil.
Der libes trank,
er shmekt zo zis.
Kum nor tsu mir,
Ikh vart oyf dir
In libes-paradiz.
Lib un ver nit mid,
zing ayn libeslid.
Lib mir nor fil,
lib in der shtil,
lib, lib, lib.

I sing you a love song./ O, how my heart glows./ O my Amour!/ I serve only you./ My Apollo!/ Listen to my tune./ Hear my song/ A harp-sound/ Of love's potion.

Chorus
Love me greatly/ Love me quietly./ Love's potion/ Smells so sweet./ Come just to me/ I wait for you/ In Love's Paradise./ Love and don't tire/ Sing a love song./ Love me greatly/ Love me quietly/ Love, love, love.

The classical citations (Amour-Cupid, Apollo) are unparalleled in the sheet music repertoire, and are comically strung together. (Recall the apostrophe to music's power from "The Jewish-American Orator," cited in Chapter 4.) The music is in the Victor Herbert mode to which Rumshinsky aspired.

A totally different type of American influence can be felt in another group of songs commenting on men and women. The Yiddish stage went through a phase of interest in the suffragette movement. There are operettas on the topic, such as *Dzheni loyft far meyer* ("Jenny Runs for Mayor"). The musical *Di sheyne amerikanerin* ("The Beautiful American Girl"), a Thomashefsky production, contains two diametrically opposed statements on the subject of women's liberation. The male chauvinist view is put forth in "Der hersher iz alts der man" ("The Man Is Still the Ruler"), while the female stance is powerfully stated in "Vayber, makht mikh far prezident" ("Women, Make Me President"):

SONG 4:
"Der hersher iz alts der man"
("The Man Is Still the Ruler")

Es meg di froy zayn klug un sheyn,
himlish raytsnd vi der velt,
es meg di froy zayn a malakh reyn,
farmegn raykhtum un fil gelt.
Meg di froy a getin zayn,
klug, gebildet vi nor zayn ken,
ir familye zayn vi fayn—
der hersher iz alts der man.

The woman can be smart and pretty/ Divinely attractive/ The
woman can be a pure angel/ Own wealth and lots of money./
The woman can be a goddess/ Smart, as well-educated as
possible/ Her family can be ever so fine—/ But the man is still
the ruler.

SONG 5:
"Vayber, makht mikh far prezident"
("Women, Make Me President")

Chorus
Nemt aykh tsuzamen vayber, makht mikh far a prezident.
Vert ir zen, vayber, vi mir haltn mener in di hent!
Nemt hent, hent!

Verse 3
Oy vayber, vayber, vayber,
kokht nit keyn diner, vayber.
Oy vayber, vayber, vayber,
Fort nit in kontri, vayber.
Ven es kumt der liber zumer,
Di zun git nor a bri,
farshlist ir shoyn ayer tsimer
un loyft in der kontri.
Oy, di mener, di mamzeyrim,
hulyen tog un nakht
un fraytik punkt vi di khazeyrim
hot zi di treyn gebrakht.

Verse 4
Oy vayber, vayber, vayber,
hot nit keyn kinder vayber.
Oy vayber, vayber, vayber,
gevald, zayt nit keyn vayber!
Zoln di mener daypers vashn,
hert ir a geshrey.
Lozt zey fun di teplekh nashn
un kinder hobn zoln zey.
Lomir zey lozn bargns ketshn
in vanemeykers stor,
un zol zey nor der korset kvetshn
khotsh tsvey mol a yor.

Chorus
Get together women, and make me a president./ You'll see,
women, how we'll have the men in our hands!/ Take hands,
hands!

Verse 3
O women, women, women/ Don't cook dinner, women./ O
women, women, women/ Don't go to the country, women./
When the lovely summer comes/ The sun starts to burn/ You
close up your rooms/ And run to the country./ O the men,
those bastards/ Frolic day and night/ And Friday, just like pigs/
The train brings them.

Verse 4
O women, women, women/ By God, don't be women!/ Let the
men wash the diapers/ If you hear an outcry./ Let them nibble
from the pots/ And let them have the children./ Let's have
them catch bargains/ At Wanamaker's store/ And let the corset
squeeze them/ At least twice a year.

The clearly American lifestyle references seem startingly modern for
1910 but are actually typical of this genre, as is the ironic tone. Perhaps
the injection of such lively, current topics was intended to attract an
audience that had tired of belabored melodramas about the past glories
and present woes of the Old World Jews. The two songs just quoted
present a contrast in linguistic styles that directly reflects their subject
matter: the conservatism of the men's side is given in un-Anglicized
Yiddish, while the women's progressive position features abundant
Americanisms ("diapers," "bargains," and "corset"). The English intru-

sions are perfectly natural here, in that they stem directly from the lifestyle depicted. No matter how even-handed the presentation of male and female positions may seem, the balance is always tipped in favor of the men. The women appear ridiculous—imagine Jenny running for mayor!—or, as in the song just cited, are presented as downright crude. "Women, Make Me President" is one of the few songs in the sheet music world to use *mamzer* ("bastard") and *khazer* ("swine"), terms we relegated to the low road. To put such words in the mouths of rebellious women is surely to undercut the credibility of their position.

More subtle Americanization creeps into the songs of marital conflict. This topic, often treated in vaudeville and the emergent comic strip (e.g., "Jiggs and Maggie"), puts a Jewish interest squarely in the mainstream. The songs, which are fairly coarse, perhaps bespeak the alienation that was widespread among couples struggling to find their footing in the New World. One such song is implicitly American in that it parodies a Yiddish song. Among Goldfadn's most widely reproduced songs during the period in question was "A yid bistu, gey vayter, gey" ("You're a Jew, So Move On"); it is a Zionist item, exhorting the Jew to stop being a driven wanderer and to find his ancient homeland. In 1914 a takeoff on the Goldfadn song, written by Isaac Reingold, was published under the title "A tremp bistu, gey vayter, gey" ("You're a Tramp, So Move On"):

SONG 6:
"A tremp bistu, gey vayter, gey"
("You're a Tramp, So Move On")

Verse 3
"Oy los mikh arayn!
Ikh shver ikh vel zayn
a guter, a voyler fun haynt.
Ikh shver dir, ikh blayb
in shtub khotsh mikh trayb;
du kenst dokh mayn gut harts, mir shaynt.
Ikh shpil shoyn—ikh shver—keyn poker nit mer,
keyn 'oke,' keyn 'pidre,' keyn 'stos.'
Un nar ikh dikh nokh, den zol mir der brokh
avekleygn do oyf der gas!"
"Ikh ken dayne shvues, ikh ken dikh gants fayn,"
derhert zikh ir shtime mit vey,
"Megst klapn biz morgn, ikh loz nit arayn,
a tremp bistu, gey vayter, gey!"

Verse 3
"O let me in!/ I swear I'll be/ Good and nice starting today./ I
swear I'll stay home/ Even if you drive me/ I think you know
my good heart./ I swear I won't play any poker again/ No 'oke,'
no 'pidre,' no 'stos.'/ And if I trick you any more, may a curse/
Fell me here on the street!"/ "I know your promises, I know
you quite well"/ You can hear her woe-filled voice/ "You can
knock until morning, I won't let you in/ You're a tramp, so
move on!"

This parody of an in-group song indicates the complexity of the material
in other ways. First, the continuity of the immigrant song tradition is
established by the fact of parody, which relies on the audience knowing
the original. Second, the parody itself is some twenty years old, indicating that self-mockery of even so sacred a topic as persecution/Zionism is
a time-tested device. Third, the song comments on the breakdown of
family life occasioned by immigration, and so has American overtones,
but at the same time mentions only one American card game (poker),
compared with three European varieties (*oke, pidre,* and *stos*) which
were apparently still very popular in Jewish homes in 1914. "A tremp
bistu" nicely illustrates the liveliness of the Jewish-American song and
at the same time proves the existence of a strong, identifiable immigrant tradition within ethnic boundaries.

Occasional Songs

Of the musical genres which Jews shared with mainstream America,
none illustrates the ambivalence of the internal-external pull more
strongly than the occasional song, consisting of items written for specific events. Some of these are purely for the in-group, such as the
funeral march played at the massive 1905 demonstration mentioned
earlier. Others comment on matters of Jewish interest that had international overtones, such as the Dreyfus case. Still a third category takes
universal events and adds a Jewish commentary (World War I, the
Russian Revolution, the sinking of the *Titanic*). Since Elizabethan
times the latest news has been put into printed song, as we noted in
connection with the broadside. During the immigrant era this old
Euro-American tradition had not yet died out; eventually, the massive
coverage of news by print and broadcast media silenced the street
singers. We will examine the *Titanic* song later, in connection with its

visual imagery. For now, we can profitably compare an internal response to a local event (the Triangle Fire of 1911) to the same group's reaction to major outside events (World War I and the Russian Revolution).

"Mamenyu! Including an Elegy to the Triangle Fire Victims" (to use its printed English title) manages to fuse the orphan topic with the theme of disaster to create an occasional song. There are two refrains, and a considerable disjunction between the song's two vantage points. The orphan section is strongly reminiscent of another Rumshinsky song, cited above (Song 2).

SONG 7:
"Mamenyu! Including an Elegy to the Triangle Fire Victims"

Vey dir, yesoymele
Bist an opgehaktes beymele. . .
Bist elent umetum. . .
Oy mama, mama, vu bistu, vu?

Woe unto you, orphan,
You're a chopped-down tree . . .
You're lonely everywhere . . .
O mama, mama, where are you?

On the other hand, the second refrain is from the perspective of the bereaved mother, seeing her daughter lying dead after the fire:

"Oy vey, kindenyu!"
Rayst zikh bay di hor di mamenyu.
"Tsulib dem shtikl broyt
hot a shreklekher toyt
geroybt mir mayn eyntsik kind. . .
Toyt ligt mayn meydele,
takhrikhim anshtot a khupe-kleydele,
vey iz mayne yor,
a kind fun 16 yor,
oy mame, mame, vey iz mir, vey!"

"Oy vey, my child!"/ The mama tears her hair./ "For a piece of bread/ A terrible death/ Robbed me of my only child . . . / My little girl lies dead/ Shrouds instead of a wedding gown/ Woe is me/ A child of sixteen/ Oy mama, mama, woe is me, vey!"

The striking double perspective of "Mamenyu" yields an almost cinematic view of the event. It would appear that the authors thought of giving two views of the tragedy, doubling the quotient of feminine sorrow expressed in similar songs. A cynic might note evidence of an interest in exploiting the catastrophe. The text, nearly identical to that of other orphan songs, carries no reference to the Triangle Fire; the songwriters may have merely appended the mother's lament to the standard orphan song, temporarily welding two genres so as to turn out a marketable item as quickly as possible. Such behavior would certainly qualify Rumshinsky & Co. as full-fledged members of the broadside ballad fraternity.

In 1917 Yiddish music publishers responded quickly to two major cataclysms. Many World War I songs express the Jewish community's complex reaction to an event that stirred all American ethnic groups. At the same time, the publishers drew on yet another major event: the Russian Revolution. Few American groups felt its impact as strongly as did the Jews. We have already noted that fierce emotions were aroused during the 1905 Revolution, and the final defeat of the czarist regime released an even stronger wave of communal feeling. American Jews envisioned the end of oppression for their relatives and *landsmen* in the Russian Empire, the hope for improvement of the Jews' lot, and, for the politically minded (who were numerous), the beginning of a new chapter in world social organization. It is hardly surprising, then, that sheet music appeared on the theme of revolution. The key song is one with words by Morris Rosenfeld, the "sweatshop poet" whose observations on street musicians were cited above. Now past his prime as a popular verse-writer, he nevertheless succeeded in finding a publisher for his ode to revolution, and for his rhapsodic call to arms to defend America. "Ruslands frayhayt lid" ("Russia's Song of Freedom") is full of allusions to Siberia, an Old World still familiar to the Jewish-Americans today.

SONG 8:
"Ruslands frayhayt lid" ("Russia's Song of Freedom")

Trogt zikh, trogt zikh frayhayts-klangn
nokh Sibir, in kalten nord.
Den tsubrokhn Ruslands tsvangen
hobn di vos shmakhten dort.
Dort, in aynzam-visten tsfon,
opgeshnitn fun der velt,
vu zey krekhtsen un zey hofen
in di toytkayt fun di kelt,

dort, ahin in yene shneyen
durkh midbores, frost un ays,
yogt zikh, trogt zikh freyd-geshreyen:
trogt di helden zeyer prayz!
Zol tsuklingen ayer gevalt
heys un kraftig, shtark un bald!
Bis di vent fun sakhalin
zol dos frahayts-lid ahin:
trogt di helden zeyer prayz!

Carry, carry, sounds of freedom,
To Siberia, in the cold North,
Since Russia's force is broken
By those who languish there.
There, in the lonely wild north,
Cut off from the world,
Where they groan and they hope
In the deadness of the world,
There, thence in those snows,
Through deserts, frost and ice,
Drive and carry the cries of joy:
Carry their prize to the heroes!
Your power should resound
Hot and powerful, strong, and soon,
To the walls of Sakhalin
Should reach the song of freedom:
Carry their prize to the heroes!

One of the most interesting and most purely in-group stanzas in the occasional songs occurs in Rosenfeld's apostrophe to the rivers of Russia. Here a purely Russian sensibility is at work: in Russian literature and folksong the turbulence and flooding of rivers has a strong emotional connotation, in part tied to the annual spring thaw.

Shlayder, Volga, dayne velen
az der breg zol zayn tsuzetst!
Du vest fun di tratf-gezelen
heren naye lider yetst.
Un oykh ir, gebentshte inden
fun der shtoltser taykh Neva:
konkonirt itst mit di vinden,
hoybt zikh oyf mit a hurra!

Oyf, du blut-getrenkter Dniester,
velkher flist durkh Volokhay:
shlog dayn flut in ayn orkestr,
dayne khvalyes zaynen fray!
Zolen Dnieper un der Bik
Royshen grusen tsum muzhik;
shturmen zol yetveyde taykh
grusen tsu mayn folk tsuglaykh:
ale khvalyes zaynen fray!

Wash your waves, Volga/ So the pier is smashed!/ You'll hear
new songs/ From the boatmen./ And you blessed billows/ Of
the proud Neva River/ Compete with the winds/ And rise up
with a "hurrah!"/ Up, you blood-soaked Dniester/ Which flows
through Wallachia/ Whip your stream into an orchestra/ Your
waves are free!/ Let the Dnieper and the Bik/ Streaming, greet
the peasants;/ Every river should storm/ And greet my people
too:/ All the waves are free!

This stanza papers over the split between the "pure" revolutionary
Jews, who evaded their ethnic identity, and those interested in the
Jewish cause: it calls for both the peasants and "my" people to be
simultaneously greeted with the news of liberation. Popular entertainment typically tries to reach the widest possible audience, if only within
a subculture.

The response to World War I also embraces a number of views.
Meyrowitz's "Tfilas milkhomo" ("War Prayer") is perhaps the Yiddish
song which best reflects the most common mainstream interest in the
war: the anxiety of the family back home. "So Long, Mother," a song
described on the cover as "Al Jolson's mother song," shows a doughboy
clutching a frail gray-haired lady. Thus, to express its feelings of worry,
the Jewish family in 1917 could choose between a Yiddish-language
song or the American song of a Jewish immigrant singer. The Meyrowitz song is almost folklike in its heartfelt prayer:

SONG 9:
"Tfilas milkhomo" ("War Prayer")

Chorus
Gotenyu, tatele, shenk undz dos glik,
breng yedn soldatele gezunterheyt tsurik.
Ver veys nokh, ver vi du mer,
vi kinder hobn kumt on shver.

Darum ze, got, undzer gebet derher:
rakhmones hob oyf di eltern,
oyb du vilst nit oyf zey.
Es iz yunge lebns, yunges blut.
Got, tu zey nit vey,
zol dayn sholem shoyn valtikn
in dem shlakht, in dem,
un besholem breng
di kinderlakh aheym.

Chorus
God our Father, grant us this happiness/ Bring back every soldier safe and sound./ Who knows better than You/ How hard it is to bear children./ Therefore God, hear our prayer/ Have pity on the parents/ If not on them [the soldiers]./ It's young lives, young blood./ God, do them no harm/ Let your peace reign already/ In the battle/ And in peace bring/ The children home.

A second major theme of mainstream American World War I songs is the spirit of the troops, most classically embodied in George M. Cohan's "Over There," the unofficial anthem of the war. This stance is echoed in Lillian's "A grus fun di trentshes" ("A Greeting from the Trenches"):

SONG 10:
"A grus fun di trentshes" ("A Greeting from the Trenches")

Chorus
Ikh breng aykh a grus fun di trentshes,
ikh breng aykh a grus fun di boyes.
Zey kemfn mit mut, mit kurazh un mit blut
un fun di daytshn lakhn zey zikh oys.
Ikh breng aykh a grus fun di semis;
dos iz der grus, dos zogn zey:
oyb mir zaynen shoyn derinen
muzn mir di shlakht gevinen,
iz der grus fun onkl sems armey.

Chorus
I bring you a greeting from the trenches/ I bring you a greeting from the boys./ They fight with spirit, courage and blood/ And laugh at the Germans./ I bring you a greeting from the Sammies/ Here is the greeting: they say/ "If we're already in it/

We must win the battle"/ That's the greeting from Uncle
Sam's army.

The line "If we're already in it, we must win the battle," sounds somewhat equivocal. But this should not be construed as a particularly
ethnic response; we saw a similar mood in "Let's All Be Americans
Now," a mainstream appeal for ethnic support.

Yet "A grus fun di trentshes" does hide deeper messages of ethnicity.
The second verse reveals a decidedly in-group stand on the issue of war,
which leads us to our second main category: songs of internal identity.

Verse 2
S'iz do a shtikl hofening,
es shaynt a shtral fun glik:
es halt derbay mir zoln krign
undzer land tsurik.
Es grindt zikh in yedn land a yidisher legyon.
Zey geyen un kemfn far der heym
fun undzer natsyon.

Verse 2
There's a bit of hope/ There's a ray of happiness/ It seems we
might get/ Our land back./ In every land a Yiddish legion is
being founded./ They will go and fight for the home/ Of our
nation.

Here the zeal of patriotism has yielded to the glow of nationalism—an
important topic, to which we now turn.

SONGS OF INTERNAL IDENTITY

Zionism

Zionism is, of course, one of the main preoccupations of American
Jewry. In the early years of the century, however, Zionism had a vastly
different significance. Today, younger American Jews partly shape a
sense of ethnic identity around the State of Israel; for the immigrants,
particularly before the Balfour Declaration (1914), "Israel" was either
an ardent dream or a stance around which to crystallize internal political activity. The sheet music songs tend to stress Zionism as an alterna-

tive for the European, but not for the American Jew. The stock figure in the song texts is the persecuted "Wandering Jew" who needs to find a snug harbor in his ancient land, rather than in the New World. This type is exemplified in the previously cited Goldfadn song, "You're a Jew, So Move On." Songs often take the argument a step further by blaming the Jew for his own troubles, as in Thomashefsky's "Shuldik" ("Guilty"):

SONG 11:
"Shuldik" ("Guilty")

Du veyst dos mistam
vi a shif oyf dem yam
varft zikh dos yidele, bruderl mayn.
Oyf der erd du krikhst,
oyf dem yam du zikhst,
dayn shif hat keyn ruder, keyn kapitan.
Kumstu keyn dorem
trefstu a shturem.
Kumstu keyn tsfon
gefinstu keyn heym.
Dayne kinder tsetribn,
vos is dir geblibn?
Zog ver iz shuldik in dem?
Ver, ver, ver, ver, ver, ver, ver?

Chorus
Shuldik bistu yidele aleyn,
na-venad bistu, elend vi a shteyn.
Koyfst dir shteyner, diamantn,
gold un zilber, brilyantn.
Vu iz dayn seykhl, dayn farshtand?
Farkoyf dos ales, bruder, shnel,
Ven nit, vet vern fun dir a tel.
Du koyf dir beser op dayn eygn land.

You probably know/ like a ship on the sea/ You're tossed, my brother Jew./ You crawl on the earth/ And seek on the sea/ But your ship has no rudder, no captain./ If you come to the south/ You find a storm./ If you come to the north/ You find no home./ Your children dispersed/ What's left to you?/ Tell me who's guilty in this?/ Who, who, who, who, who, who?

Chorus
You yourself are guilty, Jew/ You're homeless, lonely as a stone./ You buy stones, diamonds/ Gold and silver, jewels./ Where's your sense, your understanding?/ Sell them all quickly, brother/ If not, you'll be ruined./ It's better to buy up your own land.

Of particular interest here is the line "elend vi a shteyn" ("lonely as a stone"), a stock phrase of the orphan song. In a given repertoire, it is partly through a system of clichés that style is cemented. The carryover of the folksong line, already confirmed as an indicator of internal identity by its use in the sheet music repertoire, is extended to refer to the orphan state of the Zionless Jew. Thus a self-sufficient symbolic system is established for the sheet music's language. We shall see below how visual symbols parallel lyrics in striving for conceptual standardization, a process also reflected in the actual musical materials.

In social terms, "Shuldik" is similar to "A grus fun di trentshes" in its advocacy of activism: the military or economic takeover of Palestine is suggested. We begin to sense a strong, self-aware Jewish-American community flexing its muscles. Though that strength is barely hinted at in the song texts, it will grow in later decades as more assertive forms of popular entertainment emerge.

Comic Songs

Strangely, there are few comic songs in the sheet music repertoire. Items that might be considered humorous tend to represent the low road, like the "tramp" parody quoted above, or "Mayn meshpukhe" ("My Family"), a crude rundown of a lowlife family's activities. Rarely does comedy rise above this level. One comic song reflecting a purely in-group set of characters is worth quoting; it is a number from a 1914 parody, *Dos meydl fun der vest* ("The Girl from the West"), a takeoff on the popular Belasco-Puccini *Girl of the Golden West*. The operetta plays on one of the stock themes of Yiddish humor: the conflict between warring dialects. The Litvak, or Lithuanian (who cannot pronounce *sh*, so he constantly hisses) and the Galitsianer (whose southern Polish accent gives vowels a special twist) represent two cultural subtypes. Every ethnic group seems to use such internal regional/dialect differences as a base for comedy. Even in today's Yiddish vaudeville revues the Litvak-Galitsianer dichotomy is good for a laugh.

SONG 12:
"Litvak un galitsyaner" ("Litvak and Galitsianer")

Galitsyaner: hert a losn fun lutvakes,
khazer, hunt, un vakhlaklakes,
vos iz dos tsu alde klogn
vet ir hern a lutvak zogn.
Litvak: in galitsey, vi yakh farshtay,
zogt nor tomid "gey shoyn, gey,
ekh un mekh un fleysh un beyner"
—iz dos a losn? du mamzer eyner!
Galitsyaner: ven fraytik iz gedekt der tish
un s'iz vi tsuker zis;
anshtot der lutvak zol monen di fish,
mont er gor di fis . . .
Litvak: ikh veys far vos es aykh nit smekt—
it hot lutvakes gut in zinen,
ven kolombus hot nor amerika entdekt
hot er a lutvak shoyn gefunen.
Galitsyaner: gay shoyn, gay.
Litvak: s'iz azey.
Galitsyaner: Lomir fun haynt beser vern gute fraynd, yo.
Beyde: Got git yidn guts a sakh
un di goyim, makes;
vayl bay got zaynen ale glaykh—
galitsyaner un litvakes.
Ze got, vi dayne yidn
zikh raysn un baysn,
un makhn bald fridn.
Sholem brider, zol shoy zayn.
Fe! A rikh in dayn tatn arayn . . .

Galitsianer: Listen to the Litvak language/ "Khazer, hunt, and vakhlaklakes."/ "Vos iz dos tsu alde klogn,"/ You'll hear a Litvak say./ Litvak: In Galitsia, as I understand/ They always say "gey shoyn, gey/ ekh, mekh, fleysh un beyner"/ —Is that a language, you bastard?/ G: When the table is set on Friday/ And everything's sugar-sweet/ Instead of calling for the "fish"/ The Litvak calls for "feet" [*fis*] . . ./ L: I know why you don't like it—/ You think a lot about Litvaks/ Well, when Columbus first discovered America/ He already found a Litvak here./ G: Go on!/ L: It's true./ G: Well, let's be good friends from now on, yes./ Both: God give the Jews a lot/ And the Gentiles plagues/

Because before God, everyone's the same—/ Galitsyaners and
Litvaks./ Look, God, how Your Jews/ Fight and bite each
other./ And then soon make peace./ Let's have peace, brothers/
Phooey! A curse on your father! . . .

Of course, the Yiddish-speaking reader may enjoy this item more than
the outsider does; such is the nature of in-group jokes. The song raises
some interesting points for our general line of analysis. First, the dialects are not really accurately represented; they are artificial versions
of language. This is important, in that it confirms the treatment of
language we saw in *Among the Indians* and speaks to a general trend in
popular entertainment: to provide a stage world which resembles, but
does not really reflect, reality. After 1900 we are no longer in the days of
melodrama, when accurate depiction served as an anchor for flights
into fantasy. Rather, the pop media begin to seek a world they can create
themselves.

A second feature of "Litvak and Galitsianer" is its combination of
downhome, European references with an allusion to America ("when
Columbus first discovered America, he already found a Litvak here"). It
may not be accidental that the transition to the American framework
directly precedes the temporary truce between the warring dialects:
"God—give the Jews a lot and the Gentiles plagues." In America, one
can perhaps infer, older intragroup splits must cease. In a rhetorical
flourish, the two rekindle their fight in a "blackout" line to end the song;
another social message has already slipped in. Only a very close reading
of these apparently simple, even nonsensical song texts will help us to
understand the immigrants through their expressive culture. In the
language and the unconscious gestures of the texts we discover clues to
social history.

Folksong and Folkdance Arrangements

There is a small but diverse body of folk material in sheet music. Dance
tunes by far outnumber editions of folksongs, probably due to the
still-lively tradition of the *klezmer* band, which performed at weddings
and other festivities. Many of the tunes could also be performed at the
parlor piano, perhaps as a replacement for the professional group.
Traditional happy melodies—*sher, freylakhs, dobridzen*—are well represented. Of particular interest in pointing to the emergence of piano
primacy is Rumshinsky's *At a Hebrew Wedding Ceremony* (1909), a

complete suite of dances in the usual marriage sequence. For the section "Under the Canopy," a point at which music was not traditionally performed, the composer chose an interesting strategy: he interpolated the only non-ethnic-sounding number, a rather Protestant-like short chord sequence. This may augur change in the old-style wedding. At the end of the immigrant period, the Reverend Bernard Drachman, rabbi of the synagogue at which the great cantor Yosele Rosenblatt sang, wrote a song entitled "Hail Joyous Day" (1921) with an all-English text, meant to be sung at weddings.

Traditional Values

The folk tradition may not have maintained a firm musical ethnic boundary, but it did emphasize old values. So extensive are the offerings in this category that we must break it down into two parts: songs of religion, and songs of morality and didacticism.

Religion. The topic of faith itself has a twofold aspect. There are settings of liturgical texts, and songs stressing the importance of religion as a foundation for the proper life, or as consolation in times of trouble. Religious song arrangements range from florid versions of High Holiday material (e.g., "Unsane toykef" [1899], a Yom Kippur prayer) to a folk-like variant of "Got fun avrohom" ("God of Abraham" [1921], the standard women's chant at the close of the Sabbath). The wide chronological spread of these two items indicates the durability of the religious theme.

Both basic types of religious song are combined in "Likht bentshn" ("Blessing the Sabbath Candles" [1909]). A prayer in Hebrew appears within a Yiddish commentary on the importance of lighting the Sabbath candles:

SONG 13:
"Likht bentshn" ("Blessing the Sabbath Candles")

Verse 1
Mir bentshn di likht, mir bentshn di likht
lekoved dem heylikn shabes
in zkhus fun avrohom un fun itskhok un fun yankev,
zey zoln undz bayshteyn in undzer noyt, in undzer noyt.

Verse 2
Derher mayn gebet atsind, bet ikh bay dir,
helf mir almekhtiker got!

Yehi rotson milfonekho adonoy eloheynu velebey avoseynu,
oy vey, avoseynu.

Verse 1
We bless the candles, we bless the candles/ In honor of the
holy Sabbath/ Through the merit of Abraham, Isaac, and
Jacob/ May they stand by us in our need.

Verse 2
Hear my prayer now, I beg of you/ Help me, Almighty God/
Yehi rotson . . .

Songs stressing the consolation of religion are also of two types. One
simply hammers home the point that one ought to have faith. "Der
bitokhn tsu got" ("Faith in God") is from a Yiddish theater production of
1914 (Libin's *Di makht fun laydnshaft*, "The Power of Passion"):

SONG 14:
"Der bitokhn tsu got" ("Faith in God")

Verse 1
Oy, zay nit fartsveyflt, oy tatenyu,
vest zen vest nokh vern gezunt,
un hof nor tsum himlishn gotenyu
vos hert undzer betn atsind.

Chorus
Nor bitokhn ver es hot
dem nor helft dokh tomid got,
vayl bitokhn, nor bitokhn, dos iz gots gebet.
Dayn gants lebn bis in sof
shtendik mentshele nor hof,
vayl bitokhn ver es hot
dem nor helft dokh tomid got, tomid got.

Verse 1
O don't despair, dad/ You will be healthy yet/ Just hope in the
heavenly Lord/ Who hears our prayers now.

Chorus
Only the one who has faith/ Is always helped by God/ Because
faith, only faith, this is God's commandment./ Throughout your
life until the end/ Always, little man, just hope/ Because only
the one who has faith/ Is always helped by God.

The opening of the song clearly indicates its place in the drama: a sickbed scene, where a child (probably a daughter) is comforting an infirm father. This sort of "stage-setting" reference is rare in sheet music. Like its American counterpart, the Yiddish pop song is designed to stand on its own.

The second type of consolation song stresses particular rituals or objects. We have already seen how blessing the Sabbath candles can function as a focus for belief. Other songs that became particularly popular were Perlmutter and Wohl's hits "Dos talesl" ("The Prayer Shawl") and "Di tfiln" ("The Phylacteries"); these are among the very few works by composers of the immigrant period to be included in Appleton's 1968 *Bibliography of Jewish Vocal Music*,[5] indicating the durability of this particular approach to ethnicity. The strong showing of such songs in the sheet music repertoire must have two explanations. On one hand, the genre may express immigrant nostalgia for European folkways and traditions; here the songs serve to reinforce existing values. On the other hand, the songs perhaps represent an attempt to conserve older ritual in the face of rapid Americanization.

Morality and Didacticism. Closely allied to the songs of faith are those preaching the moral values of traditional Eastern European Jewish society. Among the most frequent topics emphasized is the remembrance of death. It is hard to tell just why this topic exerted such a fascination; one can only speculate that the presence of disease and bad news from the Old World led to thoughts of mortality. Meyrowitz's "Mentshele, meynst du vest eybik lebn" ("Little Man, Do You Think You'll Live Forever?" [1909]) illustrates the Yiddish *memento mori* song. The lyricist minces no words in describing the finality of death.

SONG 15:
"Mentshele, meynst du vest eybik lebn"
("Little Man, Do You Think You'll Live Forever?")

Mentshele, meynst du vest eybik lebn?
Du denkst an dayn ende gor nit.
Tayneg un gelt—dos iz dayn shtrebn,
host keyn rakhmones, fargist mentshnblut.
Du boyest paleste mit blumen a sakh
un du denkst du blaybst eybik dort;
du roybst dayne brider, vilst nor zayn raykh,
du fargest gor dos heylike ort
vu kvorim-bletelekh
vu grine grezelekh

fardekn dayn eybike ru,
un dayne gederemlekh
esn veremlekh:
es helft nit keyn raykhtum dortn.

Little man, do you think you'll live forever?/ You don't think about your end at all./ You strive for pleasure and money/ You have no pity, spill human blood./ You build palaces with a lot of flowers/ And think you'll stay there forever/ You rob your brothers and only want to be rich/ You forget the cemetery altogether/ Where grave-leaves/ And green grasses/ Cover your eternal resting-place/ And worms eat your little insides/ Your wealth is no help there.

Meyrowitz was a master of the didactic song, scoring again and again with such hits as "Krikh nit tsu hoykh" ("Don't Climb Too High") and "Mit gelt tor men nit shtoltsirn" ("Don't Show Off with Money"). Many of these songs speak directly to those Jews who had taken advantage of the "land of opportunity" to become arrogant parvenus, flaunting their social distance from their Ghetto brethren. We hear of certain thieves and fools of Europe who have become big shots in America. Didacticism is a prominent trait in Eastern European Jewish folklore, and it persisted as a major theme down to the days of the last famous *badkhonim*, the wedding jesters who were also social critics. The songs of the great bard Eliokum Zunser, who died in America, remained in circulation throughout the immigrant period (printings in 1898, 1910, and a fancy hardcover edition in 1928).

However, the attack on hypocrisy could also be comic. We have already seen Willie and Harry's comments in *Among the Indians* (1895), and songs like "Blof! Blof! Blof!" ("Bluff, Bluff, Bluff" [1905]) show the topic to be viable in the early twentieth century:

SONG 16:
"Blof! Blof! Blof!" ("Bluff, Bluff, Bluff")

Chorus
Blof! blof! blof! iz ales umetum,
blof! blof! blof! arum un arum.
Es helfn nit kayn taynes, khotsh tsum himl aroyf,
di gantse velt iz nor geshtelt oyf blof! blof! blof!

Chorus
Everywhere everything is bluff, bluff, bluff/ Bluff, bluff, bluff,

around and around./ No complaints help, even if you cry to heaven/ The whole world is based only on bluff, bluff, bluff!

An interesting topical reference occurs in the final couplet:

Und oyb ir hot in zinen
Az rusland vet di krig gevinen
Zolt ir visn, az dos iz a blof.

And if you imagine/ That Russia will win the war/ You should know that it's a bluff.

The war in question is apparently the Russo-Japanese conflict. As in the case of the patriotic American song that turned out to have a hidden Zionist agenda, one must look beneath the surface of each sheet music song text to find multiple meanings.

The song "Mentshen-fresser" ("Man-Eaters") falls into no specific category. It can be conveniently used as a transition from our present heading to the next, if we pick out two major strands of its content. As a *memento mori* song, "Mentshen-fresser" take an unusual tack: it is a commentary on tuberculosis, a dread disease of the tenements. Following Spaeth's songwriting commandments to the letter, the song has a verse in two-four and a refrain in waltz time. The juxtaposition of American structure with Jewish content is particularly striking in this song, since the oom-pah-pah of the waltz falls at the point when the text addresses microbes and bacilli, rather than appealing to a girlfriend:

SONG 17:
"Mentshen-fresser" ("Man-Eaters")

Verse 1:
In di lungen tif bagrobn
voynt di blaze pest:
di mikrobn, di batsiln
boyen zeyer nest,
fresn undzer layb un lebn,
frukhpern zikh pek
un mir muzn zelbst farshvebn
far der tsayt avek.
Un mir filn vi mir geyen
shtil un langzam oys,
un di shmertsn un di veyen
zaynen shreklikh groys.
Un di finstere makhshoves

gresern dem shmerts.
Yorn ligt der malakhamoves
tif bay undz in herts.

Chorus:
Mikrobn, batsiln, vos vilt ir?
Zogt, vemens shlikhes erfilt ir?
Ir frest di korbones
gor on rakhmones,
in bliendn lebn nor tsilt ir.
Ir bodt zikh in trern fun veyner,
ir tsit oys di markh fun di beyner.
Ir zamt di gederem, ir krikhende verem.
Mikrobn, batsiln, vos vilt ir?

Verse 1
Deeply buried in the lungs/ Lives the pale plague/ The bacilli
and microbes/ Build their nest/ They eat our bodies and lives/
And multiply greatly/ And we must fade away from the world/
Before our time./ And we feel how we expire/ Quietly and
slowly/ And the pains and the suffering/ Are terribly great./
And the dark thoughts/ Increase the pain./ For years the Angel
of Death/ Lives deep in our hearts.

Chorus
Microbes, bacilli, what do you want?/ Speak, whose errands
are you fulfilling?/ You eat the victims/ Mercilessly/ And aim
only at blossoming life./ You bathe in the tears of the weepers/
You extract the marrow from the bones./ You poison the
bowels, you creeping worms./ Microbes and bacilli, what do
you want?

The imagery is strong and relentless, down to "the marrow of the
bones." (One is reminded of the action of the cemetery worms in the
memento mori song quoted earlier.) Nevertheless, the "man-eater"
metaphor is not dropped after a single verse and chorus; as usual, the
central idea is developed in at least one other guise. Verse 4 describes
other types of "cannibals":

Verse 4
Kep gekroynte, diplomatn,
um tsu hobn zig
tsvingen undz tsu zayn soldatn,

traybn undz in krig.
Yunge mentshn in milyonen
tsoln zeyer prayz,
un es vet far di kanonen
zeyer flaysh a shpayz . . .
un tsekriplte un toyte
faln do un dort;
naye lebns ongegreyte
filn oys dem ort . . .
Un in groyse tife kvorim
pakt men laykhes fil
un di hersher, di keysorim,
shpiln shakhmat shpil!

Verse 4
Crowned heads and diplomats/ To gain victory/ Force us to be soldiers/ Drive us to war./ Young people by the millions/ Pay their price/ And their flesh/ Becomes cannon fodder . . . / And the crippled and the dead/ Fall here and there/ New lives are prepared/ To take their places . . . / And many corpses/ Are packed into big, deep graves/ And the rulers, the kings/ Play chess!

The topic of internal destruction through disease has led naturally to the issue of external annihilation via war: the "crowned heads and diplomats" are the microbes and bacilli of the human world. No punches are pulled in describing social and natural processes; Victorian euphemisms and high-flown language find little place in the naturalistic world of the Yiddish immigrant song. Unlike other ethnic groups, the Jews do not attempt to allay today's troubles with visions of a happier past. The summoning up of war victims goes beyond finger-pointing directed at the old regimes of Europe; it also speaks to the question of the Jews' lot.

SONGS OF EXTERNAL CHALLENGE
AND INTERNAL CHANGE

The Jews' Lot; War; Oppression

Of course, it is difficult to draw the line between issues of internal identity and the question of "the Jews' lot." Yet one would want to differentiate between the attempt at maintaining an in-group sense of identity, as illustrated by the songs on faith and ritual practice, and the effort to rationalize or face up to an external challenge.

General statements on the fate of the Jews tend to rely on the image of the Wandering Jew. This non-Jewish creation is accepted as part of a Jewish self-image because of consecutive expulsions and emigrations. Since we have touched on this theme before, we will only briefly consider a song of this type here, a post–World War I item (1919):

SONG 18:
"Der eybiker vanderer" ("The Eternal Wanderer")

Ikh vander, der alter reb yisroel.
Ikh vander shoyn toyznter yorn,
in goles getribn iberal.
Vi lang nokh vel ikh arumvandern
tsu zukhn mayn heym, mayn muters shoys.
Zog mir, got, vi vayt iz nokh tsum veg vos firt
fun dem goles aroys?

I wander, old Reb Israel.
I've been wandering for thousands of years,
Driven into exile everywhere.
How long will I keep wandering
Seeking my home, my mother's lap.
Tell me, God, how much longer is the road that leads
Out of exile?

Though the following stanza flirts with Zionism by mentioning the Holy Land as a possible final destination, the complaint is addressed to God, and is not couched in the rhetoric of a social movement.

A 1908 Mogulesco song, "Dos goldene rendele" ("The Gold Coin"), lists various stages along the Jewish path of suffering, culminating in the Russian excesses of the day and hoping—as in previously cited songs—that Russia will be defeated in war:

SONG 19:
"Dos goldene rendele" ("The Gold Coin")

Fun shpanyen fargest nor nit,
vifl yidish blut hot dort in gantsn land geflosn.
Shreklekh mordet men nokh haynt in vistn rusland,
es lign toyte in di gasn.

A sof hot shpanyen shoyn gehat, yetst darf nokh der despot
dershlogn vern dort bay yapan.
Un fun undzer payn un shrek zol makhn got an ende,
un brengn undz keyn tsiyon glaykh arayn.

Don't forget about Spain/ How much Jewish blood flowed
there across the whole land./ They still murder terribly today in
desolate Russia/ The dead lie in the streets./ Spain has already
met its end, and now the despot/ Must still be beaten over
there, by Japan./ And let God put an end to our pain and terror,/ And bring us straight to Zion.

One of the best-known songs about the czarist realm is Small/
Smulewitz's "A brivele fun rusland" ("A Letter from Russia" [1912]).
The strong plea to American Jewry to rescue the Russian brethren is
again reminiscent of the 1970s:

SONG 20:
"A brivele fun rusland" ("A Letter from Russia")

Brider fun di fraye shtetn, ir zayt gliklekh, ir zayt fray.
Undzer lebn iz a shotn, undzer hofenung iz farbay.
Rusland zukht oyf undz bilbulim, s'vert banayt elilas-dam;
has, ferakhtung un zilzulim, groyzamkayt fun yedn kham.
Zayt befrayer oyb aykh tayer iz dem yidns lebn aykh;
s'vet alts enger, vart nit lenger, ayer hilf iz neytik glaykh.

Chorus
A brivele der mamen fun di unterdrikte tsum amerikaner
    frayen yid:
retet, yidn brider, mir zaynen vi dershtikte, fun di gzeyres,
    fun di tsores mid.
Az eyn yid far a tsveytn shtendik iz an orev, far yemens
    shuld, der tsveyter git a fant,
helft zhe ayer fraynd, bashitst zhe ayer korev, retet undz
    fun beyzn tsarnland.

Verse 1
Brothers of the free states, you're lucky, you're free./ Our life is
a shadow, our hope is past./ Russia seeks false accusations
against us, the charge of ritual murder [of Christians for their
blood] is renewed/ Hate, contempt, and abuse, horror from every boor./ Be our liberators if Jewish life is dear to you/ It keeps
getting tighter, don't wait any longer, your help is needed now.

Chorus:
A letter to mama, from the oppressed to the free American Jews/ Save us, brother Jews, we are suffocating, weary from the evil decrees and troubles./ Just as one Jew is always a guarantor for another, one pays for another's guilt/ So help your friend, protect your relative, save us from the evil czarist land.

The "letter to mama" line, hardly motivated in this song, seems to act as a reflex-stimulator for Small/Smulewitz's aesthetic. (He wrote the famous hit using that line as its title.) Here again, a self-sufficient system of clichés is being constructed.

It is worth stepping back to view the Jewish musical approach to World War I, as opposed to mainstream American songs on the subject. Conveniently, a 1917 sheet music folio ("Hy-Sine March and One-Step") lays out the general American classification of war songs, to which Jewish practice can be compared. It lists "six different types of war songs now being sung and played everywhere":

1. "Cheer up" type: "Set Aside Your Tears Till the Boys Come Marching Home";
2. "Ballad" type: "When the Moon Is Shining Somewhere in France";
3. "Stirring march" type: "The Old Flag Never Touched the Ground";
4. "Appealing" type: "Send Back Dear Daddy to Me";
5. "Comic" type: "I'm in the Army Now";
6. "Victory" type: "There'll Be a Hot Time in the Old Town Tonight."

Of these six recognized commercial varieties, only two appear in the Yiddish tradition. "A grus fun di trentshes" ("A Greeting from the Trenches") is in the "stirring march" category, whereas "Tfilos milkho-mo" ("War Prayer") seems "appealing," though not in the cute vein represented by "Send Back Dear Daddy to Me." We find no exhortations to "cheer up," no comic songs about hapless recruits, and no romantic ballads about "The Rose of No Man's Land." Anxious worry or statements of support for America are all the Jewish-American songwriters seemed willing to compose. Perhaps this indicates, once again, that the songwriters were in touch with the community. They rarely strove to write about feelings which contradicted general opinion and sentiment.

Yet at times one senses a gentle molding of public opinion. In 1917, besides writing "Russia's Song of Freedom," Morris Rosenfeld composed words for "My America: Our New Hymn." This highfalutin tribute to the American cause exhorts Jewish youths to lay down their lives, if need be, for their new homeland. The text is hyperbolic, in both Yiddish and English, while the music is in pure Protestant hymn style. "My America" is the closest to rabble-rousing of any song in the sheet music repertoire:

SONG 21:
"My America: Our New Hymn"

A bentshung dir, du naye velt:
Dayn shvel oyf frayhayt iz geshtelt.
Amerika, ikh hob dikh lib,
un zogstu mir: dayn lebn gib,
ikh darf dayn mut, ikh darf dayn blut,
zolstu dos hobn di minut.
Ikh freg dikh nit tsu vos tsu ven;
vos du farlangst dos zol geshen.

Be thou new world by Heaven blest,
Thy threshold doth on freedom rest.
America, thou hast my love,
And if my valor thou wouldst prove
And ask my life as sacrifice,
It shall be yielded in a trice.
No wherefore and no why I ask,
I shall obey, whate'er the task.

The particularly fervid patriotism of "My America" leads us to our next major grouping, songs about the New World.

America

All the turmoil of immigration and adaptation is reflected in the sheet music repertoire. "America" is such a large topic that we need to consider its three main facets separately: pro-American and anti-American feeling, the process of immigration, and the woes of the greenhorn's life.

There are few other examples of the "My America" type. Despite the immigrants' growing success in and enthusiasm for the New World, songwriters exploited the negative aspects of their situation. An exception to this trend is a very early (1887) song, Mogulesco's "Shalakh-mones" ("Purim Gifts"), not published until 1914. The traditional gifts carried from house to house during the spring holiday of Purim relate to the central metaphor of the song, which details God's presents to Jewry. By Verse 3, Mogulesco has taken the story from Exodus to America:

SONG 22:
"Shalakh-mones" ("Purim Gifts")

Verse 3
Der driter shalakh-mones
iz oykh fun got geven
az di rusn on rakhmones
hobn zikh an undz noykem geven.
Amerika a land iz do
vos dort lebt yeder fray,
un der yidele in a guter sho
git shoyn oykh rusland a shpay.
Amerika hot shtetelakh,
hayzelakh mit kleytelakh,
ale tsuker zis.
Bal-melokhelekh yidelekh
in ale stritelekh,
oy, vi tsuker zis.

Verse 3
The third gift/ Is also God-given/ As the Russians, mercilessly/
Took revenge on us./ There is a land, America,/
Where everyone lives free/ And the Jew, in a happy hour,/
Also spits on Russia./ America has towns/ Houses and stores/
All are sugar-sweet./ Jewish artisans/ In all the streets/
Oh, how sugar-sweet.

Anti-Americanism, the more prevalent mode of commentary, encompasses the topics of immigration and adjustment. Like every other ethnic group, the Jews produced a number of songs on the actual process of arriving in the New World; there are early 78 rpm records in various languages on the subject of Ellis Island itself. A particular point of emphasis in the Jewish songs is the generally unsung problem of rejectees from America. Thousands upon thousands of prospective immigrants were turned away for a variety of reasons: failure to possess the requisite sum of money; eye disease; criminal record, including anti-czarist activity; and a host of other causes. This policy was seen as particularly cruel and capricious, as illustrated by a 1909 letter to the *Forverts* signed by one hundred immigrants, aged eight to fifty-eight, awaiting their fate at Ellis Island:

> We the unfortunates who are imprisoned on Ellis Island beg you to have pity on us and print our letter in your worthy newspapers so that our brothers in America may know how we suffer here. . . .
>
> You know full well how much the Jewish immigrant suffers till he gets to America . . . and when, with God's help, he has endured all this, and he is at last in America, he is given for "dessert" an order that he must show that he possesses twenty-five dollars. But where can we get it . . . we must have the money on arrival, yet a few hours later [when relatives come] it's too late. For this kind of nonsense they ruin so many people and send them back to the place they escaped from. . . .
>
> We are packed into a room where there is space for two hundred people, but they have crammed in about a thousand . . . men are separated from their wives and children and only when they take us out to eat can they see them. . . .
>
> God knows how many Jewish lives this will cost, because more than one mind dwells on the thought of jumping into the water when they take him [back] to the boat.[6]

As Harry Golden notes, "during the previous week, 600 detained immigrants had been sent back. And on the day the letter from the 100 was printed, they were sending back 270 people."

Given these statistics and their impact on family life, it is hardly surprising to find songs with titles such as "Der tsurikgeshikter imigrant" ("The Sent-Back Immigrant"). Small/Smulewitz's "Elis ayland" ("Ellis Island") of 1914 voices a common emotion:

SONG 23:
"Elis ayland" ("Ellis Island")

O elis ayland, du grenets fun frayland,
vi groys un vi shreklekh du bist.
Azelkhe retsikhes dos kenen nor rikhes,
du plagst di geplagte umzist.
Mit tsores gekumen, dem yam koym dershvumen,
di getin der frayhayt derzen,

do komt elis ayland, der grenets fun frayland,
zogt: halt, du kenst vayter nit geyn.

O Ellis Island, you border of Freeland/ How big and how terri-
ble you are./ Only demons can commit such outrages/
You harass the harassed for nothing./ Having come with trou-
bles, having barely crossed the sea/ Having seen the Statue of
Liberty/ There's Ellis Island, the border of Freeland/ Saying:
"Stop, you can go no further."

Once admitted to "Freeland," the immigrant voiced his disappointment and resentment at the failure of his dreams to materialize. The
phrase *goldn land* or *goldene medine* ("land of gold," or "golden land") is
rarely used as a positive epithet; rather, it is the standard vehicle for
feelings of anti-Americanism. (A similar attitude is voiced in "A brivele
dem tatn," about a father sent back to Russia, forever parted from his
immigrant son.) This negative attitude toward the new homeland is in
itself a complex emotion whose various facets are revealed in diverse
song texts. One stance found in the earlier repertoire, which we have
already suggested as a major source for didactic songs, is indignation at
the way European good-for-nothings have become American suc-
cesses. Friedsell's "Di goldene medine" (1902) displays this attitude:

SONG 24:
"Di goldene medine" ("The Golden Country")

Verse
Amerika iz a goldn land, lang un breyt no vi a rikh.
Git nor eynem in der hant, vert er an oysher gikh.
Er meg zayn a ganev fun der heym, a kolboynik mit lepke hent,
makht di khevre anshey-sdom im far a prezident.
Mit der tsayt vert er a gantser filosof,
farrayst zayn noz un kukt aroyf.
A morde frest er on vi a groyser kham,
er meynt er iz a gantser yatebedam.
Ikh zog ober, er iz der zelber ganev take vos er iz geven.

Chorus
Oy a goldn land, a goldene medine,
vilstu zayn a mentsh un leben git
in dem goldenem land, goldene medine,
vos du zest un herst, keyn kashes freg gor nit.

Verse

America is a golden country, as long and broad as a demon/
As soon as he gives a bribe, he becomes rich quickly./ He may
be a thief from back home, a scoundrel with sticky fingers/
The Society of Sodomites will make him president./
With time he becomes a regular philosopher/ He turns up his
nose and looks up./ He gorges himself and fattens his chin like
a big boor/ He thinks he's a big shot./ But I say he's the same
thief as before.

Chorus

O, a golden land, a golden country/ If you want to be a person
and live well/ In the golden land, golden country/ Don't ask
any questions about what you see and what you hear.

"Di goldene medine" is essentially a song of self-criticism, a genre
which tends to fade away as the American Dream becomes more
attainable or to take on more specific and stereotyped metaphors, such
as the eventual rise of the *schlemihl*, the Jewish Mother, and the
Jewish-American Princess. In 1902 self-criticism centered on social
inequality, rather than on the incompetence, emotional demands, or
self-satisfaction of the 1960s satire. In this respect the earlier songs
demonstrate a strong tie to the great nineteenth-century Yiddish literary and popular tradition of self-satire directed against the powerful and
the hypocrites within the European Jewish community. The connection with the earlier genre of didactic songs also shows a continuity of
European values.

A newer type of anti-American song takes on the day-to-day struggle
of immigrant life. This issue had been broached in the first American
Yiddish plays, such as Lateiner's *Di emigratsion nokh amerika* ("The
Emigration to America"), for which, unfortunately, no music survives.
One of the most striking songs of immigrant hardship is "Di nyu-yorker
trern" ("New York Tears") by Altman, published in 1910 but possibly
much older. The full text is worth reproducing because it gives a very
comprehensive account of the daily tragedies of city life:

SONG 25
"Di nyu-yorker trern" ("New York Tears")

Verse 1

In nyu-york kokht nor vi a keslgrib,
es rasht un es rudert gor on oyfher.
Fil memtshn zet ir geyn im trib,

oft mol gefint ir bay mentshn a trer.
Umglikn trefn do oyf yedn shrit,
un dokh vert der gehenem nokh frayland genent.
A familye shtelt men aroys do in strit
vayl zey kenen nit pinktlekh batsoln dem rent.
Es regnt, es gist, di trern es flist
un zey zitsn nebekh farfinstert, farvist.

Chorus
Ot dos zaynen di nyu-yorker trern
vos kenen keyn mol nit oyfhern.
A krekhts, a geshrey, a zifts und a vey,
dos kent ir nor imer do hern.
Dos iz shoyn nit nay, vu ir geyt nor farbay
zet ir di nyu yorker trern.

Verse 2
A man geyt avek fun der heym gezint,
er loyft zukhn arbet tsu trefn zayn glik.
A kar kumt on bald, tseshnayt im geshvind,
men brengt im aheym a toytn tsurik.
Di froy ven zi zet dos blaybt zi vi farshtumt,
ir ponim vert blas un di oygn royt.
Men shikt nokh a dokter, un bifor er kumt
treft er di froy az zi ligt shoyn oykh toyt,
un dos eyntsike kind shrayt nebekh atsind:
tatenyu, mamenyu, nemt mikh mit zikh geshvind.

Verse 3
Ver es hot nit gehert fun der merderay
vos hot pasirt do nit lang in mantgomeri strit:
gefunen tseshnitn hot men mentshn dray:
a man, a froy, a shviger in a taykh blut.
Un dort hert men a boy hot zayn khaver geshosn.
Kinder tsvey hobn zikh mit a pistol geshpilt.
A boy fun 14 yor, vos hot er den genosn.
Der tsveyter boy nokh yinger hot in im getsilt.
Vi er hot derfilt dem knal
shrayt er "mame" oyf a kol,
und loyfendik fun dritn flor
blaybt er lign toyt im hol.

Verse 1
New York bubbles like a pot/ There's constant tumult and
hubbub./ You see a lot of people rushing around and/ Often
you see people's tears./ Misfortunes happen here at every step/
And yet this hell is called Freeland./ They put a family out on
the street/ Because they can't pay the rent on time./ It rains, it
pours, the tears flow/ And the poor things sit depressed and
forlorn.

Chorus
That's the New York tears/ Which never can stop./ A sob, a
scream, a sigh and a woe/ That's what you hear all the time./
That's nothing new; wherever you go/ You see the New York
tears.

Verse 2
A man leaves home healthy/ He runs to look for work to seek
his fortune./ A car comes and cuts him up quickly/ They bring
him home dead./ The wife, when she sees this, stands dumb/
Her face pales and her eyes redden./ They send for a doctor,
but before he can come/ He finds the wife also lying dead/ And
the only child, alas, now screams/ O mommy, o daddy, take me
with you quickly.

Verse 3
Who hasn't heard of the murder/ That took place not long ago
on Montgomery Street?/ They found three people stabbed/ A
man, a wife, and a mother-in-law in a pool of blood./ And there
you hear a boy shot his friend./ Two children were playing
with a pistol./ A boy of 14, what has he seen of life./ The
second boy, still younger, aimed at him./ When he felt the
shot/ He screams "mama" loudly/ And, running from the third
floor/ He lies dead in the hall.

"Di nyu-yorker trern" overlaps at least two other genres on our list: the
occasional song (inspired by a specific event), and the orphan song.
Verse 2 is a strong statement of the orphan's plight, while Verse 3
mentions actual events that must have been fresh in listeners' minds.
Despite the localization, one wonders if the song is very different from
similar ballads that must have been hawked on the streets of Warsaw,
Kiev, or Odessa. Contemporaneous folksongs from those cities address
the dislocation and random cruelty of urban life; e.g., there are songs on
the deaths of factory workers due to industrial accidents. Yet however

close the parallels to European material may be, one cannot help being struck by the song's title (specifying America), by the local events (children playing with firearms; the high rate of eviction), and, most of all, by the telltale line: "And yet this hell is called Freeland." The Yiddish word, so cleverly made to rhyme with "Ellis Island" in a song examined earlier, confirms the stylized language of sheet music.

One final note on the European and American approaches to the tragedies of modern life. In the sheet music repertoire, one finds very little reference to anti-Semitism in America. There is the occasional stray item, like the broadside on the Leo Frank case; even that song, written when Frank was pardoned, took a highly optimistic view. The European songs, on the other hand, are frequently about pogroms, the ravages of war, and the sufferings brought about by the czarist regime, and topics that we have characterized as typical for American material about the Old World. One of the few anti-Gentile swipes in the New York material appears in "Der poylisher yid" ("The Polish Jew"), a commentary on Old World, rather than American, anti-Semitism.

Of all the songs on the topic of America, one is notable for its distinctive format: the bilingual "Swing Days/Men hoydet zikh in Amerika" ("You Swing in America"), with lyrics by Anshel Shorr (1908). Completely American in musical style, the song has an English text in the mainstream tradition of "School Days" and other nostalgic evocations of non-ethnic American childhood. The Yiddish text simultaneously undercuts the rosy vision by supplying an abrasive, naturalistic image of sweatshop life:

SONG 26:
"Swing Days/Men hoydet zikh in amerika"

Chorus:

Swing days, swing days,	Hoyda, hoyda,
Then were the dear happy times.	men hoydet zikh aher un ahin.
Swing days, swing days,	Hoyda, hoyda,
Days of old nursery rhymes.	meg men zayn gel tsi grin,
Oh for those dear old swing days,	mus men zikh hoyden, hoyden,
Spending our nickels and dimes	dort in a shap baym mashin.
As we used to meet near the pool	Men hoydet dos lebn aroys
And go swinging right after school.	bis es geyen di koykhes oys.

Swing, swing,/ You swing back and forth./ Swing, swing,/Whether you're yellow or green/ You have to swing, swing/ There in a shop by a machine./ You swing out your life/ Until you're all used up.

The staggering contrast between the two texts bespeaks a level of self-consciousness which might not otherwise have been credited to the supposedly unsophisticated songmakers of 1908. We have seen straightforward Yiddish parodies of American songs as far back as the mid-1890s, but the coexistence of model *and* parody as alternate texts in the same song exists only in "Swing Days." Thus, before 1910, one finds fairly elaborate means of expression for attitudes toward America, including the very irony about American life that will form the keystone of Jewish-American comedy and literature in later decades.

Social Movements

"Swing Days" is a song of social protest as much as a purely entertainment item, and it leads us to our final category. In the sheet music world, social commentary rarely made direct reference to the radical ferment of Jewish-American politics. True enough, there are editions of "The Jewish Marseillaise" and the "Internationale," the worldwide hymn of revolution. But one finds few mentions of unions, strikes, or socialism. These topics seem to have been relegated to the appropriate political body, such as the Workmen's Circle Chorus of the early 'teens, described earlier. Only with the establishment of Lefkowich's Metro Music shop and publishing house do we find a commercial enterprise taking up the workers' cause.

Nevertheless, allusions to social movements do crop up, most often in comedy numbers fresh from the Yiddish stage. We have already seen entertainment's view of feminism and the suffrage movement. In terms of socialism, "Fifti-fifti" ("50-50") can serve as a musical example. While its first verse considers broad questions of social equality, subsequent stanzas take the topic of "fifty-fifty" into the more general realm of comedy: the narrator's brother, a streetcar conductor, goes halves with the city as he collects fares.

SONG 27:
"Fifti-fifti" ("50-50")

Verse
Ikh hof, mir veln nokh derlebn kumen zol di tsayt
ven es veln mer nit zayn keyn boses un keyn arbetslayt.
Di sotsyalistn veln makhn a sof tsu orem un raykh;
di boses mit di arbeter veln zikh teyln glaykh oyf glaykh.

Chorus
Fifti fifti, oy, oy, oy, fifti!
Vanderbilt vet vi an oks
zitsn shvitsn un neyen kloks;

lomir trayen umetum
keyn tsayt farlirn un shnel aynfirn
dem fifti-fifti-skim, oy, oy, oy!

Verse
I hope we will live to see the day/ When there will be no more
bosses and workers./ The Socialists will put an end to "poor"
and "rich"/ The bosses and the workers will divide things up
evenly.

Chorus
Fifty-fifty, oy, oy, oy, fifty!/ Vanderbilt, like an ox,/ Will sit and
sweat and sew cloaks/ Let's try everywhere/ Lose no time and
quickly introduce/ The fifty-fifty scheme, oy, oy, oy!

As usual, the language closely matches the tenor of the text. We are
treated to an amusing array of Americanisms, ranging from the title
itself—"fifty-fifty," not "fuftsik-fuftsik"—through the very un-Yiddish
verb *tray* ("try") and noun *skim* ("scheme").

With this comic flourish we take our leave of the texts and topics of
the sheet music repertoire. Even so cursory a survey reveals the richness of the material, the scope of the subjects, and the complexity of the
world mirrored in the lyrics of ephemeral popular songs. Let us now
turn to the graphic imagery presented by the sheet music as artifact.

NOTES

1. This and the following quotation are from Sigmund Spaeth, *Read 'Em and
   Weep: The Songs You Forgot to Remember* (New York: Halcyon House,
   1926), pp. 1–2.
2. For a basic survey, see Charles A. Madison, *Jewish Publishing in America*
   (New York: Sanhedrin Press, 1976). The two quotations below re: Hebrew
   Publishing Co. catalogues are from pp. 79–81.
3. Lines from "Homeless Tonight, or Boston in Ashes," quoted in Lester Levy,
   Grace Notes in American History: Popular Sheet Music from 1820–1900
   (Norman: University of Oklahoma Press, 1967), p. 324.
4. Quoted in E. and C. Moore, *Ballads and Folk Songs of the Southwest* (Norman: University of Oklahoma Press, 1964), p. 366.
5. Lewis Appleton, *Bibliography of Jewish Vocal Music*, rev. ed. (New York:
   National Jewish Music Council, 1968).
6. This and the following Harry Golden quotation are from I. Metzker, ed., *A
   Bintel Brief* (New York: Ballantine, 1971), pp. 94–97.

CHAPTER 7

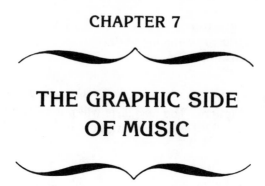

THE GRAPHIC SIDE
OF MUSIC

The great popular songs of the turn of
the century, the show tunes and
the musical movie songs have been
studied from every aspect
but the printed sheets on which they appear.
—KLAMKIN[1]

It has been estimated that over 2.5 million songs have been written and published in America. Many of these appeared in a folio form which featured a cover illustration relating directly to the song's music and text. Indeed, a piece of sheet music must be seen as a complex cultural package of various expressive and commercial media, all of which combine to create a pleasing product. Yet, as one observer has noted, "What has been published *between* the covers of popular sheet music is a subject that has been covered rather fully. However, the covers themselves are the contemporary artists' interpretation of the popular songs that they were hired to illustrate, and this aspect of popular sheet music has been largely ignored." [2] As has been aptly observed for Victorian sheet music covers, "this music-publishing industry used lithographed music covers in the same way that record sleeves are used today." [3]

For American and English sheet music, collectors' attention has been confined to the most decorative and technically proficient work of early nineteenth century engravers, or to later works by well-known artists. This highbrow approach is of scant interest to us, since we are dealing with the output of hard-pressed immigrant publishing firms that had little cash to spare for multi-color or elegantly lithographed designs. We approach the sheet music illustrations not as art, but as music-cultural evidence. They form an iconography of immigrant music that has been largely overlooked.

In the early nineteenth century, the engraving of cover illustration was part of a more general business in graphics: "Every major city had its leading engravers who did a steady business designing and printing song sheets and covers for popular music. The same engravers who printed military badges and broadsides to welcome General Lafayette on his triumphal return to this country in 1824 also published the hastily written musical pieces that were played by the bands that performed at the celebration." [4] In England, however, new developments occurred. "From the 1820s onwards," write Doreen and Sidney Spellman, "lithography began to replace engravings for music illustration." [5] They note that "the history of music illustration could be regarded as the history of lithography in England." There has been no detailed study for America; even histories of American graphic arts pay little attention to music. What is evident, however, is that by the time of the rise of Tin Pan Alley, excellence of engraving was no longer a paramount concern:

> More often than not early twentieth-century song sheet covers were printed in two colors, and the designers were faced with the challenge of devising an appealing design that could be printed cheaply. The sheet music business in the first half of this century was as important, relatively speaking, as the record industry is today. The major difference between the two industries is that the publisher was not willing to spend large amounts for the design of sheet music covers, since each sheet sold for less than a dollar and the printing and design costs had to be kept as low as possible. [6]

Earlier, celebrated illustrators like Alfred Concanen (d. 1886) or artists such as Toulouse-Lautrec (d. 1901) produced a few folios. With the advent of twentieth-century mass marketing, the relationship of the artist to his work changed dramatically: "It is obvious that most of the artists who earned a living designing covers for popular songs in this century thought very little of their work. Only a minimal amount of all the sheet music published has signed cover designs. . . . For the artists, it was a job, and they turned out thousands of handsome covers that can never be identified as theirs." [7]

The ephemeral nature of the popular song intensified the transience of music illustration. Last season's songs, printed on cheap paper, vanished into music benches, eventually to disintegrate. How much more impermanent, then, is the music of immigrants, who gave up their older songs willingly, even eagerly, once they became Americanized.

These fleeting images of a bygone musical world are of special importance for our purposes. A sheet music folio is a complex artifact; cover illustration, song text, music, and a great deal of ancillary information (publishers' catalogues, excerpts of other songs to "try on your piano") are combined into a single physical embodiment of the music culture. It is also distinctively American: as we have noted, there is little, if any, European Jewish sheet music during the immigrant period. Our survey will encompass over two dozen images as we look for patterns of meaning in the seemingly random iconography of music.

THE EARLY PHASE

When Jewish-American sheet music publishing surfaces in 1897, it boasts no coherent set of visual symbols. The inchoate nature of the repertoire is reflected in various packages for the musical product. In these early years a highly straightforward presentation is often made, as in Figure 1, from 1900. Here the Hebrew Publishing Co.'s trademark of lyre and scroll is already well established, and its ornamental style is carried over into the decoration and lettering on the upper part of the cover. Surprisingly, there appears no Yiddish whatsoever, even at this early date. Though we will attempt to identify trends in the evolution of the iconography, there is really no straight-line development which would satisfy the systematic analyst. Figure 2, an 1899 setting of liturgical music, corroborates the style just seen, with simple graphics and floral design. The heading "Traditional Religious Melodies" shows that by 1899 there was already a large Americanized audience who wished to see things labeled in English; furthermore, the transliterated title looms much larger than the Hebrew words above it. The term "Rev." rather than "Rabbi" precedes the composer's name.

Figure 3 takes us a step further by presenting a more pretentious cover illustration. Again stressing English lettering, "Zawadski/ Shoumka No. 2" adds the world of musical mythology. Surrounding the title of this 1903 item are angelic entertainers with an odd assemblage of instruments, ranging from the Greek *aulos* (the paired pipe on the upper left) through military band components (cymbals and trumpet) and Renaissance lutes up to a more modern-looking chamber ensemble on the lower right. (The trio of flute, fiddle, and bass seems more suitable for a Jewish *klezmer* band than it does for classical cherubs.) The almost grotesque faces and figures of the angels coincide with the mixed metaphors represented by the instruments. Here we have a graphic equivalent to the garbled mythology in the "Hebrew-American Orator" (King Arthur at Troy) and Rumshinsky's "Song of Love" ("my Amour, my Apollo").

In 1903, the effort to introduce Western high culture was still something of a strain; so it is somewhat surprising to find mainstream techniques self-confidently mastered within a scant five years. Figure 4 shows a 1908 example of considerable artistic competence, in a line-drawing style that is totally non-ethnic. B. Weinstock, about whom we know absolutely nothing, has created an architectural motif that will be developed in later years. He combines the symmetrically placed guitar and violin with balancing devices that extend the Hebrew Publishing logo to the upper part of the frame. What's more, a "series structure" has been established (here, "Mogulesco's Music Album") with an inset photo of the composer. This is a far cry from the design and packaging of the Mogulesco song of Figure 1, which appeared only seven years earlier. The Roman and Hebrew alphabets are nicely counterposed, though they do not contain the same data. A Yiddish phrase which appears in parentheses below the main title tells the buyer that the song is from a show called *Man un vayb* ("Man and Wife"), while the English omits this identification. Presumably theatergoers interested in the song's theatrical origin would be Yiddish-readers.

Figure 5 carries the "classical" motif to its extreme. "Chanson Russe" (1912) matches visual style and music-cultural intent very closely. This parlor piano piece has been labeled "classical" by the music culture, and is always cited that way in the publisher's listings on the backs of folios. These pieces have been given a standard cover illustration to match their defined content. The angels are by now gracefully combined with the architectural style in a series of rounded forms festooned with garlands. True, the mixture of muses, swans, cherubs, and what looks like a dramatic mask (at the very bottom) is still somewhat uneasy, and the three lyres pictured are in different styles. Yet there is a marked attempt at a balanced, "classic" form with the only Jewish reference appearing in the six-pointed star atop the center lyre. This seems a quiet way of pointing to the ethnicity raised by the publisher's name, and is an image we shall soon see again. Notice also that this publisher has had three different addresses on the folios examined thus far, reflecting the previously discussed volatility of ethnic "cottage" industries.

EVOLVING A SYMBOLIC LANGUAGE

While the question of adapting mainstream components remained open, illustrators were beginning to evolve an internal symbolic language. Very few artists are named on their sheet music. Two men, Louis Terr and Joseph Keller, begin to dominate the field, even before 1910; they are responsible for the unity of style we hope to identify. The two achieve this result largely through the line drawing, a technique no longer popular in mainstream American sheet music. Perhaps Terr and Keller use the line drawing because cheap editions could not rely on the sometimes spectacular multi-color effect of American folios, although there is no way of reconstructing the artists' motives.

Figure 6, "Khosn kale mazl tov" ("Congratulations to the Bride and Groom"), another Mogulesco contribution, shows the basic technique. The folio is undated, though the musical number dates back to the 1890s. The carefully drawn figures remain lifeless; perspective and anatomical detail are weak. Yet there is a strong attempt to convey an ethnic scene in all its richness. The bored children, officious men, fearful bride, and self-conscious matrons are all identifiable types, as if taken from the Yiddish stage. Weddings are central to the sense of ethnicity and are the focus of much in-group music-making, even (or perhaps especially) in America. The tune illustrated here is heavily Jewish in style, an identification reinforced by the drawing. The title is not translated, and the Yiddish may be somewhat more basic to the cover than is the transliteration; at any rate, it appears closer to the action depicted. Classical lyres have vanished from the publisher's logo, and the art nouveau flowers have been replaced by a more culturally anonymous crescent motif.

Terr's 1909 "Likht bentshn" ("Blessing the Sabbath Candles," Figure 7) shows a more complex statement of ethnicity. The song, which we examined earlier, stresses the importance of the basic weekly observance, combining that somewhat didactic message with a plea to God to help the Jews. Terr has carefully assembled a scene of domestic religiosity: the table is nicely set, the bread and wine are ready for the blessings, and the central image is of the candles. The housewife is Everywoman fulfilling her ritual duty. This intense vignette is centrally placed to serve as the focus of the cover, yet there is a certain conflict between this strong image and the surrounding material. Above the scene is the Yiddish title, backed by additional candles and a prayer book; the alphabet combines with the imagery to intensify the message. Nevertheless, the transliterated title is the most prominent feature, and the entire cover is surrounded by art nouveau ornamentation. The Hebrew Publishing lyre (along with the firm's fourth address) appears at the bottom, balancing the in-group information at the top. The ornamentation toward the bottom is much darker than the floral design of the upper part. It is tempting to see, in this disparity of messages, an appeal to a generation addressed by the rather didactic quality of the song. The prominence of the transliteration, which is what a prospective customer would first notice, may well be part of the marketing strategy. Mother makes a cameo appearance in order to bless the candles, literally standing behind the wall of Latin letters as if in memory.

Of course, such a reading of the iconography does not imply that Americanized customers were the only ones addressed by "Likht bentshn." The older music-buyers would merely focus on what was relevant to them, which is certainly included in the illustration. The appeal to a multifaceted audience is typical of much ethnic entertainment. Well into the 1920s, we find the famous song "My yidishe momme" recorded with a Yiddish version on one side of the disc and English on the other.

Our next two examples introduce a very different facet of our symbolic system: the cantor and the synagogue. Figure 8, "Rachmono d'one" (1912), shows J. Keller's elaboration on the theme of liturgical music. Vastly different from the spare, modest statement of 1899 (Figure 2), "Rachmono d'one" assaults the buyer with its diversity of data. The historical information itself shows how sheet music can act as a documentary source. From this cover we learn that Cantor Sirota performed this particular item on his highly successful 1912 tour. We also discover that Leo Loew, a well-known composer and arranger who later emigrated to America, was at the time musical director of the celebrated Tlomatzker Synagogue in Warsaw. Photographs of both musicians enhance the folio's historical value.

We must pay particular attention to the line drawing on the upper left, which depicts a synagogue of definitely European architecture. The cantor stands in the building, surrounded by an enormous gate. This gateway image is commonly found on Old World ceremonial objects, such as the silver plates attached to the scrolls of the Torah. Keller's architectural approach is far removed from the purely decorative structure used on the Mogulesco Music Album (Figure 4). In Figure 8, the building style is ethnic-specific, and the cultural message is transmitted by placing the cantor where he belongs, at the center of the synagogue. This is, after all, the time when the superstar cantor was a principal reason for attending services. For many congregants, this centrality of the cantor in the illustration must have jibed with their sense of the synagogue experience.

When we discussed the texts and topics of sheet music, we noted that this popular idiom tended to create a consistent "language" through format and linguistic usage. The thesis of the present chapter is that a similar development occurred in visual imagery. If the same figures and formats appear over a period of years, a standardization of visual metaphors may perhaps parallel the textual and (to be surveyed later) musical styles of the sheet music repertoire. Figure 9 should lead us toward verification of that thesis. It is a 1916 cover with no illustrator cited. Like "Rachmono d'one," "Yehi rotson" is a liturgical item featuring a well-known cantor—in this case, the most widely acclaimed and recorded sacred singer of his day, Yosele Rosenblatt. To illustrate this item, the artist has not only imitated, but even amplified Keller's synagogue. Close examination reveals that, while details remain constant (towers, triangular portico), most of the architecture has been altered. This indicates that the general concept of the synagogue, and not just a specific picture, remained in continuous use. The placement of the cantor is likewise similar to Keller's, but not identical. Instead of the full-length photo between the arches, we see an inset at the heart of the building, reduced in size to allow for the title. Again, it is not the specific format but the overall concept that carries over from 1912, reflecting more continuity than change in the matter of how to illustrate a certain aspect of the music culture.

Our next two examples round out the evolution of line drawing as a prime embodiment of ethnicity. One of the most complex pictorial representations is the graphic accompaniment to Goldfadn's Zionist "A yid bistu, gey vayter, gey" ("You're a Jew, So Move On"). Figure 10 presents this remarkable 1903 illustration (which, unfortunately, is anonymous); it is extremely detailed and comprehensive, and nothing as complicated seems to appear again. The title of the song, in Yiddish, frames the picture, while the lower two-thirds of the cover is devoted to the English-language information. Significantly, the title has been presented simply as "The Wandering Jew," encapsulating in a stock epithet the more inclusive meaning of the original. This adoption of a mainstream concept, well-known through Euro-American novels and melodrama, is an interesting sidelight of the folio. The large boldface letters in which it is written seem to appeal to the English-reading buyer; hence the suitability of an external catch phrase, rather than an ethnically oriented English name.

The illustration depicts the wanderer poised between two worlds. His feet seem to point in one direction, while he looks back as if reconsidering. He is clearly an archetypal Jew, biblically dressed with a shepherd's crook in hand, carrying the scrolls of the Torah on his back while searching for a home. To the right stretches an Oriental vista straight out of a Goldfadn musical drama, depicting palm trees, camels, classical ruins (probably the temple), and the hint of a pyramid. To the left is a fascinating characterization of America, readily identifiable by the familiar outlines of the Brooklyn Bridge. At the extreme left are shops: one is reminded of the early Mogulesco song that spoke so enthusiastically of the *"kleytelakh in ale geselakh,"* Jewish shops in every street. Just below the bridge floats a strange device recognizable as a paddle-wheel steamer. Does the river reach to Tom Sawyer's home? Such a reading would be in keeping with the mixed metaphors for America, as seen in Minikes's garbled symbolism in *Among the Indians*. At any rate, the water links the two halves of the picture, making a joint Jordan/East River which neatly summarizes the confluence of cultural concepts being illustrated.

Although it is prominent in the illustration, America does not figure in the song's lyrics. Only the incessant wandering of the Jew is cited, and the eternal command to "move on." Here the artist seems to have taken the song in hand, so to speak, clarifying its essential message: a choice between Americanization and Zionism. The fact that illustrations *can* move beyond mere depiction, toward amplification, strengthens our feeling that they cannot be omitted from any description of the music culture.

The pastoral Jew is one of the central figures of the iconography. His recurrence is no doubt fueled by Yiddish drama and poetry, based on a folksong understanding of the shepherd as an allegorical figure. Two further examples will help underscore his symbolic importance. One is the stock cover (Figure 11) designed by Keller for Joseph P. Katz's series of Yiddish folksong settings dating from the late 'teens, nearly a generation after "The Wandering Jew." In this elaborate standardized illustration, Keller simply left space for the song title, and Katz changed the ink colors with each change in title. In the 1920s the entire set was put between covers as an album.

Again palm trees, sheep, and shepherds appear as central images. Cypress trees, wheat-stalk borders, and mountains round out the picture. The candles across the top echo the symbols of ethnicity found in songs such as "Likht bentshn" (Figure 7). The series title is in Yiddish (*Yidishe folkslider,* "Jewish Folksongs"), rather than the English *Traditional Liturgical Melodies* used for an analogous series cover in 1899. Clearly, this set of songs was meant for Yiddish singers; even the tempo marking inside (*mitlmesig,* or moderato) is in Yiddish. The shepherd's lyre is now used as an integral part of the illustration, rather than as a publisher's trademark or symbol of mainstream artsiness. A Star of David can be seen rising just over the hills of Judea, corresponding to the six-pointed star above the "classical" lyre in Figure 5. The full range of graphic stylization is embodied in these carryovers and disparities. On one hand the shifts in emphasis reflect the turbulence of the immigrant period, with all its conflicts of identity and changes of taste. On the other, the long-range continuity of the candles, the Star of David and, above all, the pastoral Jew bespeaks a coherent symbolic language. Of course, this iconography was developed for commercial purposes; yet, like the texts and musical styles, it both reflected and shaped the tastes of the immigrants.

Figure 12 shows that symbols could be durable indeed. Anticipating just a bit, we see here a later development toward a stripped-down, small-format as published by Lefkowitch's important Metro Music. In this 1929 item we find a traditional Yiddish folksong, "A pastekhl" ("A Shepherd," here translated as "A Shepherd's Lament"), illustrated with the same pastoral Jew who graced the Goldfadn song of 1903. The Yiddish lettering seems to emanate from the olive trees, as if intimately connected with the biblical scene itself. Indeed, the songtext of "A pastekhl" presents the Jewish shepherd allegorically.

Only one cover illustration uses the image of the shepherd in a suitably ethnographic context. Figure 13 presents a stereotyped Rumanian shepherd who (suitably) plays a flute instead of a lyre. His garb and the forest background are of this age and place, rather than being biblical, and are reinforced by the depiction of yet another shepherd, with clarinet, on the right. The banner furled above this figure is, aptly, in Rumanian: "Album Musica Romănă," with diacritical marks intact. There is no Yiddish—it is not needed. The entire item is a comprehensive statement of the music's style and associations. This accurate portrayal of the non-Jewish shepherd acts as a perfect foil for the internal symbol of the biblical watcher of flocks. "Album Musica Romănă" also points out that musical eclecticism can be matched by diversity of illustration.

Russian-language title sheets were also published throughout the period. Figure 14 is typical, with no Yiddish and no picture. The Cyrillic and romanized titles of stock Russian songs are listed; inside, the texts appear only in Russian. Printed by Hebrew Publishing, this sort of material may indicate neighborhood music-sharing among ethnic groups. Indeed, even recently one could still find Jewish-generated sheet music in the storeroom of Surma, Myron Surmach's landmark Lower East Side Ukrainian emporium. Metro Music had a large supply of Russian and Ukrainian sheet music and records to suit all the local customers. This sort of inter-ethnic pooling of musical resources reflects Old World ties as adapted to American marketing, and was basic to early ethnic recording as well. Perhaps there are no pictures on Figure 14 because no iconography was needed, or because none would have suited every group.

POPULAR ENTERTAINMENT PICTURES ITSELF

An iconography of popular artists and the Yiddish stage gradually emerged. This trend relied on the use of photography, as was common in mainstream American sheet music. Though this tendency can perhaps be viewed as more "modern" in some sense, it nevertheless creates and relies upon standardized imagery, and hence constitutes its own tradition.

Figure 15 is an early example of the "star" mentality in imagery. It presents the canonical photograph of Goldfadn, the goateed and bespectacled father of the Yiddish theater, as captured by Mandelkern, a publicist and entrepeneur. This example is from music copyrighted 1898 (inside) and 1909 (outside). Its picture of Goldfadn was reprinted countless times, standing as a primal icon of traditional Jewish popular music. Figure 15 is also a useful example of the show album cover, with its listing of contents (often in English) for a "complete opera." The centrality of the authorial presence is obvious at first glance; the work's title takes second place. We have already seen the composer as genial guide to the music in Mogulesco's case (Figure 4). This approach was epitomized in the series entitled "Rumshisky's Music Album" (the "n" in Rumshinsky was missing from much of the music he authored). Figure 16 is taken from that series. Here Keller combines a full-length line drawing of the composer with a photograph of Dora Weissman, a stage celebrity who starred as "The Girl from the West." The dominance of the larger-than-life Rumshinsky over the elegant Miss Weissman tells us that the composer still had an important role in the music culture as late as 1911. The inaccurately sketched music that floats above the soubrette's head also stresses the music maker's prominence.

The composition of this cover for "Cheisheck" suggests yet another point. The song title itself, though central and clearly marked, is somewhat lower in the hierarchy than its composer's and performer's names. This is the great age of song-plugging, when association with a songwriter and singer generated sales; the Yiddish industry is following the dictates of Tin Pan Alley. But sheet music does not stop there in its attempt at advertising. Keller inflates the ubiquitous Hebrew Publishing lyre, making it the main frame of his graphic design. Here is an elegant reminder of why one buys sheet music: to place it, like the artist's imaginary folio, on the music rack (often lyre-shaped in those days) of the parlor piano. As we shall see again later, a cover can be, in a sense, prescriptive: it tells the customer how it should be consumed.

As firmly entrenched as the composer might seem, from the days of Mogulesco to those of Rumshinsky, he is gradually unseated by the stage personality. "Mutter un kind" ("Mother and Child"), Figure 17, spotlights the young Jennie Goldstein, later a durable star of Yiddish theater and cinema. Not only is her oversize image the visual magnet on this 1913 cover, but her name appears twice, at the top and on the left-hand side. Hebrew Publishing has cut back its logo and trimmed its flowerbed to make way for the performer's photo, and the composer receives a mere mention. This sort of visual emphasis is elaborated in various ways throughout many folios. Figure 18 is a dramatic example of how Keller yielded to the dictates of stardom. This show album from *Gots shtrof* ("God's Punishment") makes a strong appeal to the Americanized theatergoer. Jacob Adler, the reigning presence of the Yiddish stage, is described in the stock phrase "eminent tragedian." He and his lovely co-star smother Keller's favorite floral patterning. The illustrator must content himself with that frequent symbol, the radiating star— here with only five points, instead of six. Composer and contents are sandwiched into corners.

By 1914 the iconography of the actor had reached a high point. Figure 19 exemplifies a particular genre of sheet music that continued into later decades; it seems to have been distributed at the theater, since no publisher is given and the theater takes credit for the folio. The back cover lists the cast, and the music inside is crudely hand drawn, rather than typeset. In this context, it is hardly surprising to find such stress placed on the actors. To the left and right of the seventeen cameo photos we find the deathless phrase "All Star Cast." Both the producer and the theater's general manager are named—they happen to be the same man, Max R. Wilner. The playwright, composers, and lyricist are only perfunctorily listed. Apparently impatient even with such devoted friends as Hebrew Publishing, the theater industry has taken the initiative, though it cannot dispense with a pair of lyres to balance the cover's composition.

A somewhat more informative set of show tune covers depicts actual scenes from a production. Figure 20, from *A Year after Marriage*, depicts the stars of the show, clearly labeled, in typical moments from the play. The performers stand frozen into archetypal Yiddish theater poses which bear no direct relation to the song inside. While Figure 20 is a souvenir-style advertisement, Figure 21 has far greater significance as a music-cultural document. The album from *Di vaybershe mlukhe* ("Women's Kingdom") neatly summarizes the dichotomy of tradition and acculturation, in both the iconography and the linguistic component. The left-hand illustration presents the older world of Yiddish drama, as seen in Figure 20. The traditional woman is surrounded by putty-nosed, baggy-pants comedians, the classic clowns of ethnic (and mainstream) entertainment. Diametrically opposed (both literally and figuratively) is the modern image of Bessie Thomashefsky bursting in through the French windows, flashlight and pistol in hand, wearing pants, an open-necked workshirt, and a man's hat. The song titles are given in Yiddish and roman letters. Song 1, "Damaged Goods," is "demedzhd guds" in the Hebrew alphabet, a mere transliteration of the English words. The other two songs are in Yiddish in both alphabets. Inside, the musical style continues the contrasts offered by imagery and orthography: Song 1 is in an American vein, while the remainder are in the traditional European manner. Conflict of cultures is implicit in every facet of the folio, yet the sheet music is consistent in all of its components.

COMPARISON WITH THE MAINSTREAM

The question of acculturation leads us to compare images from our ethnic subculture with those of mainstream American sheet music. Figures 22 and 23 present just such a pairing, using the violin as central image. As we know, this instrument was basic to a sense of tradition in Jewish culture, as well as to the drive for upward (outward) mobility through achievement in classical music. Figure 22 is a typical Keller product of 1910, an anthology of "25 Jewish Songs for Violin." The illegible, sketched-in music, floral ornamentation, and line-drawing style are familiar from previous examples. The violin is held anonymously, as if standing for the group as a whole. The "Popular and Classical Selections" consist almost entirely of favorites from Goldfadn and later stage productions, with a sprinkling of topical and religious-didactic numbers ("Dreyfus March," "Kol Nidre"). Copyright dates range from 1900 to 1910, making this a quite inclusive album and again underscoring the durability of song genres as well as of individual items. Despite the heading, none of the works is "classical" in the accepted sense, confirming the evolution of in-group classificatory schemes.

Figure 23 also features the violin, but is an almost polar opposite to Figure 22. Dating from 1911, it is an illustration for an Irving Berlin song drawn by one E. Pfeifer and published by Ted Snyder, Berlin's first publisher (later his partner). "The Ragtime Violin" is musically and culturally in the same vein as Berlin's "Yiddle on Your Fiddle, Play Some Ragtime"; the latter is a more ethnically explicit number urging the de-ethnicization of the fiddler, written by a successfully acculturated Jewish immigrant musician. The inset of Catherine Kuhl, the singer, seems incidental to the finely worked-out image of the somewhat demonic violinist. Far from being the stereotyped ragtime fiddler, he is clearly European, with the long, delicate hands of the dreamy, artistic ethnic musician often portrayed in American popular culture. He looks more like the sensual, erotic village fiddler Stempenyu, who poured the soul of the group into his playing, than like the cardboard minstrel-show character "Mr. Brown" of Berlin's song. The use of shadow, bold striped background, and the visual trick of the performer embracing a lush art nouveau flower all show a technique far more refined than Keller's or Terr's. This is mainstream illustration at its most seductive, with the basic information—title, composer, key performer—subordinated to a message about the music itself. It is far removed from the faceless fiddler of "Jewish Favorites," though the publisher's offices were not many blocks apart. The attractive visual style may help explain why mainstream culture was so much more appealing to the immigrants' children than were the old ethnic stand-bys. That Berlin had earlier specified a "Yiddle" for his fiddle, and that the illustrator made the violinist so colorful, could be symptomatic of their interest in capturing the attention of an Americanized ethnic audience.

Our second pair of contrasting images is from 1912. When the great ship *Titanic* went down, it occasioned a vast outburst of songwriting. Nearly two hundred mainstream items were produced on the subject, many as a result of a songwriting competition arranged by a publisher. Various ethnic groups also turned out commentaries on the disaster, allowing us to compare the general and the particular responses to the event. Figure 24 is a typical all-American *Titanic* song. Put out by a regional (Chicago) publisher, it uses a newspaper illustration "by courtesy of the Chicago Record-Herald." Lifeboats flee the sinking ship as lifelines dangle from the decks. It is as close as possible to an actual photo since the artist, Schniedtgen, has drawn in a great deal of detail. The song text is typical in its largely anonymous treatment of the disaster: "Husbands were parted from loving wives," it says. The title, "Just as the Ship Went Down," comes from the song's last line,

" 'Nearer my God,' they sang, just as the ship went down." The citation of a well-known hymn can be found so frequently in mainstream *Titanic* songs that it seems to be a trademark for the genre.

The Jewish counterpart is entitled "Khorbn titanik, oder der naser keyver" ("The Wreck of the Titanic, or The Watery Grave"); the English merely says "The Titanic's Disaster." Copyrighted in 1912, this Yiddish version (Figure 25) might seem to be a copy of the mainstream product. Keller's illustration bears a remarkable likeness to the Chicago picture, including a ship listing at a similar angle, a forward mast, and four smokestacks. Yet the entire scene is arranged so as to leave room for an extremely important portrayal: two embracing figures are about to be crowned with laurel wreaths by an angel emerging from an iceberg. Despite the surface similarities, the two covers are radically different. Who is this steadfast couple? We must turn to the song text for the answer; cover and content are very closely aligned. Verses 1 and 2 are in the didactic vein: "Man, as much as you sharpen your brains, you can't compete with the sea's strength"—hardly the tack taken by most *Titanic* songs. But the final stanza provides the key to the iconography:

Ot shteyen, mit veyen,
di toyzende in noyt
un vayzn, az shtoysen
vet zey tsum grund der toyt.
Ot shrayt men "geyt zikh retn
in shiflakh, froyen, shnel,
nit vagn zol betreten
kayn man gor yene shtel."
Dokh hert a froyen-zeyle
vos ken a zog ton dan:
"Ikh gey nit fun der shtele,
ikh shtarb do mit mayn man."
Zoln eren kleyn un groys
dem nomen IDA STROYS!

There stand, in woe/ The thousands in need/ And know that death/ Will dash them down./ Then they cry, "Save yourselves/ Into the boats quickly, women/ No man dare/ Take a place there."/ But listen to one woman-soul/ Who can say,/ "I won't stir from the spot/ I'll die here with my husband."/ Let small and large Honor/ the name of IDA STRAUS!

Isidore and Ida Straus, of the old German-Jewish upper crust, went down with the ship together. Small/Smulewitz has fastened on this striking episode to fashion a didactic statement with far greater emotion than is evoked by lines like "husbands were parted from their wives." Ida Straus's exemplary conduct in the face of death is held up as a lesson; she almost joins the long list of Jewish martyrs. The ethnic reference here is two-edged. First, there is a particular moral to be learned, one that the mainstream has chosen to ignore. Second, the cover illustration strongly implies that "our" interest in the disaster is qualitatively different from "theirs." The ethnics' relationship to an event, caricatured by the punch line "but is it good or bad for the Jews?" is not just a parochial Jewish concern. Every subculture scans the news for items relating to its own concerns and reacts accordingly, interpreting signals from the outside. In America, special-interest understandings of the news are particularly pronounced, as each group has its own press and semi-official communal organizations to state the "local" point of view. The Jewish *Titanic* song, then, can stand for an entire class of immigrant songs, showing the reaction of the particular group concerned as well as answering the general question of subculture response to universal events.

But while ethnic boundaries can be maintained, they can also be eagerly erased. Sometimes the Jews identified completely with the mainstream, in terms of imagery. This occurred as early as 1910, when Hebrew Publishing launched a substantial series of titles with an identical central illustration. Figure 26 is an example of this standard music-store-window item. The Yiddish heading and transliteration and bottom data are ethnic-specific, but the icon presented is of general American origin. Indeed, the cover itself is not a Jewish design (hence no illustrator's credit), but an adaptation of a "regular" American folio design.[8] We see the by now classic image of the girl at the parlor piano, wearing a vaguely Greek flowing gown, ennobled by her pursuit of music-making. To her right, the admiring family basks in reflected glory. The only part of the picture that has been retouched to provide ethnic identity is the skullcap on Papa's head. It is of no consequence that the particular song is a Yiddish item based on and incorporating the Hebrew lament for the dead—marketing has won out over depiction of content. As in the case of Figure 16 above, a cover illustration is more a commentary on sheet music as a whole than on the particular product. "Take me home," says the folio, "let the daughter play and the family enjoy." It is no accident that this particular image is borrowed from the mainstream, since the parlor piano syndrome affected virtually every layer of American society.

STYLISTIC CHANGE

Though we have noted diverse trends that appear simultaneously in the repertoire, certain changes *can* be viewed from a chronological standpoint. A pair of songs can again stand for a general tendency. Figure 27 is a setting of the most solemn Jewish musical item, "Kol Nidre," the key song of the High Holidays. This 1913 Keller version again shows the cantor at the center, with the familiar paraphernalia of radiance, candles, prayer shawl, and prayer book. S. Schenker has even adopted the omnipresent lyre of Hebrew Publishing. This is illustration at its most stereotypically satisfying.

Figure 28, from 1922, proves that cultural distance can far exceed the few blocks between the publishers' offices (on Canal and Delancey Streets). "Kol Nidre" is now merely the heading for a heavily commercialized folio format. "The Sweetest Waltz Ever Published" was apparently not an incongruous neighbor for "Kol Nidre," nor was the "medium grade" "Poet's Vision." A. Teres is merely being the thorough businessman by maximizing the small amount of cover space to advertise his other stock. In his listing of "celebrated Jewish music" we find further reference to "Kol Nidra," which comes in "original" and "original simplified" editions. In the case of Teres, pedagogy has long since replaced affect as the principal selling point. The music inside bears further witness to this approach: he has outfitted the timeless chant of "Kol Nidre" with an "Introduction: Original Music by A. Teres." That he subjected Schubert's "Serenade" to the same treatment merely shows that the old eclecticism has not faded. The back cover is cluttered with excerpts from six other Teres specials, variously described as transcriptions, simplifications, arrangements, or paraphrases. The world of A. Teres is a comprehensive and comprehensible one which deftly subjects the diversity of the Old World music culture to the tidiness of American merchandising.

Two more examples of later iconography round out our discussion. Figure 29 is a 1926 Joseph P. Katz setting of a true Eastern European folksong. It represents the old genre of anti-Hasidic comedy (Jewish popular music was founded by freethinkers). The song text's combination of Russian, Hebrew, and Yiddish is distinctively Old World. On the surface, then, this text would appear to represent the long-term continuity of European repertoires in America; yet the "surface" of the song—its cover design—provides evidence for a changed cultural context. In the middle of the cover is a long English explanation of the song, in somewhat patronizing and condescending terms, as befits an Americanized view of European folksong: "A happy-go-lucky Chasid, considerably under the influence of liquor. . . ." The smaller details echo the overall tone of the song's presentation. The English simply labels the item "a humorous Jewish folk-song," while the Yiddish specifies that it is a "Jewish-Ukrainian folksong," dropping the mention of humor, but carefully stipulating ethnic origins. The absence of a photograph of the featured singer (Kotylansky) may indicate a greater economy of presentation of the 1920s, perhaps due to a shrinking market.

Finally, Figure 30 takes us even farther down the road to Americanization in music covers. "Three Little Lads" is the cute English title for a song whose Yiddish title can more precisely be translated as "Three Boys" ("Dray ingelakh"). The Yiddish series logo ("Kinder lider—gevidmet ale yidishe kinder") translates as "Children's Songs: Dedicated to All Jewish Children," indicating a kind of sentimental, pedagogical quality that characterizes parts of Metro Music's output. The English "Songs for Young Folks" is a bit supercilious, and complements Metro's conception of its own stock. (The back cover suggests that the customer "send for the complete catalogue of high class Jewish Music.")

It is the surrounding imagery that most strikes the eye and that confirms the real intent of the publication. A parade of moppets straight out of A. A. Milne fills the perimeter of the page. There is not the slightest trace of Jewish identity in the knickers, baseball bats, and sailor suits. These are indeed "young folks," not "yidishe kinder."

Like all our brief forays into the varied realms of immigrant music, this survey of the iconography opens up a field too broad to cover in a small space. Our main attempt has been to emphasize both the complexity and the single-mindedness of that culture of transition. Despite the great diversity of subject matter and approaches, we see the forging of a tradition of popular entertainment that represents the major expressive striving of a turbulent subculture. We have observed how content and image complement each other; now we turn to the music itself to complete our survey of the stylistic trinity of published music.

NOTES

1. Marian Klamkin, *Old Sheet Music: A Pictorial History* (New York: Hawthorn Books, 1976), p. 1.
2. Ibid.
3. D. and S. Spellman, *Victorian Music Covers* (Park Ridge, N.J.: Noyes Press, 1972), p. 56.

4. Klamkin, *Old Sheet Music*, p. 3.
5. Spellman, *Victorian Music Covers*, p. 66.
6. Klamkin, *Old Sheet Music*, p. 4.
7. Spellman, *Victorian Music Covers*, p. 64; Klamkin, *Old Sheet Music*, p. 4.
8. I am grateful to Henry Sapoznik for this information.

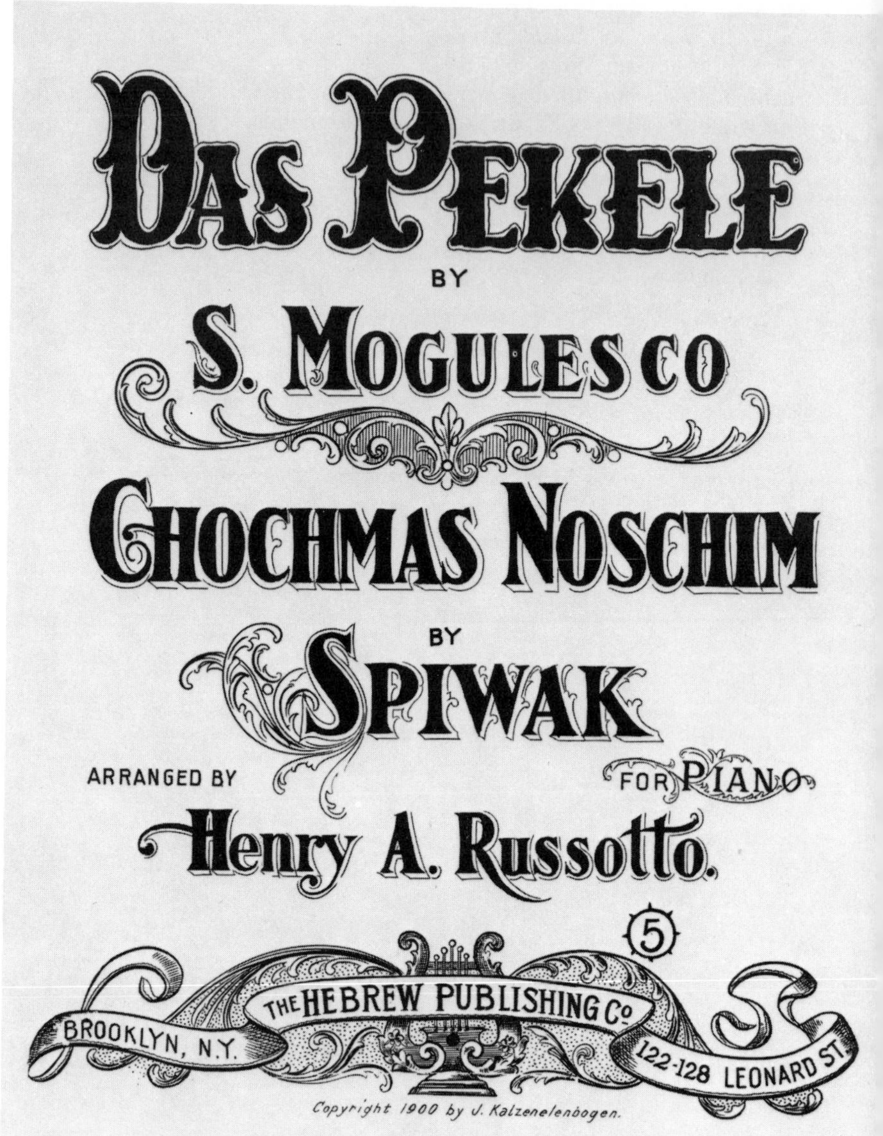

DAS PEKELE

BY

S. MOGULESCO

CHOCHMAS NOSCHIM

BY

SPIWAK

ARRANGED BY

FOR PIANO

Henry A. Russotto.

⑤

THE HEBREW PUBLISHING Co.

BROOKLYN, N.Y.

122-128 LEONARD ST.

Copyright 1900 by J. Katzenelenbogen.

FIGURE 1

TRADITIONAL RELIGIOUS MELODIES

בִּרְכַּת כֹּהֲנִים

BIRCHAS COHANIM

BY

REV. JOACHIM KURANTMANN.

VOICE & PIANO 75¢   VIOLIN SOLO 50¢

PUBLISHED BY
THE HEBREW PUBLISHING CO. 122–128 LEONARD ST.
BROOKLYN, N.Y

FIGURE 2

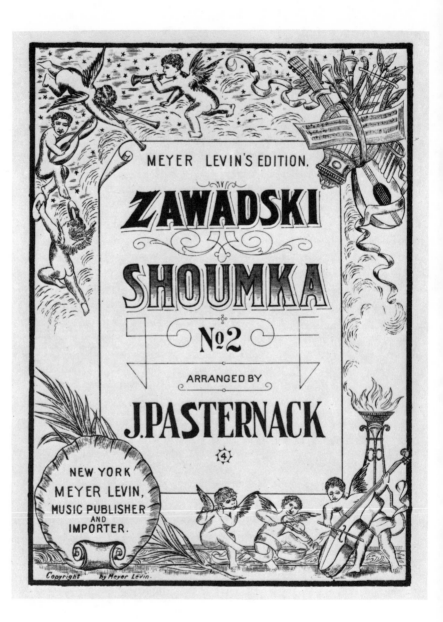

FIGURE 3

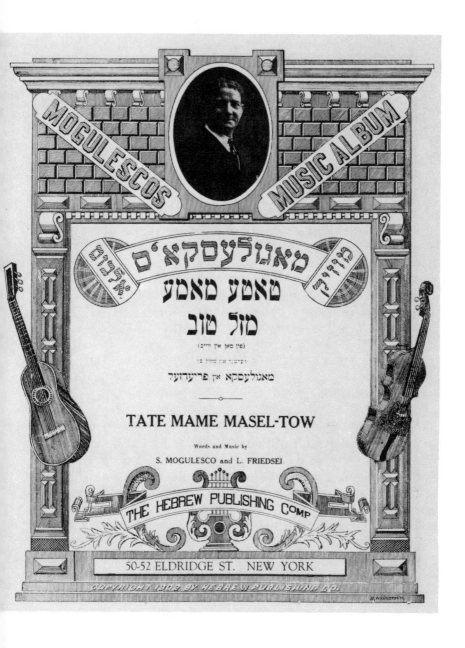

FIGURE 4

CLASSICAL PIECES FOR PIANO

CHANSON
RUSSE

By J. M. Rumshisky

HEBREW PUBLISHING CO.
83-87 CANAL ST. NEW YORK.

FIGURE 5

FIGURE 6

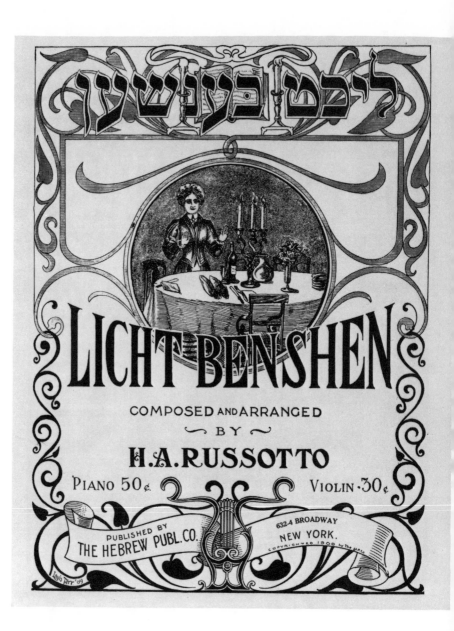

FIGURE 7

FIGURE 8

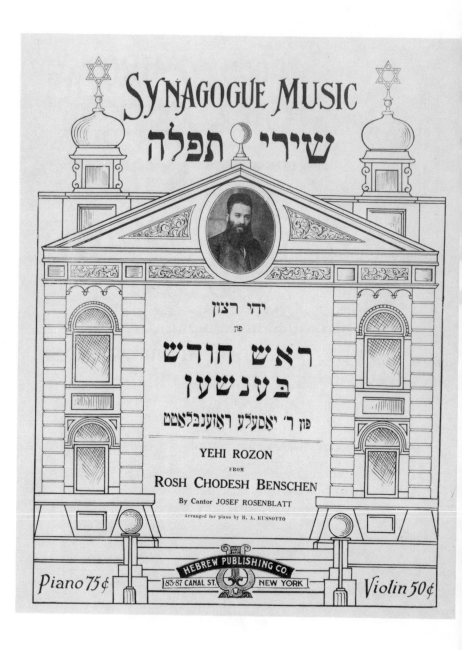

FIGURE 9

THE
"WANDERING JEW"

FROM THE OPERA

DR. ALMASADA

Words and Music by

A. GOLDFADEN

FOR PIANO   *Price 50 cents*

PUBLISHED BY

S. SCHENKER
66 Canal Street.   New York

FIGURE 10

FIGURE 11

J162

(A PASTUCH'L)

A SHEPHERD'S LAMENT
(FOLK SONG)

ARRANGED

For VOICE and PIANO

BY

HENRY LEFKOWITCH

Price 35 Cents, net

58 SECOND AVE.
NEW YORK

MADE IN
USA

FIGURE 12

FIGURE 13

ОЙ ДУБИНУШКА

Ei Dubinushka

Arr. by J. M. RUMSHISKY

ОЙ УХНЕМЪ

EI UCHNEM

Arr. by J. M. RUMSHISKY

ВО ПОЛѢ БЕРЕЗА СТОЯЛА

VO POLE BERYEZA STOYALA

Arr. By LOUIS FRIEDSELL

PUBLISHED BY

HEBREW PUBLISHING CO.

50-52 Eldridge Street, New York

FIGURE 14

FIGURE 15

FIGURE 16

FIGURE 17

FIGURE 18

FIGURE 19

THE LENOX THEATRE SUCCESS

A Year After Marriage

א יאהר נאך דער חתונה

AL TIRO AVDI JACOB

Words by SOLOMON SMALL   Music by LOUIS FRIEDSELL

S. Rosenstein   Rosa Karp   Rosa Karp   Leon Blank   S. Rosenstein

THEODORE LOHR
Music Publisher

286 GRAND STREET   NEW YORK CITY

FIGURE 20

Music from the successful Play "Weibershe Meluche"

By N. ROCKOW

in Jacob P. Adler's Peoples Theatre

„דיא וויבערשע מלוכה"

Words by L. GILROD   **Music by J. RUMSHISKY**

1. דעמעדזשד גודם
2. גוטע נאכט
3. איך האב מיך שוין איינגעטרייט

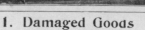
1. Damaged Goods
2. Gute Nacht
3. Ich hob mich schon eingetreit

THE HEBREW PUBLISHING CO
50-52 ELDRIDGE ST.
NEW YORK

FIGURE 21

FIGURE 22

FIGURE 23

JUST AS THE SHIP WENT DOWN

The above illustration used by courtesy of Chicago Record-Herald.

A SONG OF THE SEA

Words by
EDITH MAIDA LESSING

Music by
GIBSON AND ADLER

PUBLISHED BY
HAROLD ROSSITER MUSIC COMPANY
CHICAGO U.S.A.

FIGURE 24

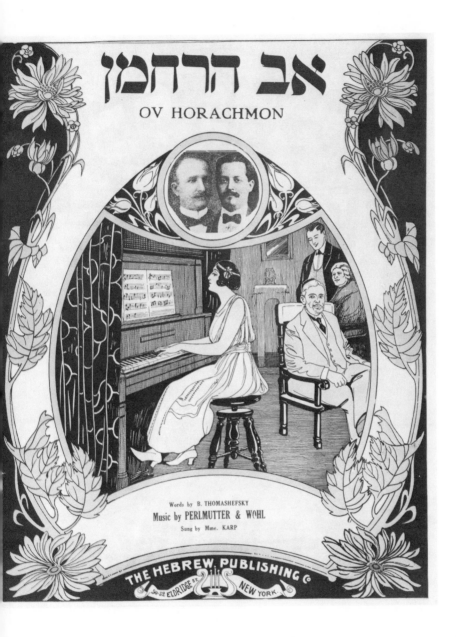

FIGURE 26

FIGURE 27

VIOLIN OR MANDOLIN

כל נדרי

KOL NIDRE

Arranged by A. PERLMUTTER

CATALOGUE OF CELEBRATED JEWISH MUSIC FOR PIANO WITH WORDS

1. A Mensh Zol Men Zein.
2. A Breevele Der Mammen.
3. Dus Tolesil.
4. Ich Benk A Haim (Dus Faigele).
5. Al Tashlichenu.
6. Gott Und Zein Mishpet Is Gerecht.
7. Sholem Beias.
8. Dus Lebedige Yesoimele.
9. Dee Yidishe Kroin.
10. Das Shaifele.
11. Ve-Yiten Lecho.
12. Dee Bloomen Krentze.
13. Isrulik Kim a Haim.
14. Lebedig und Freilach.
15. Dus Yusemil (From Ben Ami.)
17. Dus Fertribene Teibele (From Ben Ami.)
18. Videlach Bridelach.
19. Ven Men Rooft Dir Tzurikk.
20. Ver es Grubt oif Yenem a Grub Folt Alain Arein.
21. Ouf'n Preepetshok.
22. Unzer Rebeneu (Dem Rebens Naigen).
35. A Mames Verth.
23. Ich Bin A Boarder by Mein Weib.
26. Schuldig Bist Du Yiedele Alein.
37. Dem Postachil's Cholem.
42. A Folk Un A Haim.
43. Original Eli Eli.
44. Original Eli Eli Simplified.
45. A Mother's Heart.
46. Shluf Mein Kind.
47. Dus Bisile Glick.
48. Noch a Bisel In Epes Noch.
49. Weh Dem Kind When a Mame Felt.
50. Honig Shabes.
52. Tzurik Kein Zion (Back to Zion).
53. Leben Zol Columbus.
54. Gedenk Mine Kind Der Mammes Trehen.
56. Original Kol Nidra.
57. Original Kol Nidra (Simplified).
58. Hatikvoh (Jewish Folk Song).
62. Schenk mir Mine Mame.
68. Mine Leebster Freind Is Mine Mamenu (A Mamme's Lyde).
72. Wie Zennen Meine Kinder.
75. A Kind Is Dus Glik Auf Die Welt.
80. A Chover In Leben.
81. A Kind Un a Heim.
84. In 100 Yohr Arim.
85. Leebe Tzu Kinder (Kinder Leebe).

THE SWEETEST WALTZ EVER PUBLISHED

A POET'S VISION (Twilight Shadows) Valse in D minor (Medium Grade) by J. S. Deutsch, Op. 50   price 25¢ net

Valse lento cantabile

Twi-light sha-dows fall - ing   Soft thy voice is call - ing,   Call-ing ev - er   call-ing me from o'er   the mystic sea.

Copyright MCMXXII by Albert Teres, International Copyright Secured

2nd Part
Ev-er   dearer   sweeter   far   Is the charm that lies In thy loveli't eyes. Let   thy   dear   pre - sence   Ever and always be   near   me,—

3rd Part

Published by A. TERES   MUSIC DEALER and PUBLISHER
159 DELANCEY ST., NEW YORK

FIGURE 28

FROM THE REPERTOIRE
OF
CHAIM KOTYLANSKY

"V'NASHEY RASSEYI"

HUMOROUS JEWISH FOLK-SONG

AS ARRANGED AND NOTATED BY

"V'NASHEY RASSEYI"

A happy-go-lucky Chasid, considerably under the influence of liquor, is recounting in a mixture of Russian and Hebrew the order of the prayers and the manner of their performance.

One starts, he believes, in the middle of the night with "Negel-Wasser" and ends with "Oleinu" and a little "L'Chaim". The ceremony connected with the prayers is so dear to him that in his most happy moments he makes it the subject of his hilarity.

Ch. Kotylansky and H. Russoto

„וו'נשיי ראַסייאַ"

אידיש-אוקראיניש פאָלקס-ליעד

Made in U. S. A.

Published By
Jos. P. Katz
101 E. Broadway. New York

PRICE 50 NET no discount

FIGURE 29

מינדער לידער
געווידמעט אלע אידישע קינדער

דריי אינגעלאך

THREE LITTLE LADS

VERSE BY

GOICHBERG

MUSIC BY

N. L. SASLAVSKY

SONGS FOR YOUNG FOLKS

No. 3

PRICE 75¢ IN U.S.A.

Made in U. S. A.

FIGURE 30

CHAPTER 8

BETWEEN THE SHEET MUSIC COVERS: STYLE

"It is in his blood," wrote Irving Berlin's first biographer in 1927, "to write the lugubrious melodies which, in the jargon of Tin Pan Alley, have a tear in them. Back of him are generations of wailing cantors to tinge all his work with an enjoyable melancholy." [1] Here Alexander Woolcott repeats the tired truism that all Eastern European Jewish songs are sad. Like any ethnic stereotype, the myth of musical melancholy is grounded in the misperception of an ethnic group's way of doing things. To understand why this caricature developed, we must look into the final, most expressive component of the sheet music universe: the music between the covers. A culture lays out its musical credo in a set of stylistic preferences: we'll use these intervals in these combinations to make our scales; here are the types of trills, shakes, and turns that will ornament our tunes; and only those basic meters will do. Not too fast except for dancing, lots of songs in the key of E minor— these and other prescriptions are part of an in-group musical language. As with any language, only an insider can perform it properly and really feel the subtleties. Outsiders like Woolcott could only see gross features and interpret them according to their own preferences.

If this Jewish music is unabashedly and exuberantly eclectic, as I have repeatedly demonstrated, how can we presume to define a basic ethnic style? The answer is simple: look to the musical situations where the group takes style most seriously. Seek the musical symbol. A musical symbol is hard to define but easy to identify. No one can miss the cultural message of "The Star-Spangled Banner" as played by the Marine Band at the White House; nor was it hard to understand what Jimi Hendrix meant when he played the same song at Woodstock in

1969 as a virtuoso solo for electric guitar, punctuating the melody with the scream of falling bombs and the wail of sirens. In these two cases, context as much as melody defines the symbol. But it is no accident that the American national anthem is in the major mode: for Western European and American ears, the major is affirmative, and the minor mode negative. In short, a successful symbol must combine context with musical content in a potent package.

In this chapter we will touch only lightly on the increasing Americanization of Yiddish popular song. Instead, we mean to search out the in-group symbols which provided Woolcott with his stereotype, and which gave the immigrants their sense of musical identity.

Just because outsiders can easily identify a symbol does not mean that insiders regard it as relevant. The minor mode is a good case in point: in Eastern Europe, it is not automatically considered sad. A good deal of Russian, Ukrainian, Rumanian, and other folk music happens to be in minor, while the bulk of Polish, Czech, Austrian, and other Central European music is in other modes, principally the major. The major clearly predominates in most of Western Europe. Not all the Eastern songs are sad, nor are all the Western melodies happy—the choice of mode is just one of the preferences that define style. An American listening to Jewish music, then, uses his Western European ears in responding to Eastern habits, and usually concludes that "their" music is melancholy.

Some musical turns of phrase are neither major nor minor. In Western and Central Europe, pentatonic tunes also abound (e.g., "Auld Lang Syne," which can be played on just the black keys of the piano). In the East, people favor still other tonal structures, ones which provide exactly the material we need in order to examine Jewish musical ethnicity. These structures have just the right character to help form an ethnic boundary: they sound familiar to Jewish-Americans but exotic to others. This allows them to function as musical symbols in the fullest sense.

To grasp this rather intricate aspect of a music culture, we must go back to the mountains, valleys, and steppes of southeastern Europe, and begin by defining our musical material. The major and minor modes are made up of two sizes of steps, or intervals, between pitches of a melody; these are commonly called half and whole steps. One deviant form of the minor (the "harmonic") has a giant step made of three half-steps and called the augmented second. Throughout the history of classical music, this interval was something of an outcast. It lends some of Vivaldi's slow movements their poignant airs, and Bach used it occasionally. Haydn, Mozart, and Beethoven tend to ignore this interval as a melodic device, using it in its harmonic (hence the name) rather than in a tuneful sense. Later in the nineteenth century, exotica combined with nationalism to make a new ethnic sound fashionable. Liszt and Brahms rediscovered the augmented second in the cafe music of gypsy fiddlers, while Tchaikovsky introduced it as a Slavic sound ("Marche Slave"), even though Russian folk music generally avoids the augmented second.

Of course, we cannot thoroughly survey the tangled history and distribution of the augmented second in its Eastern European homeland. What interests us is its melodic appearance in two easily recognizable phrases, which we will call "melody-types." They look like this:

EXAMPLE 1. The Two Augmented-Second Melody-Types of Jewish Folk Music

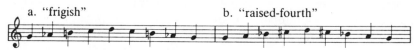

Type A has the augmented second between the second and third pitches of a tune. Jewish folk musicians called it *frigish*, apparently reminded of the medieval Christian church mode called the Phrygian, in which the second pitch of the scale is a scant half-step away from the first. However, the Phrygian mode does not have the augmented second; rather, the third note is only a whole step away from the second:

EXAMPLE 2. The Phrygian Mode

While the Jewish fiddlers' term *frigish* is not exactly accurate in terms of church practice, it does underscore that key opening half-step that defines part of an ethnic sound.

Type B places the augmented second between the third and fourth pitches, elevating the latter above its customary spot in the minor scale; we will call this the raised-fourth variety, since there is no folk term for it. It bears some resemblance to the synagogue mode called *Mi sheberakh*, while Type A is related to another important liturgical sound, the *Ahabah rabah* mode. These distinctive tunes appeared not just at weddings or in folksongs, but in sacred song as well.

These melody-types were not ethnic-specific across a wide region of southeastern Europe. The Bulgarians and Ukrainians sang them extensively, particularly in certain areas, as did the Rumanians, especially where there was a heavy Jewish population (Moldavia, Bukovina). The melody-types are less common among Slovaks and Poles and are quite rare in the songs of Hungary, Russia, and Belorussia. The Jews used them extensively: for the raised-fourth melody-type, one study [2] gives a figure of 4-5 percent in folksongs and 10-12 percent in dance tunes. There are strong ties to Middle Eastern music. In Arab and Persian lands, the *Hijaz* mode incorporates our melody-type A. This does not mean that the Jews, as "Orientals," brought this sound with them from their ancestral homeland in the Middle East during two thousand years of migration. Rather, merely living among southeastern Europeans probably helped them get used to the sound of the augmented second. Even a leading scholar of Jewish music does not attempt to pinpoint how the *frigish* infiltrated European folk music. It was introduced, Werner says, in different places: for example, via "Spain, Sicily, the Balkans, Ancient Greece, Armenia, Russia (almost certainly the Black Sea) and North and East Africa." [3]

Fortunately, we need not settle these thorny musicological issues. We merely want to observe how Eastern European peoples, including Jews, tended to use our melody-types, so we can assess their impact on American musical life with the Old World context in mind. In Eastern Europe the *frigish* and the raised-fourth tunes were used selectively. Melodies either feature them throughout or use them only in specific sections. Example 3 is from a Yiddish song, in which the *frigish* appears consistently. Example 4 is a Ukrainian counterpart [4] in which the raised-fourth melody-type is constantly visible:

EXAMPLE 3. "In droysh geyt a regn" (singer: Lifsha Schaechter Widman, 1954, tapes of YIVO Jewish Folksong Project)

Az in droy- sn gey-et a re- gn   ver-en di Shteyn-de- lakh nas___

Un az a mey-de- le shpilt_ a___ li- be vern ir di be- ke-lakh nas.

This approach is perhaps a bit unusual. Often singers or fiddlers choose to use the augmented-second sound as coloration, to break up a uniform tonality. A musician might make a sharp break between one section of a dance tune and another, or might mark off phrase endings in this fashion. Another pair of melodies, Jewish and non-Jewish, show the common practice. Example 5 is a Yiddish melody in the minor, the most common mode for such folksongs. Toward the cadence, the *frigish* creeps in to underscore a musical moment. In Example 6, a Moldavian fiddler [5] makes a similar move from minor to *frigish*, in this case dividing a piece into two well-defined sections.

EXAMPLE 4. "Oi na gori kalina"

EXAMPLE 5. "Shluflid" (Widman, 1954)

Shluf mayn kind___ in a glik-li-khen shluf.___ Shluf___ un-ter a

lid.   Di_bist nokh tsi ying___ tsi er- fi-len dayn shtruf___

der-far vos du bist___ a yid._

EXAMPLE 6. "Florichika"

Other types of selectivity are also at work in the Old World tune traditions. One is the geographic and musical limitation on our melody-types; as mentioned earlier, one variety occurs more commonly in Jewish instrumental than in vocal music, and the types were unevenly spread across the terrain. For some reason Eastern Carpathian Ukrainians are fonder of the raised-fourth sound than are their compatriots on the western slopes; among Rumanians, Moldavians are particularly interested in the same melody-type.

Now we are equipped to take on the weighty question of symbolism.

Granted that Jews and their Gentile neighbors share certain preferences in tonality, do they have a particularly Jewish way of understanding these musical beliefs? After all, a musical unit is a symbol only if a given group decides it is. Jews *do* attach specific values to our melody-types, which allows note patterns to deliver deep cultural messages. Eric Werner has stated that, in the eighteenth century, the *Ahabah rabah* liturgical mode (our *frigish*) was "supposed to be the perfect expression of penitential contrition and deep lament—the theological ideal of a cantor's effect upon the worshippers." The musicians had absolutely no doubt that this melodic structure was Jewish property: "In spite of musicologists, the Eastern European hazanim [cantors] are still firmly [and wrongly] convinced that the Ahabah Rabah is principally theirs, and that all other appearances are borrowings from the world of Eastern Jewish chant." [6] This ethnocentric approach to shared musical material is particularly strong evidence for the existence of an ethnic boundary. Werner claims that 85 percent of Hasidic songs use this tonality, and he concludes that "the diffusion of the Ahabah Rabah, particularly its exorbitant popularity with the singers and their listeners, deserves a special study."

The other melody-type, the raised-fourth, is also a vehicle for strong expression, but is a somewhat more complex symbol. Beregovski, whose statistics we cited earlier, found that two radically different sentiments are conveyed by the raised-fourth sound: lament, grief, and separation on the one hand, and satire and comedy on the other.[7] This may be partly due to the fact that satire is often directed at the Hasidim, who are particularly fond of this melody-type. Using their own sound against them is effective parody indeed.

Before we leave the Old World, we must mention the early use of our melody-types in Yiddish popular song while the choirboy generation was still in Europe. Fortunately, Goldfadn was very explicit in discussing his deliberate introduction of the *frigish* sound. Commenting on his general eclecticism—lifting a cantorial nugget here, an operatic gem there—he says:

> I did it exclusively because I wanted to raise the musical taste of the broad masses of my people. But, unfortunately, the taste of the lower layers of the Jewish population was so contaminated that they simply couldn't bear European music. . . . I had to renounce these pointless attempts and take another path. I limited myself to preserving a particular Jewish folk music, characterized by a certain Phrygian mode, and this approach was crowned by great success.[8]

Of course, Goldfadn underrated segments of his audience, some of whom were already adopting classical music into their folk repertoire, and all of whom matched or surpassed him in eclecticism. His early popular music, however it is defined, is unquestionably close to a folk base. So it is particularly useful for us to examine his major works to see how he employs our melody-types. Do his instincts lead him toward a folk pattern of preference? On the whole they do, as the following examples indicate.

Two arias from *Akeydas yitskhok* ("The Sacrifice of Isaac") show strong links to the folk's musical habits. The first is the touching "fantasy" aria of Abraham, sung as he ponders how lonely a man is without children: who will take care of him when he is sick, or accompany him along the last journey? The use of the *frigish* is consistent throughout the song, as often happens in folk usage, and as is also consonant with the folk attitude. It is a wail of despair, of deep lament to God:

EXAMPLE 7. Abraham's "Fantasy" Aria, *Akeydas yitskhok* (Goldfadn)

In another section of the same opera Goldfadn applies the folk principle of switching melody-types to fit the mood. In a long duet, Abraham and Sarah decide they must turn to God for help to remedy their childless state. The pathos of the augmented-second sound is introduced, once more in the *frigish*, the liturgical symbol of the penitent seeking consolation. Later in the same number the two affirm God's power to help in times of need. The tonality changes, and we are in the more usual Yiddish song mode, the minor. Significantly, the minor in this case remains within the internal Jewish symbolic system. Here it means not sadness, as it would in European classical music or American popular music, but affirmation. Example 8 gives excerpts from the duet, showing the two tonal orientations.

In addition to supporting folk usage, Goldfadn also stretches the conventional musical frame. His early major works blaze dramatic and musical trails that his choirboy colleagues follow. Example 9 is an exotic "Turkish Chorus" from *Di kishefmakherin* ("The Sorceress"). To portray Turks, Mozart and Beethoven tended to rely on the minor mode and a drone-like accompaniment; Goldfadn, on the other hand, actually uses a Middle Eastern tonality. This allows him to have the best of both worlds. While the stage action and musical context allow the aug-

EXAMPLE 8. Abraham & Sarah's "Duet," *Akeydas yitskhok* (Goldfadn)

EXAMPLE 9. "Turkish Chorus," *Di kishefmakherin* (Goldfadn)

mented-second sound to ring foreign, the basic melodic style remains familiar: it sounds Hasidic.

Our melody-types tend to crop up at certain times when a nationalistic, *yidishkayt* ("Jewishness") feeling is demanded. Both melody-types appear when the angels, disguised as wanderers, speak to Abraham (*Akeydas yitskhok*), or when shepherds dance around the fire as they sing of the pastoral life (*Shulamis*). In our discussion of iconography, we noted that biblical and pastoral images play an important role in the Jewish self-image projected by popular culture. Sarah's lullaby to the infant Isaac, which predicts his future greatness (and hence that of the Jewish people), is in *frigish*. This is probably the effect to which Goldfadn refers when he writes of appealing to the masses with a "certain Phrygian mode."

Non-Jewish contemporaries of Goldfadn did the same thing. As Avenary has observed, "The Ahavah Rabbah . . . has also been used for the musical characterization of the Jewish nation by Mussorgsky, Anton Rubenstein, and other composers." [9] These Eastern European artists could make an accurate ethnomusical statement. American observers, less well equipped, sometimes misunderstand ethnic musical styles.

Tin Pan Alley's attempts at exotica were often unsuccessful, and commentators like Woolcott, quoted at the beginning of this chapter, frequently came to wrong conclusions about the music's meaning.

It is worth taking a closer look at Goldfadn's work habits. In his seminal work on the thinking of tribal man, the French anthropologist Lévi-Strauss[10] conjures up the image of the *bricoleur*, the Sunday do-it-yourselfer, who rebuilds and recycles the spare parts around his workbench to create new artifacts for the job at hand. Lévi-Strauss tends to limit this approach to "primitive" peoples, when in fact much of folk and even popular culture follows similar practice. Goldfadn was a consummate master of *bricolage*. One of his most familiar songs is the aria "Ot der brunen, ot der" ("That Well over There") from *Shulamis*. The newfound lovers Shulamis and Avesholem agree to a sacred vow of betrothal before the only witnesses they can find in the desert: a well and a wildcat. The musicologist A. Z. Idelsohn[11] has identified the tune of "Ot der brunen" is based on Violetta's aria "Ah fors'e lui" from Verdi's *La Traviata*. While we have no supporting evidence for this claim, it certainly seems likely that Goldfadn might have borrowed a bit of melody from the Verdi opera. Let us look at the two arias (Examples 10, 11); note that Goldfadn uses the augmented second.

EXAMPLE 10. "The Oath," *Shulamis* (Goldfadn)

EXAMPLE 11. "Ah fors'e lui," *La Traviata* (Verdi)

Now we can tackle the question of how this flourishing musical style was transplanted to American soil. We must recall that, for Jewish composers and audiences of the 1880s and 1890s, the move from Odessa to New York occasioned no great break with their budding pop music tradition; rather, the shift in cultural context suddenly imposes a whole new layer of meaning on their creative work. To an immigrant ear, the sound of *frigish* or of the raised fourth took on a new meaning.

No longer could the listener associate a particular tonal configuration with the Ukrainian band that played at a Jewish wedding, or with the Rumanian shepherd picutred on a sheet-music cover (Figure 13). In America the immigrants heard sentimental Irish tenor songs, Sousa marches, "gay nineties" ballads, and Caruso opera renditions. All of these lacked the familiar resonance of southeastern European music, where Jewish styles were not all that different from the mainstream.

Where might we turn to seek out the musical symbolism of the immigrants? Liturgical music provides some continuity. After all, the great cantor Rosenblatt vied with Caruso for record sales in Jewish homes. Yet one has the sense that voice quality, and not specific musical material, was the main selling point in both cases; everywhere one reads of the general decline of standards for cantorial music. For insights into the new system of musical symbolism, we must again turn to popular music, beginning with the work of the choirboy generation. While they continued the folk and Goldfadn approaches, these composers also subtly began to stretch the limits of the symbolic system.

Mogulesco used the augmented-second sound in the tried and true folk manner, featuring our melody-types in both comic and pathetic songs. Example 12 is the drunken servant Noah's song from *Dovids fidele*, the 1897 melodrama analyzed earlier. "Noah's Song," a comic number, emphasizes the *frigish* and is modeled on Lot's inebriated tune in Goldfadn's "Sacrifice of Isaac." Here we see how popular musical styles create their own traditions, as Mogulesco leans on Goldfadn's precedent.

EXAMPLE 12. "Noah's Song," *David's Violin* (Mogulesco)

Perlmutter and Wohl, leading stage composers, tend to use our melody-types sparsely but effectively. In Example 13 they illustrate the pathos of the Jewish exile with a *frigish* cadence very much in the folk vein. It falls on the words "When will the end of exile come?" in "Dos goles-lid" ("Song of Exile"), from an opera on the Exodus from Egypt. This partial usage, at a cadence, reaffirms the folk sense of how the augmented-second sound should be applied.

Slowly the choirboys and their successors, notably Rumshinsky, began to expand the *yiddishkayt* ("Jewishness") side of musical sym-

EXAMPLE 13. "Dos goles-lid," *Yetsias mitsraim* (Perlmutter & Wohl)

Vi lang o- rem   yi-   de- le   vet nor el- end   shmerts_ un   payn

zayn dayn go- les   li-   de- le?   Ven   vet der sof fun   go-les zayn?

bolism. It was inevitable that, on the Lower East Side, the music of southeastern Europe would become more usable for evoking nostalgia than for displaying current practice. In the period of extreme cultural stress we have been surveying, our melody-types live on in America as echoes of home, and hence as symbols of a bygone pattern of life. For urban Jewish-Americans, the augmented second forms part of a downhome sound.

A particularly striking example of this emerging approach can be found in Perlmutter and Wohl's opera *Der poylisher yid* ("The Polish Jew"). Works about the Old World would certainly seem likely to use symbolic musical material. In the title song, the composers set the following text:

> Umetum vi ikh kum her ikh shrayen alts dem goy
> Az der yid is nit git, treft far vos dos iz azoy:
> Vayl der yid iz erlikh frim, shabes yomtov hit er op
>   zayn tish;
> Dem goy gits dos in boykh a grim ven er zet dem yidn
>   esn fish.

> Everywhere I go I hear the Gentile shout
> That the Jew's no good—just guess why:
> Because the Jew's honestly pious. Sabbath and holidays he
>   cherishes his table.
> It makes the Gentile's stomach turn to see the Jew eat fish.

The text makes a rather naive case for anti-Semitism based on observance of holidays and the eating of the Sabbath fish. This is not accidental; in America, holiday customs and gastronomy become basic badges of ethnicity, more than do other forms of in-group activity.

"Der poylisher yid" is not the first Yiddish song to speak to differences between Jew and Gentile. "Shiker iz der goy" ("The Gentile's Drunk") is a traditional folksong:

Geyt der goy in shenk arayn.
Trinkt er dort a gleyzele vayn.
Oy, shiker iz der goy.
Shiker iz er, trinken muz er
Vayl er iz a goy.

Geyt der yid in bes-medresh arayn.
Kuket er dort in a seyfer arayn.
Oy, nikhtern iz der yid.
Nikhtern iz er, lernen muz er
Vayl er iz a yid.

The Gentile goes into the tavern.
He drinks a glass of wine there.
Oy, the Gentile is drunk.
He's drunk, he has to drink,
Because he's a Gentile.

The Jew goes into the House of Study.
He looks into a book there.
Oy, the Jew is sober.
He's sober, he has to study,
Because he's a Jew.

In this folksong the ethnic difference is explicitly spelled out in patterns familiar from the European context. However, the traditional melody makes no correlation between text and tune. Both stanzas are in the major mode, despite the sharp character contrasts. Perlmutter and Wohl, writing in an American context, handle matters differently, as shown in Example 14. To underscore the shift from a Gentile to a Jewish perspective, they shift the musical means of expression: they set up an ethnic boundary. The first eight bars are *moderato* and in major; the rest of the excerpt quoted is marked *andante* (creating a tempo stress) and is in minor, with raised-fourth cadence. The crossover occurs in the third line of text, when the Jew's lifestyle is described.

Precisely because the songwriters were in New York, they may have felt obliged to make the musical ethnic boundaries as clear as possible. In the case of the folksong, there was no particular need to switch idioms: Jew and non-Jew shared the same tonal resources, so content alone could convey the message. In America, the musical symbol has a new role to play. At one time the melody-types served as musical bases with strong liturgical and ethnical significance. They expressed penitence, pathos, and laments—or they were mock-religious, in the case of the Hasidic parodies. Now they have become vehicles for self-identification in a world where they can no longer be taken for granted as part of a familiar musical ecology.

This trend toward self-identification is clear even in strongly acculturated pieces. In 1899 Russotto, that most versatile of musical *bricoleurs*, turned out an item entitled "Dreyfus March Two-Step," cashing in on Jewish concern over the Dreyfus affair. As we might expect, this quickie displays a portrait of its hero on the cover. Musically, however, the piece is almost completely nondescript, a standard march with trio section. Only one transitional passage marks the ethnic boundary: a short phrase which features the augmented-second sound.

Ironically, Dreyfus probably would not have understood this musical tribute. As a French Jew and an officer, the augmented second would likely have been lost on him—and surely the use of the "Marseillaise" as a socialist Jewish rallying-cry would have disturbed him.

We can round out this brief study of style by summarizing the fate of our melody-types in the post-immigrant years. The musical symbols we have been tracing become ever more prominent as Jewish ethnicity grows more visible in American society. The stereotyping of ethnic groups that had been part and parcel of American popular culture since the 1820s reached its apogee in the early years of the record and film industries. Popular entertainment was the spotlight which relentlessly followed the ethnics as actors on the stage of American public life; only the stress on unity and fear of racism engendered by the events of the 1930s and 1940s softened the glare. An interesting case in point is the soundtrack of the first successful talking picture, *The Jazz Singer* (1927), which we will briefly examine for its stylistic content.

The Jazz Singer was an important Broadway play of 1925, starring George Jessel, one of the Lower East Side boys who made good in mainstream entertainment. When the struggling Warner brothers (also ghetto kids) decided to film the show, they turned first to Jessel, who wanted too much money; then to Eddie Cantor, who wasn't interested; and finally to Al Jolson, the third former street urchin on their list. Although the plot bore little resemblance to Jolson's life, *The Jazz Singer* became the "official" biography of a quintessential, if mythical, immigrant who faces the conflicting pulls of ethnic roots (synagogue music) and Broadway. The film was wildly successful, made Warner Brothers into moguls, and solidified the talking picture as the definitive form of movie-making.

Musically, *The Jazz Singer* is doubly important. First, the story spins the legend of the immigrant entertainer's rise and acculturation.

Second, it has the first full-length musical soundtrack in Hollywood's history. Technically, the film straddles two worlds: the voices of Jolson and other singers introduce sound, while the rest of the plot unfolds in old silent-picture format, titles and all. This problematic mixture of media and of emotional content is held together by a straightforward technique: stereotyping. Emotions are trademarked by themes, as in other films of the day. Tchaikovsky's "Romeo and Juliet" indicates mother and son's love; Jolson's pseudo-Irish sentimental song "Mother o'Mine" implies the same affect; ragtime is used in the show business scenes—all fairly predictable. But what will the industry choose when the Jewish scenes and characters appear? The ethnic music must be easily identifiable, since Jewishness (or lack of it) is what the film is about.

There are two "Hebrew" themes on the soundtrack. The central piece is "Kol Nidre," holiest chant of the Jewish liturgical year. The story demands that the Jolson character choose, on the eve of the Day of Atonement, either to replace his sick father as cantor or to make his Broadway debut. "Kol Nidre" does not feature the augmented-second sound directly; it is a mixture of modes, a musical pastiche that scholars have repeatedly (and unsuccessfully) tried to dissect. But then there is no need here for a specific melody-type: in context, the tune of "Kol Nidre" itself will be easily recognized. The more revealing moment, in terms of stereotyping, comes with the entrance of a Lower East Side character named Yudelson. A family friend and "kibitzer," as he is called, this stock vaudeville clown would have been equally at home in the Yiddish theater or in American vaudeville. He is accompanied with one of the mock-Hasidic tunes, in *frigish*, that Goldfadn and Mogulesco perfected. An ethnic stage tradition now five decades old has become embedded in one of the major works of American popular culture. (See Example 14.)

EXAMPLE 14. "Kibitzer's Theme," *The Jazz Singer* (1927)

etc.

Looking nearly forty years ahead, we will examine a much more ambitious attempt to create an ethnic musical image in mainstream America. *Fiddler on the Roof* (1964), a landmark of both Jewish-American and Broadway history, displays all the eclecticism of Goldfadn or Hollywood. It intends to be traditional, and has become so among Jews—and many non-Jews—the world over. *Fiddler*'s success is remarkable in that it tries to be much more ethnic than works like *The Jazz Singer*. The 1927 film dealt with Americanization, which won out in the final sequence of the film: Jolson, in blackface, belts out "Mammy" to his beaming mother. *Fiddler*, on the other hand, falls back on the Old World as setting. The imitation Eastern European musical style hinted at in *The Jazz Singer* is replaced, in *Fiddler*, by a highly sophisticated blending of Broadway and ethnic sounds.

How *Fiddler* distorts the stories of Sholom Aleichem, on which it is based, to Americanize the myth of the Old World is a separate subject. We will target the one aspect of style that is our present concern: the sound of the augmented second. By 1964, the brand-name melody-types had become a bit shopworn. The composer Jerry Bock makes the customary bow to the older trademarks, but mostly in secondary material or counter-melodies; he tends to be more interested in the minor mode and the characteristic opening half-step (but not the following augmented second) of *frigish*. One example will suffice. The first music heard in *Fiddler* is, suitably, the solo violin. It enters with a tune which seems to call for the *frigish* sound, but instead the tune avoids the augmented second and makes the bare, final half-step send the message of exotica.

EXAMPLE 15. Opening theme, *Fiddler on the Roof* (Bock)

As this tune is repeated, a counter-theme sneaks in. This curious melody insinuates itself around the augmented second, and finally takes the plunge. Our melody-type does eventually find a home in Broadway's *shtetl* (Example 16).

EXAMPLE 16. Counter-melody, opening theme, *Fiddler on the Roof* (Bock)

The fiddler, for whom the show is named, is not the one who introduces our melody-type—that job goes to the Broadway pit orchestra. It is as if the mainstream wanted to force the musical stereotype on an unwilling, captive Old World *klezmer* who knows he is merely one of the stage props. Indeed, in the final scene of the show the fiddler packs up and takes his instrument to America.

We have strayed far from the old sheet music legacy. It is difficult to stem the flow of our material, which represents the expressive statement of an ethnic group in motion, working hard at defining itself while simultaneously claiming a niche in American society. In a final chapter we can only sketch in some of the blank pages which appear in the Jewish-American family album, between the immigrant portraits and the Broadway publicity photos. A couple of snapshots will have to substitute for the reels and reels of ethnic footage that could only be covered in another full-length study.

NOTES

1. Alexander Woolcott, *The Story of Irving Berlin* (New York: Putnam, 1925), p. 86.
2. M. Beregovski, "Izmenennyi doriiskii lad vi evreiskom muzykal'nom fol'k-lore (k voprosu o semanticheskikh svoistvakh lada)," in I. Zemtsovskii, ed., *Problemy muzykal'nogo fol'klora narodov SSSR* (Moscow: Muzyka, 1973), pp. 367–82.
3. Eric Werner, *A Voice Still Heard . . . : The Sacred Songs of the Ashkenazic Jews* (University Park: Pennsylvania State University Press, 1976), p. 56.
4. Example from V. A. Vakhromeiev, *Ladovaia struktura russkikh narodnykh pesen* (Moscow: Muzyka, 1968), p. 90.
5. Example from T. Stoianov, *500 melodii de zhokul din Moldova* (Kishinev: Kartia moldoviniaske, 1972), p. 252.
6. This and the following quotation are from Werner, *Voice Still Heard*, p. 57.
7. Beregovskii, "Izmenennyi."
8. As quoted in Z. Zilbertsvayg, *Leksikon fun yidishn teatr*, I (New York: Aetna Printers, 1931), "Goldfadn" entry.
9. H. Avenary, "Shtayger," *Encyclopaedia Judaica* (Jerusalem: Keter, 1971), VIII, 1463–66.
10. Claude Lévi-Strauss, "The Science of the Concrete," *The Savage Mind* (Chicago: University of Chicago Press, 1966), pp. 16–19.
11. Cited in Zilbertsvayg, *Leksikon*.

EPILOGUE

In the first two decades of the twentieth century, the New York Jews were "a group splintered by dogma, culture, localism, and class." [1] This was not a uniquely Jewish problem. Writing about the immigrants of the early nineteenth century, Robert Ernst has noted: "The immigrant community lacked cohesiveness in several essential respects. A wide gulf separated the educated from the uneducated. . . . Another element of disunity among the immigrants was the surviving provincialism which set natives of the same country against one another." [2] Yet the Jews groped for a sense of community that would defy internal fragmentation. For, despite the divisions, all Jews "did possess a single broad culture—the Yiddish-speaking culture of Eastern Europe—all had suffered from czarist oppression, and now all shared the common lot of the newcomer. In brief: the preconditions existed for a reconstruction of community or for its fragmentation." [3]

It is in these terms that the historian Arthur Goren explains the formation in 1908 of the New York Kehillah, a broadly based communal organization. By this time America entered World War I, that effort would fail: "Modernism in Europe weakened the communal fabric; immigration to America's burgeoning urban society tore it to shreds." [4] Eventually the Jews, like all other ethnic groups, would have to find purely American solutions to New World problems. The structure of Jewish-American communal life as we now know it rose from the ruins of the Kehillah.

We have seen that the Jews, like the Irish, had already found a certain path toward consensus during the immigrant years: through popular music and entertainment. Couched in language, music, and graphic symbolism which cut across regional, class, and ideological barriers, this powerful expressive world served its public well during a transitional period, when Europeans were turning into Americans. There was, in effect, a community of song which lasted as long as the Ghetto stayed intact, and as long as a fresh flow of immigrants could replenish the sources of talent and the audience. This situation had to change, for two reasons. First, the Jews' successful push toward security in America meant moving away from the old neighborhood, physically and concep- tually. Second, the restriction of immigration by Congress in 1924 stemmed the tide of newcomers, making nostalgia an attractive alterna- tive to the more difficult task of acculturating the greenhorns.

Jewish popular culture in the 1920s became increasingly defined in terms of its relationship to the mainstream of American life. To rely on the continuity of internal traditions became ever more risky, as the ethnic thread was stretched thinner and thinner. The Holocaust accelerated this process catastrophically by simply removing Europe from consideration. Once nostalgia turned to nightmare, the older communal tie was replaced by an Americanized fiction of European life, evident both in *Fiddler on the Roof* and its best-selling pseudo- ethnographic counterpart, *Life Is With People*.[5] By the 1970s, the Lower East Side itself has become, for third- and fourth-generation Americans, a kind of Old World to be recalled in a rosy haze.

We cannot take the story up to the present in this study. Here we can merely examine a pair of songs that nicely illustrate the growing Amer- icanization of the repertoire. Both songs of the 1920s that have parallel Yiddish and English texts; one describes the exploits of a now-forgotten Jewish hero, while the other is on the timeless topic of mother. Suitably, both were issued on records, which begin to replace sheet music as a dominant ethnic entertainment medium in this period. Though dispa- rate in subject matter, the two songs share certain cultural assumptions that mark them off from the immigrant era. Among these is the use of bilingualism. Earlier, we saw two songs with parallel texts, each approaching the format quite differently. One was the heavily satirical "Swing Days," which pitted immigrant sensibilities (in Yiddish) against mainstream American naivete (in English). The other was "My Amer- ica: Our New Hymn," a patriotic song which had an equally bombastic text in both Yiddish and English. The two other songs now under discussion utilize the bilingual structure somewhat differently. Both mean to convey roughly the same message in each language, but end up un-self-consciously introducing cultural discrepancies as part of the contemporary social context.

Let us take the heroic song first. Charles A. Levine is hardly a household name in America, even among members of his own ethnic group; yet in 1927 he became the first Jew to fly across the Atlantic nonstop, as the passenger of Clarence Chamberlin, a well-known pilot. Levine, who has been described as "a capitalist interested in aviation," [6] had dillydallied so long in assembling a team for the trans-oceanic flight that Lindbergh beat him to it. Wanting to regain his stature in the aviation world, Levine decided to extend Lindbergh's distance record and simultaneously show his own personal bravery by flying along with Chamberlin to Berlin. The thirty-year-old Jewish millionaire kept his plans so secret that his wife fainted when she saw him take off into the dawn. While Levine proved an inept navigator (the plane missed Berlin), the men managed to break the long-range flying mark.

According to Molly Picon,[7] "Levine and His Flying Machine" was originated by Charles Cohen, a veteran Yiddish vaudevillian who was outraged that President Coolidge received Chamberlin, but not Levine, at the White House. The song, issued on Victor 79434, shows how music can serve as a cultural reservoir, retaining information which would otherwise be lost. One suspects that few Jewish-Americans remember Levine's exploits, yet the song makes it possible for us to uncover and recapture the enthusiasm his adventure aroused within his ethnic community. We can almost imagine Jews adopting the ditty to balance out the many Lindbergh songs sweeping America. A standard component of American ethnicity involves the celebration of in-group heroes who succeed in the mainstream; indeed, other minority songs about aviators (Italian, Hungarian, etc.) were also recorded in this period.[8] So there should be nothing surprising about the Levine song, other than its complete lapse into obscurity, along with its subject.

Musically, the song is in a sort of standard American up-tempo march rhythm, softened by smooth strings. It is the text that draws our attention. We hear the Yiddish words first, then the English:

> Es flien helden iber groyse yamen
> Un men zingt fun zey fil umetum.
> Nor eyn yidn darf men nit farzamen,
> Zingen [unclear], zingen vegn im.
> Levine, Levine, bist der held yetst fun Yisroel,
> Levine, Levine, vi di oves fun amol.
> Ven Chamberlin iz gekimen dort
> Bist du geven mit im.
> Levine, Levine, nisht geklert un nisht getrakht,
> Host du dayn nomen groys gemakht.
> Fun brokhes on a tsol [fun shir?] dayn Yisroel,
> Levine mit zayn flaying mashin.

Levine, Levine, you're the hero of your race,
Levine, Levine, you're the greatest Hebrew ace.
We got a thrill when Chamberlin flew
But you were right there too, we're proud of you.
Levine, Levine, just an ordinary name
But you gave it everlasting fame.
We welcome you home from over the foam,
Levine in your flying machine.

The form of the song is worth a second glance. Instead of two equal consecutive stanzas, the song consists of longer Yiddish and shorter English segments, with the "flying machine" line making the linguistic transition. A translation of the Yiddish stanza follows:

Heroes fly over the great oceans
And they're singing about them a lot everywhere.
But you shouldn't forget one Jew,
Sing [unclear], sing about him.
Levine, Levine, now you're the hero of Israel,
Levine, Levine, like the Patriarchs of yore.
When Chamberlin reached there,
You were with him.
Levine, Levine, not deliberating and not reflecting,
You made your name great.
From countless blessings, from [your Israel?]
Levine, with his flying machine.

The Yiddish seems to need more space, to cover the topic from an older point of view. The Yiddish text makes a point of maintaining the self-image of the Jew as biblical personage. The songwriters stop at nothing short of Abraham, Isaac, and Jacob when they compare Levine to Jewish heroes. The phrase about "making your name great" is reminiscent of Sarah's lullaby to the infant Isaac in Goldfadn's *Akeydas yitskhok*, forging a link to traditional Jewish popular music. The blessings of Israel that accompany the hero on his flight also resonate with archetypal emotions. This sentiment is reinforced by the Yiddish-only song on the flip side of the record, "Levine, der groyser held" ("Levine, the Great Hero"), which contains the following couplet:

Di gantse velt hobn gehaltn oygen ofen
Nor gotes oyg hot im bahit far katastrofn.

The whole world watched with open eyes
But God's eye shielded him from catastrophes.

   Yet all this ethnic fanfare is framed by a clear minority-group statement: they're singing about heroes everywhere (a clear reference to
Lindbergh)—but don't forget that one of our own has made it, too.
Jewish-Americans experienced the same feeling when Mark Spitz won
seven Olympic gold medals in 1972; feats of physical prowess evoke
particular pride among the intellectually oriented Jews. The boosting of
Levine, then, is not an isolated event, but a typical statement of what it
means to become an actor on the American stage. In the long run, one
celebrates the falling of ethnic boundaries. At its core, a song like
"Levine" says: Take us seriously—we can do anything you can. This
message, addressed both to the mainstream and to the group itself,
reflects an attitude of the post-immigrant phase and displays a good deal
of self-confidence in the group's upward struggle.
   The English verse about Levine uses the now-jarring terminology of
"Hebrew race" that was standard until Hitler's shadow fell across
American ethnicity. The narrator now takes the stance of mainstream
culture, informing Levine of his rightful status as "hero" and "greatest
Hebrew ace," going on to welcome him "from over the foam," just like
Lindbergh. It is almost unclear whether the welcoming group consists
of Jews or of the general public. This confusion is implicit in the
previous line: "just an ordinary name." Is this self-effacement by the
group, or a comment by the dominant culture? The songwriter is
donning the mask of the majority, seeing Levine from the mainstream's
point of view. The ethnic contribution lies in ignoring the fact that
Levine was passenger, not pilot—hardly an "ace." This desire for
acceptance is proof positive of the Americanization of Jewish popular
culture. It is a long journey from "Swing Days" to "Levine and His
Flying Machine."
   Our second song is infinitely better known than the Levine item. One
of the favorite songs of Jewish America, it has crossed over into the
majority culture, being recorded by such singers as Connie Francis.
Even more important is its association with a particular performer: it is
hard to dissociate "My yidishe momme" from Sophie Tucker.
   Sophie Tucker's life, colorfully and frankly detailed in her
autobiography,[9] is both typical and anomalous. In her meteoric rise to
fame, she so closely followed the path of male Jewish colleagues and has
so few female counterparts that one is constantly surprised. Starting in
blackface, then establishing her own performer's persona, she became

a show-business legend like Jolson, Cantor, and the rest, influencing many younger entertainers (notably Mae West). At the same time, like her male co-religionists, she felt a tie to her ethnic identity, which she often readily acknowledged. Eddie Cantor was quite involved in Jewish causes; and even Al Jolson pressed a record of "Hatikvah," the Israeli national anthem, backed by "Israel," a buoyant praise of the new Jewish state, in 1948. But, even more than male stars, Sophie Tucker made a point of playing for Jewish audiences to "touch the earth" and gain strength.

Sophie Tucker introduced "My yidishe momme" in 1925, when *The Jazz Singer* was opening on Broadway. In the still new and uncertain post-immigrant era, statements about ethnicity were both acceptable and commercially viable in American popular culture. Still, they had to be couched in terms familiar to the general audience, which could mean using the gray-haired mother as bridge from minority to mainstream. This is exactly what *The Jazz Singer* did, and it is the whole message of "My yidishe momme." Tucker should not have been surprised at the international success of the song: nostalgia for mom and for what are called "childhood bygones" is nearly universal in the industrial age. English and Yiddish versions were issued on two sides of a single 78 rpm recording (Decca 23902).

"MY YIDISHE MOMME": *English version*

Of things I should be thankful for I've had a goodly share
And as I sit here in the comfort of a cozy chair
My fancy takes me to a humble East Side tenement
Three flights up in the rear to where my childhood days were
    spent.
It wasn't much like Paradise, but 'mid the dirt and all
There sat the sweetest angel, one that I fondly call:
My yidishe momme, I need her more than ever now,
My yidishe momme, I'd love to kiss that wrinkled brow.
I long to hold her hands once more as in days gone by
And ask her to forgive me for things I did that made her cry.
How few were her pleasures, she never cared for fashion's
    styles.
Her jewels and her treasures, she found them in her baby's
    smiles.
Oh, I know that I owe what I am today to that dear little lady
    so old and gray,
To that wonderful yidishe momme of mine.

I see her at her daily task in morning's early light
Her willing hands forever toiling far into the night.
I hear the quaint old lullabies that haunt my memory,
Each plaintive note, each tender word, a Mother's prayer for
    me.
What have I that I would not give to cross the trails of Time
Back to those childhood bygones, back to you, Momme mine.

Translation of Yiddish version
As I stand here and think my old mother comes to mind.
No made-up, well-dressed lady, just a mother,
Bent over from great sorrow, with a pure Jewish heart
And with cried-out eyes.
In the same little room where she's gotten old and gray
She sits and cries and dreams of long-gone days
When the house was full with the sound of children's voices
And the kitchen smelled of roast and dumplings.
You can be sure our house did not lack poverty,
But there was always enough for the children.
She used to voluntarily give us bread from her mouth
And she would have given up her life for her children as well.
Millions of dollars, diamonds, big beautiful houses—
But one thing in the world you get only one of from God:
A yidishe mama, she makes the world sweet
A yidishe mama, oh how bitter when she's missing.
You should thank God that you still have her with you—
You don't know how you'll grieve when she passes away.
She would have leaped into fire and water for her children.
Not cherishing her is certainly the greatest sin.
Oh, how lucky and rich is the person who has such a beautiful
    gift from God:
Just an old little yidishe mama, my mama.

Tucker sings the English version without accent. This is clearly not an ethnic caricature item like Fannie Brice's contemporary songs ("Second-Hand Rose from Second Avenue"); instead, we hear the confident voice of a celebrity performer who feels free to acknowledge her ethnicity. Indeed, the "humble East Side tenement" of the third line directly states the group and milieu. (As usual, it is mythical: Tucker was born and raised in Hartford, Connecticut.) But beyond this opening frame, only the adjective "yidishe" has an exotic ring. The balance of the text is in slightly "high-class" English with a Victorian flavor, recalling the heyday of Tin Pan Alley ("at her daily task in morning's early light": "across the trails of Time"). This approach allows the songwriters, Yellen and Pollack, to draw on two sentiments simultaneously. By recalling older American sheet music traditions, they gain automatic credence with the general audience. At the same time, the resolutely American tone of the text can appeal to the immigrants' children, the listeners most directly addressed by the song's message. A line like "quaint old lullabies" shows the intersection of these two modes: it is condescending in the manner of parlor song, but catches the Americanized Jew's attachment to the songs of childhood with equal skill. Musically, "My yidishe momme" also straddles the fence. It is in the minor (hence exotic) mode, without the truly ethnic sound of the augmented second described earlier. The gentle, implied tango rhythm is also colorful in an uncommitted way.

The Yiddish version of the song differs radically from the English, in ways that transcend language alone. Every ethnic aspect is invoked and dwelled on: gastronomic delights, family ties, and moral values are heavily underlined. The emotional climate is immeasurably heavier than in the English version, invoking "cried-out eyes" and poverty. The song rises to a pitch of pathos when the mother's imminent death is suggested ("how bitter when she's missing"), and it sends a strong message of guilt about neglect of the aged parent: "not cherishing her is the greatest sin." The two texts are poles apart expressively, and nearly seem to be for different songs. Behind her ready identification with the song lies the fact that Sophie Tucker left home at an early age and felt guilty over abandoning her parents.[10] Similarly, Jolson's ambivalence about his own success and Americanization provides much of the electricity of his performance in the film version of *The Jazz Singer*. Both Tucker and Jolson changed spouses frequently and failed to sustain a stable family life. How can one tell the singer from the song?

With this brief insight into the ethnic headliners, we close our study of the immigrant generation. A great many archives need unpacking, trunks and piano benches need to yield their cargo, and the perspective of many Jewish-Americans needs to be broadened before we can have a full and well-balanced view of the expressive side of music from 1880 to 1920. Here we could only hope to demonstrate the remarkable richness and diversity of the material, which is just beginning to be noticed by young Jewish musicians. Bands reviving the old wedding tunes are springing up on both coasts, as the fiddler is taken off the roof and put back where he belongs, in the midst of the dancers. The last melodic flow of the nineteenth-century Jews is being tapped from older folk-singers. Revivals of Yiddish shows are increasing, fed not only by nostalgia but also by a younger generation studying Yiddish at some three dozen college campuses. More than ever, the group seems determined to look back and measure the ground covered in the last sixty years.

One hopes that this new awareness will flow directly into the cross-ethnic interest in musical roots now taking hold in such national institutions as the Library of Congress and the Smithsonian Institution, and that it will soon trickle down to local studies across the country. The Jewish case is certainly a special one, and it can shed a great deal of light on general patterns of ethnic expression and on the development of popular culture in America. At the same time, the tenement songs of the immigrant era were not sung only in Yiddish. A truly comprehensive study of American music can only emerge when we jointly reclaim our neglected musical heritage.

NOTES

1. Arthur Goren, *New York Jews and the Quest for Community* (New York: Columbia University Press, 1970), pp. 3–4.
2. Robert Ernst, *Immigrant Life in New York City, 1825–1863*, 2d ed. (Port Washington, N.Y.: Ira J. Friedman, n.d.), pp. 177, 181.
3. Goren, *New York Jews*, p. 12.
4. Ibid.
5. Mark Zborowski and Elizabeth Herzog, *Life Is With People* (New York: International Universities Press, 1952). Some later editions of this book try to capitalize on its affinity with the Broadway musical by saying "if you like *Fiddler on the Roof*, you'll love *Life Is With People*."
6. A thorough account of the flight, apparently based on Chamberlin's own account, is given in Chelsea Fraser, *Heroes of the Air* (New York: Crowell, 1927), pp. 459–74. Chamberlin's feelings about Levine may be gleaned from the following passage (p. 472), about the pair's encounter with German peasants when they force-landed in a field. The villagers "refused to believe that the new arrivals had just dropped down from a trip from New York. They could see that Chamberlin was some sort of a foreigner, but they suspected Levine of coming from some place not so far away."
7. Molly Picon, personal communication, 1979.
8. I am grateful to Richard Spottswood for this information.
9. Sophie Tucker, *Some of These Days: The Autobiography of Sophie Tucker* (Garden City: Doubleday Doran, 1945).

10. However, it should also be pointed out (ibid., pp. 169–73) that, after the death of her father, Tucker did remember her own "yidishe mama," paying her tribute with mink coats and spotlighted appearances at the Palace Theater on Broadway.

INDEX

"Marche Slave," 184
Matthews, Charles, 51
"Mayn kales apetit," 101, 104–6
"Mayn libster fraynd iz mayn
mamenyu," 125–26
"Mayn meshpukhe," 141
Melodrama. See Popular entertainment,
forms of
The Melting Pot, 56–57
Mendele Mokher Sforim, 20
"Mentshele, maynst du vest eybik legn,"
146–47
"Mentshen-fresser," 148–50
Menuhin, Yehudi, 46
Meshoyrer (Jewish choirboy), 15, 16, 19,
21, 33–35
Metro Music, 172–73, 180, 186
Dos meydl fun der vest, 141
Meyrowitz, David, 137, 146–47
Minikes, Yakov-Khanan: Tsvishn indian-
er/Among the Indians, 99, 108–14,
147, 171; mentioned, 123
Minstrel show. See Popular entertain-
ment, forms of
"Mit gelt tor men nit shtolsirn," 147
Mlotek, E. and J., 99
Mogulesco, Sigmund, 32, 33–36, 39, 40,
47, 95, 96, 167, 168, 169, 170, 173,
174, 191, 195
"Mom and Dad's Friendship," 101
Moscow, 6
Moscowitz, Pearl, 25–26
"Mother Machree," 61, 125
"Mother of Mine," 61
"Motke," 106
"Mourning Song of the Great War,"
100–101
Music, Jewish: art music, 43; folk instrumental music, 15, 143; folksongs,
13, 22–30, 126–27, 179–80; sacred
music, 19–21, 23–24, 33–35, 37, 40,
69–71, 144, 184, 187, 191, 194–95.
See also Badkhn; Khazn; Klezmer; "Kol
Nidre"
Music, non-Jewish: Austrian, 83; Belo-
russian, 185; Bulgarian, 185; church
music, 35, 39–40; Czech, 183; German, 15, 16; Polish, 37–38, 40, 183,
185; Rumanian, 20, 172, 183, 185,
186, 191; Russian, 16, 37–38, 39, 173,

185; Slovak, 185; Ukrainian, 19, 33,
173, 183, 185, 186, 191
Music publishing: Jewish, 122–23; other
ethnic, 122, 164; popular, 164–66
"Mutter un kind," 174
"My America: Our New Hymn," 154,
199
"My Best Friend Is My Mama," 125–26
"My Country 'Tis of Thee," 56, 57
"My Fiancee's Appetite," 101, 104–6
"My yidishe momme," 61, 125, 169,
202–5

"New York Boy," 101
"New York Tears," 158–61
Nirenberg, Mariam, 26

Odessa, 6, 14, 20, 40, 77, 92, 160, 190
Olcott, Chauncey, 61
Old World, 12
Olshanetsky, Alexander, 32
Opera. See Popular entertainment, forms
of
Operetta. See Popular entertainment,
forms of
"Ot der brunen, ot der," 190
"Over There," 138

"A pastekhi," 172
Pastor, Tony, 49–50
Peerce, Jan, 40
Perets, Y. L., 1
Perlmutter, Arnold, 5, 32, 83, 121, 146,
191–93
Philadelphia: Jewish entertainment in,
71–76
Piano: spread and use of, 44–46, 68, 178
Picon, Molly, 7, 30
"Poet's Vision," 179
Pogrom: response to, 6, 77, 82–83, 125
Polish-Americans, 58
Popular entertainment, forms of: broad-
side song, 99–107, 119; ethnic theater
(non-Jewish), 84, 86–88; melodrama,
73–75, 84–88, 122; minstrel show, 4,
51, 113; opera, 20, 26, 35, 43–44;
operetta, 35, 41; vaudeville, 49–50, 73,
108–14, 141; Yiddish theater, 72–74,
83–86

• 211 •

Popular entertainment, topics in: didacticism, 146–48, 168; disasters, 60, 87, 134–35; ethnic stereotyping, 49–56, 60–61, 85–86; flight history, 200; hypocrisy, 112, 147–48; immigration/ emigration, 58–60, 87, 154–59; marriage and weddings, 89, 94, 124, 132–33, 168; mother, 60–61, 122, 124–26, 203–5; nostalgia, 58–60, 87, 122, 124–25, 161; orphans, 60, 126–28, 134–35, 160; parody, 101, 133, 141, 161–62; persecution and oppression, 125, 133, 150–53, 192–93; religious faith, 144–46, 168; romantic love, 128–29; temperance, 60; women's rights, 129–31; World War I, 137–39, 153–54; Zionism, 132–33, 139–41, 148, 151, 171
"Der poylisher yid," 161, 192
Prostitution, 96, 103–4, 107, 112
"Purim Gifts," 155

"Rachomo d'one," 169, 170
"The Ragtime Violin," 176
Recordings, 3, 21, 27–28, 41–42, 88, 100, 119, 155, 200, 203
Reingold, Isaac, 132
Revolutions, Russian, response to: of 1905, 76–77, 79, 135; of 1917, 135–37
Riis, Jacob, 127
Roosevelt, Theodore, 56
Rosenblatt, Yosele, 93, 144, 170, 191
Rosenfeld, Morris, 68–71, 135–37, 153
Roth, Philip, 104
"Rozhinkes met mandlen," 30
Rubenstein, Arthur, 45
Rumshinsky, Joseph, 4, 11, 12, 13, 14, 21, 25, 32, 34, 36–45, 47, 121, 127, 167, 173, 174
"Ruslands frayhayt lid," 135–37, 153
Russotto, Henry, 43–44, 194

Sachs, Curt, 22
St. Petersburg, 13
San Francisco, 72
Sandrow, Nahma, 84
Saturday Night Fever, 76
Schenker, S., 179
"Second-Hand Rose from Second Avenue," 62, 204

Secunda, Shlomo, 32, 40
"Send Back Dear Daddy to Me," 153
"Shabes koydesh," 100
Shaefer, Jacob, 46–47
Shakespeare, William, 87
"Shalakh-mones," 155
Shapiro, Sani, 100, 101
Sharrow, Anuta, 26
Shepherd: as Jewish symbol, 171–72
"A Shepherd's Lament," 172
Di sheyne americanerin, 129
"Shiker iz der goy," 192–93
Shir hashirim, 128
"Shlof mayn kind," 30
Shlossberg, Yitskhak, 93
Sholom Aleichem: Stempenyu, 16–18, 20; mentioned, 16, 30, 80
Shorr, Anshel, 161
Shtetl, 2, 28
Shulamis, 69, 189
"Shuldik," 140–41
Siberia, 135–36
Small/Smulewitz, Solomon, 152, 153, 156, 178
Socialism and communism, 25, 78, 162–63
"The Song of Love," 128, 167
Spaeth, Sigmund, 121–22, 126, 148
"Star-Spangled Banner," 182
Stern, Isaac, 46
Straus, Ida and Isidore, 4, 177–78
"The Strawberry Blonde," 50
"The Stray Sheep," 101
Streisand, Barbra, 62
Surmach, Myron, 172
"The Sweetest Waltz Ever Published," 179
"Swing Days," 161–62, 199

"Dos talesl," 146
"Tate mames frayndshaft," 101
Teres, Alberg, 179
Terr, Louis, 168, 176
"Tfilas milkhomo," 137–38, 153
"Di tfiln," 146
Thomashefsky, Bessie, 175
Thomashefsky, Boris, 4, 21, 34, 50, 72, 110, 129, 140
"Three Little Lads," 180
Tin Pan Alley, 120, 165, 173, 190, 205

Early American Music Engraving and Printing:
A History of Music Publishing in America from 1787 to 1825
with Commentary on Earlier and Later Practices
RICHARD J. WOLFE

Sing a Sad Song: The Life of Hank Williams
ROGER M. WILLIAMS

Long Steel Rail: The Railroad in American Folksong
NORM COHEN

Resources of American Music History: A Directory of Source
Materials from Colonial Times to World War II
D. W. KRUMMEL, JEAN GEIL, DORIS J. DYEN, AND DEANE L. ROOT

Ozark Folksongs
VANCE RANDOLPH
Edited and Abridged by Norm Cohen

Tenement Songs: The Popular Music of the Jewish Immigrants
MARK SLOBIN

A NOTE ON THE RECORDING

A one-hour cassette recording of songs discussed in this book has been prepared. It includes the following selections:

Side 1.
1. "Der yidisher troyer-marsh." Naomi Amos, pianist. See pp. 82–83.
2. "Dor holekh, ve or bo." From 78 rpm recording by Maurice Mishelof. See p. 96.
3. "Dos lid der libe." Lydia Saxton, soprano; Naomi Amos, pianist. See p. 128.
4. "Vayber, makht mikh far prezident." Saxton and Amos.
5. "Ruslands frayhayt lid." Phyllis Bruce, soprano; Ann Beutler, alto; Victor Vogt, tenor; Stephen Crites, bass. See p. 135.
6. "Tfilas milkhomo." From 78 rpm recording by Joseph Feldman. See p. 137.
7. "A grus fun di trentshes." From 78 rpm recording by Louis Birnbaum. See p. 138.
8. "Shuldik." From 78 rpm recording by Kalman Juvelier. See p. 140.
9. *At a Hebrew Wedding Ceremony*. Naomi Amos, pianist. See p. 143.

Side 2.
10. "Mentshen-fresser." Saxton and Amos. See p. 148.
11. "My America: Our New Hymn." Bruce, Beutler, Vogt, and Crites. See p. 154.
12. "A brivele dem tatn." Saxton, Amos. See p. 157.
13. "Swing Days/Men hoydet zikh in Amerika." Saxton, Amos. See p. 161.
14. "Fifti-fifti." Saxton, Amos. See p. 162.
15. *Doina*. Naomi Amos, pianist. See p. 172 (Figure 13).
16. "Der poylisher yid." Saxton, Amos. See p. 192.
17. "Levine mit zayn flaying mashin." From 78 rpm recording by Charles Cohen. See p. 200.

#5 and #11 recorded live at Wesleyan University, April 17, 1977. #1, #3, #4, #9, #10, #12, #13, #14, #15, #16 recorded in studio at Wesleyan University, July 16, 1981.

The cassette is available separately from the University of Illinois Press (ISBN 0–252–00962–2).